THERESA REBECK
Volume II

Complete Full-Length Plays

1999–2007

THERESA REBECK

Volume II
Complete Full-Length Plays
1999–2007

CONTEMPORARY PLAYWRIGHTS
SERIES

A Smith and Kraus Book

A Smith and Kraus Book
Published by Smith and Kraus, Inc.
177 Lyme Road, Hanover, New Hampshire, 03755
www.smithandkraus.com / (888) 282-2881

First Edition: July 2007
10 9 8 7 6 5 4 3 2 1
Manufactured in the United States of America
Cover and text design and production by Julia Hill Gignoux, Freedom Hill Design
Cover image: Ted Marcoux, Pun Bandhu, Christopher Innvar in The Bells. *Photo by T. Charles Erickson*

The Library of Congress Cataloging-In-Publication Data
Rebeck, Theresa.
[Plays]
Theresa Rebeck: collected plays. —1st ed.
p. cm. — (Contemporary playwrights series)
ISBN-10 1-57525-444-1
ISBN-13 978-1-57525-444-9
I. Title. II. Series.
PS3568.E2697A19 1998
812'.54—dc21 98-53027

CONTENTS

FOR ARTHUR AND TINA, DAVID AND DAVID,

DANIELLA AND JOHN, AND

EVERYONE ELSE AT THE LARK

WHO TOOK SUCH CARE WITH ME AND MY PLAYS.

INTRODUCTION

First, a confession: I was late to the Theresa Rebeck party. In 1992, when *Spike Heels* premiered in New York and Rebeck's name was on everybody's lips, I had just moved to Tokyo where I was busy re-learning how to speak, searching the grocery store shelves for a product I could recognize as floor cleaner, and desperately trying to figure out how to work on Western plays with Japanese actors. In short, I was far far away from the hot new writing in American theater. When I got back to the U.S. a few years later, though, I found out what the celebration was all about.

Reading my way through a giant stack of scripts in the literary office at Seattle Repertory Theatre, I encountered an early draft of a new Theresa Rebeck play then titled *The Assistant*. It was a revelation. Characters leapt to life, vivid and recognizable, their dialogue crisp and truthful, their struggles messy and painful and human. Best of all, in a world of contemporary plays with quick little black-out scenes that avoided any real conflict, here was sustained dramatic action. I hadn't realized how hungry I was for it until I'd tasted it again.

The Assistant became *The Butterfly Collection*, Rebeck's combustible drama about family and the capacity of human beings to both hurt and heal one another. The action takes place in the upstate Connecticut home of a Nobel Prize–winning author and his family, during the summer that everything changes. People go too far, say too much, cut too deep, and pride, stubbornness, family baggage, ambition, and desire swirl together in a nasty brew that nearly poisons all concerned. Yet in the wake of all that pain, something beautiful emerges: A young writer is born. Is the beauty worth the pain?

In *The Butterfly Collection* — indeed in all the plays in this anthology — Theresa Rebeck asks big questions: What does it mean to be human? How do we hold onto our humanity? What's it like on the dark side? What are the limits? What do we risk? What are the consequences? What endures? In marriage? Family? Art? The world? Her questions are epic in scope, but rooted in specific people, places, and events, all with the tang of lived history.

In Rebeck's 1998 drama *Abstract Expression,* a woman supports her aging father by toiling as a cater-waiter at wealthy people's dinner parties.

Thoughtless remarks and unwanted scrutiny are the price Jenny pays to put food on the table (even if it is rich folks' leftovers), but her labor helps protect something precious. Her father, a once-famous Abstract Expressionist painter, hasn't shown his work in years but has steadfastly continued to pursue his vision, creating works that are seen by no one but Jenny. With biting humor and a deep undercurrent of love and sorrow, father and daughter are forced to face what happens when art and the marketplace collide. It's a classic Theresa Rebeck play: life as we know it, but heightened, deepened, and sharpened to a knife edge.

Her characters are human beings with all that makes them human. Whether it's a character whose wit and charm we'd all like to possess (like Haley in *Bad Dates*), someone who forces us to face our own dark potential (like Helen in *The Water's Edge*), or one who actively courts self-destruction (like Charlie in *The Scene*), Rebeck's characters get under the skin. Their passions, their tenderness, their rage, their weaknesses, their joys become our own.

I met Rebeck in 2001, when she was invited to the Women Playwrights Festival to work on *The Bells*, her epic play about the Alaskan Gold Rush. With her ready laugh, fierce clarity of vision, and joyous embrace of actors' ability to bring the work to life, Theresa made missionaries of us all in the service of her story. The project began as an adaptation of Leopold Lewis's classic nineteenth-century melodrama about haunting guilt (made famous by Henry Irving), but Rebeck's reflections on the harsh Alaska wilderness and the extremes human beings will venture in pursuit of wealth gave her play its own momentum and identity. She listened intently to the public reading at Seattle's ACT Theatre, then traveled with a small group of playwrights and dramaturgs to Hedgebrook, a Whidbey Island writers' retreat, where she went for long walks on the beach, silently watched the eagles, joined in lively conversation over dinner, and took refuge in the solitude of her forest cottage to contemplate and rewrite. Each morning I awoke to the sound of new pages being slipped beneath my door.

That's Theresa Rebeck: attuned to her heart, dedicated to her craft. Read these plays and, if you can, get them on the stage where they belong.

Christine Sumption

Christine Sumption is a freelance dramaturg who makes her home in Seattle, Washington.

ABSTRACT EXPRESSION

ORIGINAL PRODUCTION

Abstract Expression was originally produced at Long Wharf Theatre November 13, 1998. It was directed by Greg Leaming and had the following cast:

CHARLIE . . . . David Wolos-Fonteno
SYLVIA . . . . Beth Dixon
LILLIAN . . . . Kristine Nielsen
EUGENE . . . . Bray Poor
LUCAS/RAY . . . . Larry Gilliard Jr.
PHILLIP/JORDY . . . . Glenn Fleshler
JENNY . . . . Angie Phillips
KIDMAN . . . . Jack Willis
WILLIE . . . . Mark Nelson

Scenic Design . . . . Neil Patel
Costume Design . . . . David Zinn
Lighting Design . . . . Dan Kotlowitz
Original Music . . . . Fabian Obispo
Sound Design . . . . Matthew Mezick
Wigs . . . . Paul Huntley
Production Stage Manager . . . . Kevin E. Thompson
Artistic Director . . . . Doug Hughes

CHARACTERS

CHARLIE: Black, mid-fifties
SYLVIA: White, early sixties
LILLIAN: White, late thirties
EUGENE: White, forty
JENNY: White, twenty-eight
KIDMAN: White, early fifties
RAY/LUCAS: Black, late twenties
PHILLIP/JORDY: White, late twenties
WILLIE: White, thirty

SET

The locations vary between Charlie's apartment, quite small and meager, on the Lower East Side; Sylvia's elegant apartment on the Upper East Side; the kitchen of Kidman's artist's loft; and the office of Lillian's gallery.

ACT I
SCENE ONE

Lights up on a man at a table. He is unloading a bag of groceries and talk-ing to a small bird in a cage on top of a very small television set.

CHARLIE: Who needs money? Long as we can eat and watch a little television now and then we be OK, hey sweet pea. Look at this, dollar ninety-nine for toilet paper, you believe that? Plus they raised the coffee again, I don't really care long as I don't have to drink that stuff tastes like nuts and berries. Four ninety-nine a can. That's a crime. If I was making the rules, I'd keep down the coffee, that's what I say. Only sure way to stave off the revolution. Yeah, don't look at me like that, I got your peanut butter.
(He pulls it out of the bag and looks at it.)
Reduced fat. They charge the same and take things out, that's the way the world, huh. Everything just shrinking down, well, we don't mind. You and me and a good cup of coffee, little television, who needs money. Like a kingdom in here.
(He looks at his mail and stops at a letter. Considers it, then goes back to the can of coffee.)
Make me some coffee.
(He studies the can. Blackout.)

SCENE TWO

Lights up on a dinner party. Eugene, Sylvia, Lillian, Lucas, and Phillip are finishing their desert and coffee.

SYLVIA: I just think the whole thing is much ado about nothing. I mean, the city has been going to hell as long as I can remember, I just think it should go there in style and I'm not going to apologize about that.
EUGENE: Don't be ridiculous Mother.
SYLVIA: I'm not being ridiculous, it's absolutely everywhere in the news again. The gaps between the rich and poor, as if this were a noteworthy situa-tion, or an actual social condition or something. When it's really noth-ing more than a definition. I mean, it's just what the words mean, isn't it? Some people are rich, and some are poor, and the poor ones don't have as much money. How is this news? This is some idiot's idea of news.

LILLIAN: Sylvia. You're just trying to be controversial.

SYLVIA: But I'm not! This isn't even original, what I'm saying. I mean God, people have been — who was it who said that thing about poor people being around all the time —

PHILLIP: The poor will be with you always?

EUGENE: That was Jesus Christ, actually.

SYLVIA: There, that's what I mean. Even he was saying it and he liked them.

(Jenny enters and starts clearing plates.)

LUCAS: Your point being what, Sylvia? I mean, I'm not saying I disagree with you, but this is starting to make me uncomfortable. I am a person of color after all —

SYLVIA: Oh don't start that. That's not what I'm talking about and you know it. I'm just saying how bad is it really, being poor? Don't you think they're exaggerating, at least a little, the source of all our social problems et cetera, et cetera, well I know plenty of rich people who have social problems. And if the rich are as bad as the poor, socially I mean, or any other way for that matter, well. Then all this fuss is really over nothing.

EUGENE: All what fuss? I don't even know what you're talking about.

SYLVIA: You do too, and don't use that tone with me, young man.

EUGENE: I'm not using a tone, Mother, you're just rattling on about nothing as usual —

SYLVIA: *(Overlap.)* Oh really, and may I say your manners are lovely, at your own engagement party, which I am paying for I might add —

EUGENE: Oh for God's sake —

SYLVIA: Well, honestly, you're turning into one of those people who hate their own money and I don't have anyone else to leave it to —

EUGENE: Mother —

LILLIAN: Eugene does not hate money. I won't let him.

(She kisses his hand.)

EUGENE: *(Good-natured.)* Of course I don't hate money, that's ridiculous. I'm just uncomfortable with the assumption that just because you have it that means you know something about social conditions.

PHILLIP: Well why shouldn't it mean that?

EUGENE: When in fact I happen to know that she personally has never spoken to anyone whose trust fund is smaller than two mil on a good day in the market.

SYLVIA: Oh that's not real money —

LILLIAN: *(Laughing.)* Sylvia —

EUGENE: *(Animated.)* Meanwhile we live in a city where people are starving, literally starving, if the newspapers are to be trusted at all —

PHILLIP: Which they're not —

SYLVIA: Oh, nobody starves on Manhattan. Manhattan is thirty-four square miles of room service, my father used to say that.

(They all laugh.)

EUGENE: Not that I care, I don't care. I just don't know why you keep going on about it.

SYLVIA: Oh, now you're upset.

EUGENE: I'm not upset.

LILLIAN: What about you, are you poor?

(She looks at Jenny. Jenny stops her cleaning for a moment and looks up, surprised.)

PHILLIP: *(Amused.)* Oh really, Lillian.

LILLIAN: What's it like?

EUGENE: Lillian.

SYLVIA: Oh no, that's not what I meant at all. I don't want to know what it's like, that's not the point.

LUCAS: No, I think it is.

(Jenny starts for the door, carrying plates.)

LILLIAN: Where are you going? I asked you a question.

JENNY: *(Surprised.)* Oh.

LUCAS: You're serious.

LILLIAN: Eugene has a point. I don't see how we can talk about this, consider ourselves informed on any level, if we're not willing to confront the reality of poverty in the city.

(To Jenny.)

So what's it like? Can you tell us?

SYLVIA: Yes but she's not poor. Look at her, she's clearly educated. You're educated, aren't you, you're an actress or something.

LUCAS: Actresses are poor.

JENNY: I'm not an actress.

SYLVIA: But you're educated.

(There is an awkward pause at this.)

JENNY: I've been to high school.

SYLVIA: Not college?

JENNY: No.

LILLIAN: But you graduated high school.

JENNY: *(A slight beat.)* I haven't, actually. Excuse me.

(She heads for the door, with the plates.)

SYLVIA: Oh, you dropped out, is that it? To be an actress, or something?

EUGENE: She already said she's not an actress, Mother.

(To Jenny.)

I'm sorry. You need to finish up, and we're keeping you.

SYLVIA: All of a sudden you're so sensitive, well, she can just answer the question before she goes. What is it like to be poor?

(They stare at Jenny. She considers this.)

JENNY: It's like not having enough money.

SYLVIA: This is my point . . .

JENNY: You worry a lot.

SYLVIA: You worry? Well I worry.

EUGENE: You worry about your nails, and whether or not you can get theater tickets.

JENNY: Did you need anything else?

LILLIAN: Stop trying to run off, this is interesting.

JENNY: It's not interesting. It's not. It's just, you don't have enough money. That's all it is. You skip breakfast. You buy cheap shoes. You stand in the drugstore and try to figure out how much it costs per aspirin if you buy the big bottle instead of the little one, and all you can think is of course it's better to just spend the money and have the big bottle because then you've paid less per aspirin, but if you do that, there won't be enough left to go to a movie and sometimes you just want to go to a movie. You'd be amazed at how long you can think about that. Then you think about other cities where movies don't cost eight dollars and you get mad, 'cause eight dollars is a lot, for a movie, it's . . . It's boring, really. A lot of boring things stick in your head for a long time. You just, you think about money all the time.

EUGENE: *(Dry.)* So in one way at least, it is like being rich.

SYLVIA: Don't your parents help you?

JENNY: My mother's dead.

PHILLIP: What about your father, doesn't he work?

JENNY: No, he does work, he works very hard. But he's, actually, he's an artist.

LILLIAN: An artist? You mean a painter?

JENNY: Yes.

SYLVIA: Oh, that's different. Her father's an artist. So she's poor, but it doesn't count.

EUGENE: Why not?

SYLVIA: Artists are supposed to be poor. It helps their art. And don't argue with me about this, I'm right about this.

LILLIAN: *(Interested.)* What's his name?

JENNY: Walter Kidman.

LILLIAN: Mac Kidman?

(There is a surprised stir at this. Jenny is clearly startled.)

LUCAS: *(Amused.)* My God, Lillian. You know this man?

LILLIAN: Is it him?

JENNY: *(Now truly uncomfortable.)* Yes, actually.

LILLIAN: No one's heard from him in years. He's still painting?

JENNY: Of course he's still painting. That's what he is, he's a painter.

PHILLIP: *(To Lillian.)* Is he any good?

LILLIAN: There was some debate about it, but he had something of a career, what, fifteen or twenty years ago. My uncle reviewed one of his shows. He didn't much like that particular batch, but he always felt he had talent.

JENNY: Your uncle?

LILLIAN: Yes, he was the art critic for the *Times*. You must've been a child, I'm sure you don't remember.

JENNY: Of course I remember. It was his last show.

LILLIAN: Was it?

JENNY: I have to go.

(She suddenly turns and heads for the door.)

LILLIAN: *(Calling.)* But your father's still painting?

JENNY: *(Tense.)* Yes. He is.

LILLIAN: I'd love to see what he's doing these days. I have a gallery. Lillian Paul. My uncle had terrific respect for your father. He just thought he was going down the wrong track, I think.

(A beat. Jenny doesn't respond. She finally turns and goes.)

SYLVIA: Well, that was rude.

EUGENE: For God's sake. You were examining her like she was some kind of bug!

SYLVIA: We were expressing interest. How is that a bad thing?

PHILLIP: This Kidman was good, you say?

LILLIAN: Not likely but for God's sake you can't say that to the man's daughter. What kind of a bitch do you think I am?

(They laugh. Blackout.)

SCENE THREE

Kidman's loft. Kidman and Charlie sit at a table, getting drunk on Jack Daniels. They are looking at a painting.

CHARLIE: I like it.
(Kidman goes to the painting and turns it so that it now stands horizontal, which is the correct way to look at it.)
KIDMAN: It's shit.
CHARLIE: No, it's good.
KIDMAN: No, I mean, yeah, it's good shit. But Jesus, this bullshit —
CHARLIE: That part, looks like a duck?
KIDMAN: What?
CHARLIE: It looks like a little duck in a lake, or one of those birds with the legs. And the things over there . . .
KIDMAN: What things?
CHARLIE: You know, those things grow out of the water. Bullrushes.
KIDMAN: *(Annoyed.)* Those aren't — this is not a duck, all right?
CHARLIE: Then what is it?
KIDMAN: It's abstract. It's not anything.
CHARLIE: If it's not anything, it can be a duck.
KIDMAN: No it can't.
CHARLIE: That's what you said before. Before, you said —
KIDMAN: It's abstract.
CHARLIE: So, it's an abstract duck.
KIDMAN: It's nonrepresentational!
CHARLIE: *(Overlap.)* I'm just pulling your leg. You get all worked up and start using words, I'm just having a conversation here. Good Lord.
KIDMAN: *(Overlap.)* I'm having a conversation. Am I not having a conversation? I'm just saying it's not a duck.
CHARLIE: Yeah, OK . . .
KIDMAN: This line is shit. Look at this, it's like some giant worm.
(He looks for a brush.)
CHARLIE: Leave it alone, I like it.
KIDMAN: You think it looks like a duck! I mean Jesus, you're like some fucking German expressionist, why don't I just put a woman and a tree in there, that would really make it good —
CHARLIE: Oh cut it out.

KIDMAN: Those idiot Germans acting like they invented the moon, when they didn't even —
(He starts to smudge something.)
Fucking philosophical shit heads. Look at this. Aw shit.
CHARLIE: Leave it alone!
KIDMAN: Hey, who's the painter, you or me?
CHARLIE: I'm just saying —
KIDMAN: Who's the painter?
CHARLIE: Don't pull that shit on me. You want to fuck that up, be my guest, but all I'm saying you should calm down, stop being such an asshole and just accept the fact, that's a damn duck.
(Kidman sits and stares at it.)
KIDMAN: Fuck, I'm fucked. It's a fucking duck.
(He laughs. Charlie laughs, too. Kidman pours another round of drinks and stands to put the painting away.)
CHARLIE: Well, I like it.
KIDMAN: You want it?
CHARLIE: You mean to have? You throwing that away?
KIDMAN: I'm not throwing it away. I'm giving it to you.
CHARLIE: Don't you throw that away. That's good, I'm telling you.
KIDMAN: I'm not throwing it away, I'm giving it to you.
CHARLIE: 'Cause a lot of people might like a picture like that.
KIDMAN: You don't want it?
CHARLIE: I didn't say that. I been saying I like it.
KIDMAN: But you don't want it.
CHARLIE: I'm just saying you could sell that for a lot of money.
KIDMAN: What are you, nuts?
CHARLIE: They sell pictures, people make a lot of money off pictures like this.
KIDMAN: Really? No, really?
CHARLIE: Yeah I know you being smart with me. All I'm saying, one day, we'll be singing and dancing 'cause you gonna be rich.
KIDMAN: 'Cause the market for paintings of ducks is about to take off.
CHARLIE: That's what I said.
KIDMAN: Too bad it's not painted on velvet, that would make it really good.
(They laugh. Jenny enters, still in her catering outfit, carrying a large paper bag of leftover food.)
JENNY: Hey Charlie. Hi, Daddy.
(Charlie whisks the bottle off the table and holds it between his legs on the floor. Happily involved in her own news, Jenny doesn't notice it at first.)

CHARLIE: Hey, honey.

KIDMAN: Hey, where'd you go? I turned around and you were gone.

JENNY: I took this catering gig at the last minute, I so did not want to do it but they were begging, and I thought, well maybe I can work this into a favor from Bernie sometime, so I went and I was the only one working, right, and these people are kind of a nightmare but they could not care less about the leftovers, which is like, I mean, excuse me. Chicken with mustard tarragon sauce.

CHARLIE: Oh my goodness, how 'bout that.

JENNY: Stuffed acorn squash.

KIDMAN: Oh, this is fantastic.

JENNY: Crème brûlée. I love even just saying that, crème brûlée. Crème Brûléee. I got all of it, most of these people are, they're all so worried about getting fat they've completely forgotten how to eat. Crème bru — *(She sees the bottle of whiskey on the floor. The mood changes. Charlie looks embarrassed. Kidman becomes immediately defiant, openly picking up the bottle. He takes a mug full of paint brushes off the table, knocks the brushes out and makes a show of pouring a large drink.)*

CHARLIE: I guess we gonna have a feast, huh?

(Beat.)

Just come up to watch the game. My TV busted.

JENNY: *(Still trying to recover.)* Oh, huh?

CHARLIE: *(Tap-dancing now.)* Picture don't even come in, just scramble, you know. So I come up here, saying I'll just watch on your set, then Mac, he can't even find it. Put it away somewhere, he don't even know.

KIDMAN: It's here somewhere.

JENNY: So you couldn't find the TV, so you decided to get trashed.

(A beat. Charlie is embarrassed. Kidman is not.)

CHARLIE: Oh now.

KIDMAN: That's right, we took your hard-earned money and said what's the surest way to piss that girl off? What's gonna really tie her up? How can I make my long-suffering daughter suffer even more?

JENNY: Daddy. You promised.

KIDMAN: "Daddy, you promised."

JENNY: *(Patient.)* Yes, you promised, and I don't know why you'd, it's been months, and everything's fine, you were doing, we're —

KIDMAN: Oh now I have to justify myself to my daughter? Is that where we're at? I'm such a sorry hack I have to lie to everybody when I want a drink or you're what, you're gonna cut off my allowance —

JENNY: You told me —

CHARLIE: We was just having one drink, Jenny.

JENNY: Charlie, half the damn bottle is — I'm not — no.

(She dumps the food and heads for the next room, trying not to lose it.)

KIDMAN: *(Yelling after her.)* You're an old woman!

JENNY: You're a drunk!

KIDMAN: Oh you really cut me. That's a hit. Oh my —

JENNY: I can't believe this. I've been working like an animal, serving eight courses to assholes so we can pay for some heat in this — I can't even — I'm begging scraps of food and you're back here killing yourself! You know that stuff will kill you, and —

KIDMAN: Christ you need to get laid.

JENNY: *(Losing it.)* I WOULD get laid if I had a life instead of —

(Beat.)

I'm such an idiot. I'm just a complete fucking idiot.

KIDMAN: That's my girl.

JENNY: Fuck you.

KIDMAN: Yeah, fuck you too.

CHARLIE: No, now, Jenny! You know, we was just having a nip.

(There is a terrible pause while Kidman glares at her. She doesn't know what to do. She sits, finally. Kidman prowls. Charlie looks at them both, nervous.)

CHARLIE: *(Continuing; tap-dancing again.)* Did I tell you? Got a letter from my sister's boy, Ray. He's finally gettin' out of the joint. I say that's a good thing, you know, but he been in there upwards four years, so who knows. Wants to come stay with me, I'm thinking, well, I don't know about that. Ain't exactly a palace down there. Don't have the kind of room you all got. Plus the TV's on the blink. Well I told you that.

(He stops, unhappy, wondering what the others will do. Jenny wipes her eyes and finally looks up, resigned.)

JENNY: Ray? Did I meet him once?

CHARLIE: Well maybe you did. You remember that, you got a good head on your shoulders, 'cause that would be a long time ago. 'Course you got a good head, we know that.

(Jenny sobs, briefly.)

Oh now honey. You're OK.

(Kidman prowls, restless.)

KIDMAN: I don't ask for this. You want to take off, take off. No one's begging you to prostrate yourself on the altar of filial devotion. Your brother had the balls to leave. You want a life, go get one.

JENNY: I'm going to bed.

KIDMAN: Just don't come home expecting people to genuflect, you're so holy, you're so good. Your life is your own.

CHARLIE: You're going to bed? I thought we was gonna have a party. All this nice food.

JENNY: You eat it.

CHARLIE: Oh now Jenny.

JENNY: I just don't know why I even — these people were hideous, they — and you think that's nothing? That I have to stand there and take it, the whole time I'm just thinking, pay me. I'm doing the job, why can't you just pay me, you sons of bitches, why do I have to be humiliated to just get the damn MONEY.

(Beat.)

Fuck it.

(She heads for her room, speaking as she goes.)

Oh. By the way. One of them knew who you were. Her uncle was that critic who said your sense of color was preadolescent.

KIDMAN: Asshole.

JENNY: She wants to see your work. She has a gallery, Lillian something.

KIDMAN: You didn't even get her damn name?

JENNY: Lillian Paul, all right —

KIDMAN: Yeah, Lillian Paul, and I'm supposed to jump, is that it? They're coming crawling now, I'm supposed to go pay obeisance to some cunt wouldn't know a real painting unless she pissed on it —

JENNY: Never mind.

KIDMAN: Did you tell her she can go fuck herself? Did you tell her that?

(There is a short beat while Jenny looks at her father.)

JENNY: No. I didn't.

(Blackout.)

SCENE FOUR

It is the middle of the night. Kidman sits at the table, totally drunk, surrounded by half-open boxes of left-overs and the now near-empty bottle of Jack Daniels. Jenny enters, in a T-shirt and old pajama bottoms. She looks at him, in the half-light.

JENNY: It's three in the morning. You should go to bed.

KIDMAN: All this food. I was gonna . . .

JENNY: Just go to bed.

(She starts to put away the food.)

KIDMAN: That stuff is shit. It's shit anyway. I was in Pisa, with your mother, we had crème brûlée, that was the real stuff. Got in a fight with some asshole on the street, he's screaming at me in Italian, right? I did something, who knows, your mom gets so embarrassed, she starts screaming back at him in German. He's yelling Privato! Privato! And your mom is, she was embarrassed, so she starts talking German, so this guy doesn't know we're American idiots. Ich ben Deutch something, wasser bitte, shit like this.

JENNY: And then you had crème brûlée.

KIDMAN: She did. I ordered . . . pear tart with avocado sauce. She hated pears. Only ever had two in her life, that she liked. One was in France. The other . . . Spent years, trying to get her to eat another pear. Big thing with her. The search for pear number three.

(Beat.)

You got that from her. This thing for food. The woman would take a bite of something and swoon. Thought a corn dog was a gift from God.

JENNY: Well. Corn dogs.

KIDMAN: She was like that. Skinny as a twig. Loved food. Any food. Except pears.

(Beat.)

JENNY: How was it?

KIDMAN: Huh?

JENNY: The pear tart with avocado sauce.

KIDMAN: It was Italy. Pear number three.

JENNY: *(After a beat.)* You should go to bed.

KIDMAN: I was gonna paint. You went to bed and I was, but I can't . . .

JENNY: It'll be OK tomorrow.

KIDMAN: *(An apology.)* This is — I didn't — It's just, the painting is shit right now —

JENNY: It's not, Daddy.

KIDMAN: You don't know.

JENNY: I do know. There's no light now. You can't, you're drunk, and —

KIDMAN: Don't you fucking throw that at me —

JENNY: Daddy, there's no light! It's three in the morning. There's no light.

(The force of this argument actually gets through to him. He nods.)

KIDMAN: That fucking prick. Preadolescent.

JENNY: *(Patient.)* He was an asshole.

KIDMAN: Dead now, you know. That's the only good thing you can say about critics. Eventually, they're gonna die, just like everyone else. They come up with these words, preadolescent, it's primitive, we're doing something, but ever since Picasso, you can't use that word as an insult so they come up with something else because they don't want to spend half a brain cell thinking what someone's trying to do.

JENNY: Daddy, your paintings are beautiful. It doesn't matter what he said.

KIDMAN: That's what I'm saying.

JENNY: They didn't stop you. You still did it. And they're beautiful.

KIDMAN: They tried to stop me.

JENNY: They lost.

(Beat.)

KIDMAN: I'm murdering you.

JENNY: No.

KIDMAN: There's such light in you.

JENNY: There's light in you, Daddy. There's light in you.

(He cannot look at her. Blackout.)

SCENE FIVE

The office of Lillian Paul. Lillian sits at her desk. Charlie stands before her, holding a painting.

LILLIAN: Where did you get this?

CHARLIE: My friend give it to me. Walter Kidman, he's a friend of mine.

LILLIAN: Really.

CHARLIE: See I know him and his girl Jenny, who said she met you and you said, you wanted to see what kind of painting Walter was making, 'cause you remembered him from before.

LILLIAN: And he sent you as his emissary.

CHARLIE: He don't know I'm here.

LILLIAN: Such a surprise.

CHARLIE: 'Scuse me?

LILLIAN: No, continue.

CHARLIE: Well, he's a little contentious on account that's just how he is, but he give me this painting, and when Jenny said you remembered Walter I thought maybe I could sell it.

LILLIAN: This is yours to sell?

CHARLIE: Yeah, he give it to me. It's a present.

LILLIAN: He gave you a present, and now you're selling it? That's not very nice.

CHARLIE: Well, I'm way out of cash, and that's a fact. My nephew's coming to stay with me, my TV's busted, and now they's these cuts the government keeps talking about. I don't know. Spent two years in Vietnam, that don't seem to mean much to people, but can't change the world, I guess.

LILLIAN: I guess not.

(She looks at the painting. Charlie watches her, nervous.)

CHARLIE: 'Cause see, I really like it. Don't get me wrong about that. That's how come I'm here, Jenny said you expressed interest, and I thought, she don't even know, on account nobody's been seeing what all Walter can do for how long. This is a fine piece of work. I think it looks like a duck. *(A beat, then, as she doesn't respond.)*

'Cause you can see him, swimming on the lake, with those things, look like bullrushes to me. I know, you're not supposed to do that. Decide what it looks like.

LILLIAN: Why not?

CHARLIE: I don't know. Walter, he just gets worked up sometimes, when you suggest stuff like that.

LILLIAN: And how much are you asking?

CHARLIE: 'Scuse me?

LILLIAN: Your price. How much would you like me to pay for it?

(There is a bit of a pause at this, as Charlie never quite expected to get this far.)

CHARLIE: Oh, I don't, you know. You'd know more about that.

(She shrugs. He looks about, uncomfortable, then decides to go for it.)

CHARLIE: *(Continuing.)* It's art and all, so that's worth something. That's all I'm saying.

(Beat. She waits.)

CHARLIE: *(Continuing.)* I was thinking six hundred dollars. Maybe seven, even.

LILLIAN: Which, six or seven?

CHARLIE: Seven.

LILLIAN: Six.

CHARLIE: Whoa, really? OK. Six.

LILLIAN: Sold.

(Charlie grins, having hit the jackpot, and even laughs a little. His laugher becomes uncomfortable. Blackout.)

SCENE SIX

Sylvia's apartment. Lillian is laughing. Eugene is looking at the painting. Sylvia bustles about, serving tea.

SYLVIA: Well, I just don't know what you're saying.

LILLIAN: I'm saying I bought a painting, a very good painting.

SYLVIA: From that girl's father? That cater-person who told us what it's like to be poor, and then went on and on —

LILLIAN: *(Overlap.)* Oh God, I feel terrible about that. I was drunk —

SYLVIA: Why do you feel terrible? She was very well-paid. And she took all the left-overs, I think we treated her very well.

LILLIAN: *(To Eugene.)* Yes, but what do you think?

EUGENE: I . . .

LILLIAN: You don't like it?

EUGENE: No, I do, I just . . .

LILLIAN: Because I love it. Look what he's doing with perspective, it's like the whole thing moves, look —

EUGENE: This isn't my forte, Lillian. I mean, you never show this stuff.

SYLVIA: No one's interested in Abstract Expressionism, because you can never tell if it's any good. That's the problem with it.

LILLIAN: You can tell. This is good.

EUGENE: He actually showed up, then? The father?

LILLIAN: No, God no. This is fabulous. This old black man showed up, dressed like you wouldn't — I mean, I almost called security, this guy looks like he's living on the street, but he's carrying this painting. Turns out they're friends, and he needs cash.

EUGENE: How much did you give him?

LILLIAN: Six hundred dollars.

SYLVIA: For that? No. Really? You paid six hundred dollars for that?

LILLIAN: I'm telling you, Sylvia, I love it. And not only that, I think it's going to be worth something.
(She goes up behind Eugene and hugs him, enthusiastic. He looks at her, bemused.)

EUGENE: I haven't seen you like this, ever.

LILLIAN: *(Laughing.)* I know! I'm just so . . . you get so sick of this damn bull-shit, putting together group shows, schmoozing the fucking critics, just to get them into an opening once in a while, following who's showing what in some stupid gallery in Minneapolis for God's sake, forcing a sale out of a friend so that you can generate some little bit of heat for someone who's really good, it's all just, nothing is a bit of fun since Black Thursday, when the hell are we going to recover from that, that's what I want to know. And then to have something different happen, something really different. You should have seen this guy. And what did that girl say, this guy's been out there for years, painting, he's been painting for fifteen years in some garret, probably, and not showing anywhere. Abject poverty, blah blah blah —

SYLVIA: *(Interested.)* You mean like Van Gogh?

EUGENE: Not Van Gogh again, when are we going to —

LILLIAN: Come on, this is a story, Gene. I can do something with this.

EUGENE: A story. And here I am, thinking you liked the painting.

LILLIAN: I love the painting. The painting is fantastic, that's what makes the story so good. If the painting's no good, the story is just pathetic. But the painting is fantastic.

SYLVIA: How can you know that? It's abstract. Who can tell if those things are any good?

(Lillian is now looking for pen and paper.)

LILLIAN: We have to find Kidman. Sylvia, that catering company, what's the phone number. We have to track that girl down.

EUGENE: I already did.

(Lillian looks at him, surprised.)

EUGENE: *(Continuing.)* I felt bad. Forgot to give her her tip.

(He hands a card to Lillian. She considers this, and him, as Sylvia speaks.)

SYLVIA: *(Preoccupied, looking at painting.)* Don't be ridiculous. I tipped her the way I always do.

EUGENE: Exactly.

SYLVIA: *(Rattling on.)* Plus I let her take all that food, she did very well by us. Well, I just don't see it, Lillian. I'm glad you're excited, but I have to say, if I'm going to hang something on the wall, it should look like something. Well, I suppose you could say that's a bird, or a duck over there. I suppose you could say that.

(Blackout.)

SCENE SEVEN

Kidman's apartment. Eugene stands at one side, casually disinterested. Jenny waits, nervous.

EUGENE: They've been in there for a while.

JENNY: Yes.

EUGENE: She was very enthusiastic. About the one painting. She doesn't get this way.

(Beat.)

How many does he have? I mean, I just got a glimpse. Looked like quite a few.

JENNY: Yes.

(She paces.)

EUGENE: Hundreds, even. Fifteen years worth, I guess.

JENNY: Look, why are you here?

EUGENE: She liked his work. It's not unusual for gallery owners. Visiting an artist in his studio, that's —

JENNY: No one has been interested in him for years.

EUGENE: So this is a good thing. Right? Which is why you're so cheerful.

JENNY: I just think you should go. I mean, I didn't say anything, at that dinner party, but, this isn't, you don't know what —

EUGENE: Look. I wanted to apologize about that. The way people spoke to you was inappropriate, and —

JENNY: No. I'm not —

EUGENE: Well, I wanted to apologize.

JENNY: I'm not —

(Beat.)

You know, does your girlfriend know you were hitting on me at your own engagement party?

EUGENE: I was what?

JENNY: Oh, you weren't hitting on me. In the kitchen.

EUGENE: No.

JENNY: "What's that perfume you're wearing?"

EUGENE: I wanted to —

JENNY: I wasn't wearing —

EUGENE: So you said. I asked a question, you answered it. That's hardly —

JENNY: "Do you want to go have a drink sometime." That's not —

EUGENE: It was an honest —

JENNY: *(Starting to laugh.)* Oh my God. It was your own engagement party and you were, and now —

EUGENE: Lillian wanted to see your father's paintings, and I came along. I admit I find you interesting. That's not a crime.

JENNY: Interesting? What? I'm what?

EUGENE: Interesting. You seem —

JENNY: Interesting?

EUGENE: Yes. Interesting.

JENNY: *(Matter-of-fact, confrontational.)* Don't you mean "pretty?" That I seem pretty?

EUGENE: I mean what I said. You seemed interesting.

JENNY: Then I'm not pretty.

EUGENE: Of course you're pretty. That's not what I was talking about.

JENNY: *(Finally defiant.)* So you would find me just as interesting if I weren't pretty? If I were some sort of huge fat person? Or some little nerdy boy with greasy hair and glasses, but the same person, I'd be just as interesting to you?

EUGENE: If you were those things, you wouldn't be the same person.

JENNY: Funny, somehow I knew you were going to say that.

EUGENE: Do you think I'm hitting on you?

JENNY: No. I think you find me "interesting."

EUGENE: *(Growing amusement.)* Yes, you grow more interesting by the second.

JENNY: Oh good.

EUGENE: You weren't like this at all the other night. I mean, you're very —

JENNY: *(Frustrated finally.)* What?

EUGENE: Nothing. Interesting.

(Lillian and Kidman reenter the room. Kidman and Lillian are deep into it. Lillian is happily enthralled.)

KIDMAN: Yeah, it's possible he wasn't a complete vegetable, I'm just saying, people admit he didn't even paint —

LILLIAN: Unquestionably, his assistants were doing some of the work. But there's plenty of critical discussion about —

KIDMAN: Don't you fucking talk to me about critical discussion. I'll kick you out of my fucking studio, you —

LILLIAN: But that's not what we're talking about. We're talking about what you think.

KIDMAN: About de Koonig.

LILLIAN: Yes.

KIDMAN: Yeah, see, I don't think that's what we're talking about.

(He looks at her. She gives him a slight nod of acknowledgement.)

LILLIAN: I think that many things inform an artist's work, and many things taint it. Your work is untainted but not uninformed. I would say it's a tragedy that you haven't been showing all these years, but I don't think you could've done this otherwise. The sense of privacy and turbulent isolation, it's absolutely stunning. My future mother-in-law says the problem with Abstract Expressionism is that no one understands it, but it's impossible to misunderstand the greatness of your paintings. Really, I haven't any words.

EUGENE: And yet.

LILLIAN: *(Excited, oblivious.)* Yes, and yet I could go on! But I won't. I'm going to show these paintings, Walter. And I'm not talking about next year; I'm talking about now. Next month. This is absolutely the right time, no one's seen anything like this in years. Fuck de Koonig, we've got Walter Kidman back from the dead! These paintings make the post-post-modernists I've been showing look like pure bullshit —

KIDMAN: They look like that anyway, Lillian.

LILLIAN: *(Laughing.)* Oh, Walter. This is going to be fun.

(She takes his hand and smiles at him. He doesn't quite know what to make of this.)

JENNY: Well, that's just —

LILLIAN: What?

JENNY: Crazy. I mean, this is just — crazy.

LILLIAN: I don't think so.

JENNY: Well, but, so are we supposed to clap? No one's even spoken to him in fifteen years and now we're supposed to jump up and down because you like his paintings?

KIDMAN: What's your problem?

JENNY: Dad, they're not even — they didn't even come over here because — oh, shit.

LILLIAN: Oh.

JENNY: I mean its . . .

KIDMAN: *(Offended.)* What? It's what?

JENNY: *(Defiant.)* It's crazy.

KIDMAN: Since you know so much about it.

JENNY: Dad.

KIDMAN: I mean, I thought I was the one painting my guts out for fifteen years. I didn't realize —

JENNY: Oh, for — you're the one who said it! All this time —

KIDMAN: *(Overlap.)* You were the great genius behind the throne.

JENNY: *(Overlap.)* You've been doing this for fifteen years without them!

KIDMAN: Don't you fucking talk to me like an idiot —

JENNY: You're the one who, you keep saying, what do you need them for?

KIDMAN: It's not a question of needing them. I don't need them.

JENNY: Exactly. You did that, before, and they treated you — You did what she's talking about, the galleries, and the critics, and it almost killed you!

KIDMAN: Oh no no.

LILLIAN: The critical environment is very different now, if you're concerned about —

KIDMAN: We're not concerned.

EUGENE: We should go.

KIDMAN: No. She's nuts. She's got like no life, she's a nun in training, it's made her —

JENNY: No one would take your damn phone calls! Sending slides out into the void, galleries couldn't even be bothered to send a rejection letter! All because one asshole in *The New York Times* —

LILLIAN: It's a little more complicated than —

JENNY: It wasn't more complicated to us. My mother died. We had no health insurance, we had no heat —

KIDMAN: *(Cutting her off.)* She had cancer!

LILLIAN: *(Alert.)* Your wife died of cancer?

EUGENE: We can come back.

JENNY: Don't. This doesn't have anything to do with you. All those years, you left us alone, and it almost killed him, but then it didn't, and that's what he did. Now all a sudden, you show up, and he's supposed to jump? You can forget it. He doesn't need you. He doesn't need anything you can offer. He doesn't need it.

(There is a silence at this. Lillian looks at Kidman, who looks down. She nods.)

LILLIAN: All right, look. This was very sudden. I'm a little, I can't say I'm enthusiastic by nature, because I'm not, so maybe I got carried away. Why don't you think about it for a few days.

(She waits a beat, then looks at Eugene and turns to go.)

KIDMAN: *(To Jenny.)* Yeah, we're not thinking about this, 'cause I'm gonna do it. I mean, what are you, insane? Are you completely insane?

(Beat.)

LILLIAN: Is there someplace we can go and talk?

KIDMAN: Let's go get a drink.
> *(To Lillian, as he goes.)*
> My friends call me Mac.
LILLIAN: Well, Mac, how about some champagne?
> *(She laughs and they go, leaving Jenny alone. Eugene stops for a moment, wanting to say something. She looks at him. Blackout.)*

SCENE EIGHT

Charlie's apartment. Ray, energetic and edgy, looks around the small room.

RAY: This is great, Uncle Charlie. Fantastic.

CHARLIE: *(Cautious.)* It ain't big or nothin'. I mean, you gonna have to maybe sleep in the couch.

RAY: Kitchen floor do for me. Hey, you got a bird. What's your name, bird?

CHARLIE: That's Swee'pea.

RAY: Swee'pea. That's nice.

CHARLIE: *(Lecturing.)* And I know you're gonna work hard and meet your obligations. It's not easy comin' out of the slammer, and I told Charlotte I'd give you a hand, but you gonna have to work. She says that's part of the parole. You want to rest your coat?

RAY: No, I'm OK. And Uncle Charlie, trust me, you don't have to worry 'bout that other stuff, 'cause I am not going back. I'm a reformed person. Look at this, a new TV.

CHARLIE: *(Uncomfortable making small talk.)* Yeah, the other one it just finally busted. My friend Mac give me a picture he painted, and I had to sell it for the money. Woman give me six hundred dollars for it.

RAY: Six hundred dollars? For a picture of what?

CHARLIE: It's not that kind of picture.

RAY: What kind of picture is it?

CHARLIE: It kinda looks like a duck.

RAY: Six hundred dollars for a picture of a duck. And probably she woulda paid a lot more, that's how those things work. White woman, right?

CHARLIE: *(Uncomfortable.)* She was white, sure, but she didn't seem like she was taking advantage. I mean, I wouldn't say that.

RAY: That picture was probably worth two or three thousand dollars. You think she gonna pay you what it's worth? I don't think so. Black man comes to her with something she wants, she ain't gonna say let's do the right thing for this black man. She gonna say, how much can I steal this for. 'Cause that's what they like to do. It ain't worth it to them 'less they rob you.

CHARLIE: I don't think that's what it was. 'Cause she give the whole six hundred. Paid for the whole television out of that. Plus a toaster oven and a microwave.

RAY: If she give you six right out, that's 'cause she don't want you thinking about it! You got that money in your pocket, you ain't thinking about nothin', that's what they like! She don't want you thinkin', how come she's trying to get rid of me so fast? Maybe six hundred isn't such a good deal now. White women, that's how they work. Lookin' to make you a fool, that's how they work.

CHARLIE: Well, I don't know about that.

RAY: You got peanut butter? 'Cause all I'm saying, you got to be aware of what the white man's tryin' to do to you. I spent four years in prison for a robbery I didn't even do, and I regret none of it, you know why? 'Cause it taught me 'bout the world. Now I see what's comin', 'cause of what the white man and the black man mean to each other. There is going to be a racial explosion and that's just a fact. Other than that, the only solution is a complete separation between the black race and the white race.

CHARLIE: Some of them OK, now.

RAY: They's some tarantulas OK too, only I don't want 'em sleepin' in my bed. Look at this place, all you got's four walls and a bird, that white woman won't even let you buy a decent TV. That's all I'm saying. You went to Vietnam.

(There is a pause at this, as Ray eats peanut butter.)

CHARLIE: (Finally.) Little more money, I coulda got cable, I guess.

RAY: That's what I'm sayin'. That's all I'm sayin'.

(He continues eating peanut butter. Blackout.)

SCENE NINE

Sylvia's apartment. Another dinner party is in full swing. This time, Kidman is one of the guests. They are looking at a painting.

SYLVIA: Do you like it?

KIDMAN: Like? I don't know. It's hard to talk about paintings that way.

SYLVIA: How would you talk about it?

KIDMAN: Well, I wouldn't go so far as to say that it's bad. For instance, it's not that I wouldn't piss on it if it was burning. But that's sort of the general area I'd use in discussing it.

SYLVIA: Oh really.

KIDMAN: It's just not my kind of thing.

PHILLIP: Why don't you like it?

KIDMAN: You mean, besides the fact that it's ugly?

LILLIAN: It's never been my favorite, either, Sylvia —

SYLVIA: What do you mean, you never told me that.

EUGENE: I think —

SYLVIA: You stay out of this. Well I don't care. I like it very much. This artist is very successful.

KIDMAN: Oh yeah, well then what do I know.

PHILLIP: Not only that, but this particular piece has been especially well-reviewed.

KIDMAN: Oh, the asshole critics like it, there you go. That means it's art.

SYLVIA: No, it's not just that, although they're professionals, I don't see why I shouldn't take their recommendations. I do take their recommendations, and besides that, I like it a great deal.

LILLIAN: That's what matters.

KIDMAN: No it's not. I mean, this is — can I have more of this?

(He holds up his glass. Eugene refills it.)

SYLVIA: It doesn't matter that I like it?

KIDMAN: No, because you don't know anything.

SYLVIA: Lillian!

LILLIAN: *(Trying to save this.)* Maybe we should eat.

(She steers them to the table, where they sit.)

SYLVIA: Well, I don't like abstract paintings. So clearly, there are just different opinions on this matter.

KIDMAN: Yeah. Right ones, and wrong ones.

LUCAS: You've hurt her feelings, she doesn't mean it. You like some abstract paintings, Sylvia. I took you to the de Kooning retrospective, you loved it.

SYLVIA: I was being polite. Oh some of it was all right, I like the colors. I just don't like it when I can't tell what a picture's about.

LILLIAN: It's about whatever you want it to be about. However it makes you feel.

SYLVIA: I know, I know, but I don't like that.

KIDMAN: *(Fed up.)* Then don't look at it.

SYLVIA: Well, that's no answer.

KIDMAN: Yes it is.

SYLVIA: Well, I have to look at it. If I don't I won't ever know if I can like it.

KIDMAN: You just said you didn't.

SYLVIA: Maybe I'll change my mind.

KIDMAN: *(Getting fed up with this.)* Who cares if you change your mind? You're a moron!

SYLVIA: Oh really!

LILLIAN: *(Again trying to save this.)* I think what Mac means is he doesn't particularly feel the need to defend his idiom. Nor should he. It's like a Frenchman defending the fact that he speaks French.

SYLVIA: If he were speaking French, I'd like him much better.

PHILLIP: Well, I think that Sylvia might have a point.

SYLVIA: Thank you.

PHILLIP: That's not to say that I object to Abstract Expressionism per se. But if the subject of American art is in fact "The New," as Hughes posits, then how do you justify it's return, a mere thirty years after its flowering?

LILLIAN: It's American Neo-classicism. The only significant movement that was absolutely defined by American artists is, after all, Abstract Expressionism —

PHILLIP: Oh Lillian. Andy Warhol is spinning —

LILLIAN: I don't care; Pop Art was a dead end. The whole scene just turned into one huge disgusting crowd of poseurs and hypocrites, and I ought to know. People are hungry for art again, real art, beauty, truth, and everything else holy and good that got tossed out in the eighties. That's what we're going to give them.

LUCAS: You are so good.

LILLIAN: Thank you, and I've barely even begun. Mac and I are planning on making a ton of money, aren't we Mac?

KIDMAN: A ton of money. That sounds about right.

LUCAS: Careful, Mr. Kidman. You're very close to admitting that you very much care if people like your paintings after all.

KIDMAN: I only care if they buy them. The only one who has to like them is me.

LUCAS: Ah. A romantic distinction.

PHILLIP: Really, well, forgive me, but I think you'll care if the critics like them.

KIDMAN: *(Starting to lose it.)* Yeah, OK —

PHILLIP: Am I wrong? Because from what we heard you stopped showing because of one or two bad reviews —

KIDMAN: You don't know dick about it, asshole.

PHILLIP: Have I touched a nerve?

KIDMAN: *(To Lillian.)* Who are these people?

LILLIAN: Leave the critics to me.

SYLVIA: You see, I was right. You care if the critics like you.

KIDMAN: Hey, I didn't ask to come here. I mean, this is horseshit —

LILLIAN: All right, Mac, thank you —

KIDMAN: This fucking homo trying to tell me something about my work. I
    mean —

PHILLIP: *(Outraged.)* Excuse me? What did you call me?

LILLIAN: All right, that's enough! No more talk about art, or artists or critics.
    Let's talk about something else. Eugene —

EUGENE: *(Awakening from an ironic stupor.)* Yes —

LILLIAN: Another topic, any topic.

LUCAS: Except poverty.

LILLIAN: Yes, except that.

EUGENE: Oh, all right. I was reading the other day about serial killers —
    (All react.)
    — Yes, and how psychologists have observed that these killers have actu-
ally driven themselves mad with self-loathing, and so the only time
they're not in pain is when they're inflicting pain on others. The pleasure
of murdering another human being is the only thing that makes life liv-
able to them. And when I read this, I thought, my God, serial killers are
just — critics. It's exactly the same thing.
    (There is a terrible silence at this. Kidman suddenly roars with laughter.)

LILLIAN: *(Dry.)* Thank you, Eugene.

EUGENE: You're welcome.
    (Blackout.)

SCENE TEN

*Kidman's apartment. Jenny sits at the table, trying to do homework for her
GED class. Willie, her brother, is there bothering her. He is an entertaining
jerk.*

WILLIE: So he's gonna do it? He's really gonna show? And you're gonna let
    him?

JENNY: Oh, like he listens to me.

WILLIE: This is insane. It's suicide. Do you remember what happened the last time?

JENNY: Of course I remember —

WILLIE: Jesus, Mom ended up in jail.

JENNY: It wasn't her fault.

WILLIE: Of course it wasn't her fault. It was all his fault. I'm just saying, Jesus. It's going to be a bloodbath. He's gonna show? What moron decided to give him a show?

JENNY: Some woman.

WILLIE: Is he screwing her?

JENNY: No. I don't know.

WILLIE: Do women still like him even? He's always seemed so repulsive to me. Like some big disgusting cowboy. Why you stay with him, I will never understand.

JENNY: Somebody has to. He'll starve.

WILLIE: Good riddance. What a jerk. Remember when he got drunk and locked us in for three days? Remember that? What an asshole. Why do you stay here?

JENNY: It wasn't three days, it was one day.

WILLIE: It was one and a half days, because Charlie came up and heard us yelling and picked the lock. As you'll recall, Mac didn't come back for three entire days. He didn't know Charlie had picked the lock. As far as he was concerned, which wasn't very far —

JENNY: Willie, could you — God. I mean, I'm glad to see you, I am, but do you have to —

WILLIE: I'm just saying, Jesus. Look at this, you're still studying for your GED, that's pathetic.

JENNY: Oh well, thank you, I appreciate the support.

WILLIE: I mean that in a good way. I mean, it's pathetic, he's feeding off you like some sort of giant bug, why don't you leave him? Come live with me. You're my sister, I love you, come live with me.

JENNY: You just want me to live with you because you hate him and you want him to starve.

WILLIE: Hey, if he starved, I'm not saying I wouldn't enjoy that. He's an asshole. He murdered Mom.

JENNY: He didn't —

WILLIE: Why do you defend him?

JENNY: I'm not defending him. It's just, you know, I was there too. I was there more than you. And I know he made a lot of mistakes, but Mom died of cancer, and I just don't — why can't her death just be hers? Why does it have to be part of him?

WILLIE: You don't think he had anything to do with her getting sick, and when he was too drunk to take her in for chemo —

JENNY: Oh God, Willie. Let's just have a good time, huh? I hardly ever get to see you. It's so great, you came over, and I just — I just don't want everything to always be about him.

WILLIE: That's what I'm saying. You shouldn't let him do this show. He'll be insufferable. And drunk. And then he'll get so worked up, we'll have to listen to him go on about the critics ad infinitum, aye yi yi —

JENNY: He's already started.

WILLIE: See? See?

JENNY: Please, he never stopped. Drinking, sometimes I can get him to stop drinking. But obsessing about the critics, no way.

WILLIE: Why do you stay with him?

JENNY: He's a really good painter.

WILLIE: That's not a reason.

JENNY: Do you want a drink?

(He looks up at this, startled. She grins at him.)

WILLIE: A drink?

JENNY: A gin and tonic. Would you like a gin and tonic?

WILLIE: A gin and tonic?

JENNY: Have you ever had one?

WILLIE: Yes I've had a gin and tonic. You don't drink.

JENNY: I drink. I started drinking; I drink gin and tonics. Do you want one?

WILLIE: I'm stunned.

(She finds gin and tonic in the refrigerator and starts making a couple drinks.)

JENNY: Oh why? Everybody in the world drinks. I got tired of not drinking. Everybody else just does whatever they want, I should be able to have a drink once in a while.

WILLIE: No, of course, you were just so against it. You're so good.

JENNY: I don't want to be good anymore.

WILLIE: I don't think it's optional with you.

JENNY: I'm not saying I'm going to go out and, and start being mean to people.

WILLIE: Heaven forbid.

JENNY: I just want to relax a little. What's wrong with that?

WILLIE: Nothing. Does this mean you're going to start dating?

JENNY: Maybe.

(She hands him a drink.)

WILLIE: The entire West Side just heaved a huge sigh of relief.

JENNY: (Laughing.) Yeah, here's to it.

(They toast. There is a knock on the door. Jenny goes to answer it.)

JENNY: (Continuing.) Who's that? Charlie?

(Eugene enters, carrying Mac. Both are drunk.)

EUGENE: It's me.

KIDMAN: (Drunk.) This is a great guy, Jenny. You need to talk to this guy. He's fantastic.

JENNY: Dad, would you — aww Jesus.

(She helps him sit, annoyed.)

EUGENE: Who are you?

WILLIE: Who are you?

JENNY: His name's Eugene. He's, his girlfriend is the woman who's giving Mac his show.

KIDMAN: What's that, gin? You're drinking gin?

(To Eugene.)

Let's have a drink.

WILLIE: Yes, have a drink. That's what you need. Because as usual you are nowhere near drunk enough.

KIDMAN: Shut up. You're never here, I don't have to listen to you.

JENNY: I'm here all the time. Will you listen to me?

KIDMAN: No. We saw the gallery, Jenny. It's amazing. It's amazing.

WILLIE: Yeah, I heard you were showing. What a great idea, Walter, that was so much fun for everyone, when you were doing that.

KIDMAN: Fuck you.

WILLIE: Fuck you too.

EUGENE: Who are you?

(To Jenny.)

Who is this?

JENNY: This is my brother, Willie.

EUGENE: You have a brother?

JENNY: Of course I have a brother.

EUGENE: You never talk about him.

(To Willie.)

They never talk about you.

WILLIE: They both wish I was dead.

JENNY: That is so not true!

KIDMAN: I wish he was dead.

WILLIE: Yeah, see, Mac wishes I was dead, and Jenny wishes I didn't wish Mac was dead. It evens out.

KIDMAN: *(Again on his own track, making drinks.)* We went to the gallery. It's nice, it's not great —

EUGENE: But it's big. Bigger than it —

KIDMAN: *(Overlap, agreeing.)* Bigger than it looks.

EUGENE: *(Overlap.)* And we hung like six of them. It's — man, you should —

KIDMAN: *(Overlap.)* Drinking and hanging paintings, you should see it, Jenny.

EUGENE: They look amazing.

KIDMAN: Amazing, right?

EUGENE: They look amazing.

JENNY: Dad, don't drink anymore.

(She tries to take the drink from him.)

KIDMAN: This was here! I didn't buy it!

JENNY: I bought it, I bought it for me, and —

KIDMAN: *(Amazed.)* You're drinking? You shouldn't drink.

JENNY: You shouldn't drink.

KIDMAN: No no, I drink all the time.

JENNY: Dad, give me the drink.

KIDMAN: You're so good.

JENNY: I am not good.

EUGENE: Yes you are.

JENNY: I am not good!

KIDMAN: *(To Willie.)* He thinks she's interesting.

WILLIE: I just bet he does.

EUGENE: *(Off Jenny, drunk.)* She's interesting. What's so wrong, all I said was she's interesting.

JENNY: *(To Eugene.)* Could you leave, please? I have to get him to bed.

KIDMAN: No, no! He came to see you.

EUGENE: *(To Kidman.)* I came to bring you home.

KIDMAN: Oh please. I been wandering this city drunk for more years than you were born. You shoulda seen it, Jenny. The gallery. They look great on those walls. You're gonna love it. I know you don't want me to do this, but they look great, the paintings look like, you know, fuck you! All of you, they look fucking amazing, and we are gonna make a ton of money, I'm gonna take you to Italy, Jenny —

(To Willie.)

— Not you because she's the one who stuck it out, and I'm gonna take you to Italy and I'm gonna feed you pear number three, you think you know food, but you don't know food because you've never been to Italy, and we're gonna — you — we —

(His mood suddenly drops.)

I'm a piece of shit.

WILLIE: Oh, there's a news flash.

JENNY: Willie.

KIDMAN: *(Brightening suddenly.)* No, he's right. So what, I'm a piece of shit. Those are great fucking paintings, and they look great and you can quit your fucking day job, because I am going to make a ton of money. Do they look great or what?

(He laughs, delighted. He throws his arm around Eugene, who laughs too at his sudden good humor. Mac takes Eugene's drink.)

EUGENE: They look fucking amazing.

JENNY: Don't give him that.

KIDMAN: You don't believe us? Believe me, darling, 'cause this time the truth will set you free. Those paintings are damn fucking good.

(He hugs her. She starts to laugh, finally infected by his mood.)

JENNY: I know, Dad, I've been telling you that for years —

KIDMAN: They're fucking great.

EUGENE: It's true. I've seen a ton of these shows, and this is a great show. It doesn't matter what the critics say.

KIDMAN: No, 'cause they're idiots. *(Laughing.)* They're serial killers, that's what we figured out.

(Eugene and Kidman are laughing.)

WILLIE: Well then you should all get along fine. Killing Mom, killing me, killing Jenny, you have much more in common than anyone thought.

JENNY: Willie —

WILLIE: I'm kidding! You have no sense of humor. You're too good.

JENNY: I'm not good!

KIDMAN: You are good, my sweetie pie. You're my good girl.

(He kisses her on the forehead, and then slumps on her. She helps him in a chair, and takes the bottle of gin from him.)

JENNY: Oh, Daddy.

EUGENE: He's all right.

JENNY: He's not all right. I mean, why do you think he's drinking like this? He's scared to death.

(She takes the glasses to the sink, annoyed now.)

EUGENE: No, you should have faith. It really is a great show. If he keeps his mouth shut and doesn't insult the wrong people, he'll be the next big thing.

WILLIE: So how much did he drink?

EUGENE: Not that much. Some, you know, wine with dinner, and some scotch, this gin here, then at the gallery people had, tequila, I think.

JENNY: Oh that's really great.

EUGENE: He's the one who brought it.

JENNY: And you just let him drink as much as he wanted.

EUGENE: Oh, you try telling him what to do.

JENNY: I do.

EUGENE: Yes, and I see how successful it is.

JENNY: You should go. Could you just go? Willie, give me a hand.

(She goes to Mac and tries to help him stand.)

JENNY: *(Continuing.)* Come on, Daddy.

(He slumps over.)

EUGENE: I'll help.

JENNY: It's fine.

EUGENE: Come on, let me help.

WILLIE: It's not fine, Jenny.

(He has picked up a cellophane packet that fell out of Mac's pocket. Jenny looks over, startled, as Willie looks in Mac's face.)

WILLIE: *(Continuing.)* Mac? Come on, Dad, what is this stuff?

JENNY: What is it?

WILLIE: I don't know. Come on, Mac, talk to me.

(But Mac is completely out. He slumps to the floor. Willie tries to hold him up. Jenny looks at the pills, horrified.)

JENNY: What is this? What is this?

EUGENE: *(Startled.)* I don't know. I didn't — I don't know where he got that.

JENNY: Call 911.

EUGENE: I didn't know.

JENNY: Call, would you call?

(Desperate, Willie looks for the phone.)

JENNY: *(Continuing; to Mac.)* Dad? Come on, Dad. Talk to me, Dad. Daddy?

WILLIE: Where's the damn phone?

JENNY: Come on, Dad. Oh no. Daddy come on. Please.

(She holds him. Blackout.)

END OF ACT I

ACT II
SCENE ELEVEN

Charlie's apartment. One of Ray's friends is there, completely comatose from the crack they are both smoking. The microwave is gone. Ray takes a hit off the crack pipe.

RAY: If negroes were actually citizens, we wouldn't have a racial problem. There is going to be a racial explosion. The only solution now is complete separation between the black race and the white race. Just as the white man has the right to defend himself, we have the right to defend ourselves. We don't hate him. We love ourselves. For the white man to ask the black man why do you hate us, is like the wolf asking his victim, do you like me? The white man is in no moral position to ask us anything.

JORDY: *(Mumbling.)* Yeah, OK.

RAY: Look at you. Your sorry white ass wasted on crack, nobody in their right mind be smoking this shit no more, but here's you and me suckin' it down, what you think's gonna happen if we get busted on this? You get sent to rehab and I'm back on Rikers for selling it to you.

JORDY: *(Correcting him.)* I sold it to you.

RAY: I'm talking white man's logic, fool. White man goes down on an O.D., everybody talks what a tragedy, big fucking articles in the newspapers. This happened right here, I'm talking right in this building, piece of shit white man gets himself fucked up on pills and booze and everyone's all upset. Black man O.D.'s, you think it's gonna show up in the papers? More like they try to arrest his dead ass. Dead white man, he's in the newspaper, meanwhile I'm still on parole for a job I didn't even do.

JORDY: You did that job.

RAY: That's not the point. I'm trying to tell you something.

JORDY: And I'm trying to tell you, you're full of shit, and you know why? Because O.J. walked.

RAY: You want to talk to me about O.J.?

JORDY: I don't want to talk about O.J.

RAY: You want to talk about O.J.?

JORDY: I don't want to talk about O.J.

RAY: 'Cause in case you failed to notice, O.J. was found innocent in a court of law. That man is a hero and I'm not saying he didn't do it, what I am sayin', he got himself a fair trial, which is something that has hitherto been denied to the black man. The only way the black man can earn respect in a white man's world is by having money, and that is what O.J. knew, and he stood up before this entire nation and said, I'm not your nigger, I am a rich man and I am going to buy me some justice, just like you white men been doing for hundreds of years. That is what O.J. did. And don't get me started on Nicole, 'cause that's not to say she wasn't asking for that shit —

JORDY: Aw come on, I don't want to talk about O.J.!

RAY: Yeah, white people don't want to talk about O.J. 'cause they don't like to hear the truth.

JORDY: Fuck the truth,

RAY:. Come on.

(Jordy offers him the pipe.)

RAY: There's gonna be a race war. Count on it. Now, gimmee that.

(Ray takes it and takes a hit.)

RAY: *(Continuing.)* This is good shit.

JORDY: It is indeed.

(They laugh. Blackout.)

SCENE TWELVE

Jenny's apartment. Eugene is there, talking to Charlie.

EUGENE: How is she?

CHARLIE: Not so good. Well, you know. It's a shock for everybody. I don't know what I'm thinking half the day.

EUGENE: Yes.

CHARLIE: All those years he was just a wild man, this never happened. Don't seem right, things finally looking up. You were here, they said.

EUGENE: Yes.

CHARLIE: They said he went real fast.

EUGENE: Yes.

CHARLIE: Yeah, that's what they said.

EUGENE: I'm here . . . I have something for Jenny.

CHARLIE: *(Awkward.)* She said nobody but me and Willie. Plus she's sleeping, I don't . . .

EUGENE: Of course.

(Explaining, awkward.)

It's just, she's going to need money. Funerals, and the hospital, emergency rooms are expensive. Death is expensive.

(*He holds out a check.*)

CHARLIE: I don't think she's gonna take that.

EUGENE: It's hers.

JENNY: Hey, Charlie, it's OK, I'll talk to him.

(*She stands in the doorway, sleepy, looking at the men. She clutches a sweater, which she wears over a nightgown.*)

JENNY: (*Continuing.*) What is that?

EUGENE: It's from the show. The paintings, some of them were pre-sold. This is your money. I just thought, you'll probably need it.

(*She steps forward and looks at the check, confused.*)

JENNY: The show isn't until next week.

EUGENE: Tonight, actually, it's tonight.

(*A beat, explaining again.*)

But some of the paintings are sold already. It's something the galleries do sometimes; they let important collectors come before the opening when there's a sense that it's potentially a big show.

(*He is increasingly embarrassed. Jenny is confused.*)

JENNY: What do you mean, a big show? How would they know? No one knew who he was.

EUGENE: (*Apologetic.*) They know these things. There's a machinery. Publicists, you know.

JENNY: (*Ignoring him.*) Yeah, but this can't be right. Look at this, Charlie, this is a lot of money.

(*She shows the check to Charlie.*)

CHARLIE: They paid that for Mac's paintings?

EUGENE: Actually, that's only 50 percent. That's Mac's cut. It's your money.

JENNY: Well, I don't need that. I'd rather have the paintings back.

(*She puts it on the table.*)

EUGENE: The paintings are sold.

JENNY: So, give them their money back.

CHARLIE: Can I get my picture back?

EUGENE: I don't think you understand. This is an important event. What's happened? The show is an important show.

JENNY: Oh yeah, now he's important, now that he's dead.

(*She sits, miserable.*)

CHARLIE: You want anything, honey? How 'bout I fix you a sandwich?

JENNY: Maybe some water would be good. I don't know.

(She looks around, honestly perplexed.)

Doesn't it seem weird, he's not here? It's like, I can't believe how much it looks like the same place. Look, the walls, they're the same walls, and the door is the same door. That night, when we came back from the hospital, I found a tube of paint behind the coffee machine. Burnt Umber. He dropped it there, sometimes, he would get in the middle of something and then go for something else and lose his paint. You know, he did that. So his paint's still here. I can't quite figure it out.

EUGENE: Jenny. You're going to need somebody to help you.

JENNY: Help me what?

EUGENE: Things are going to start to happen.

JENNY: *(On a different track again.)* I don't understand why I can't get those paintings back. I mean, what's the point, he's not here, what's the point of having the show?

EUGENE: The paintings have been sold. People think he's important.

JENNY: Stop saying that. He wasn't important when he was alive. He's not allowed to be important now.

CHARLIE: Don't talk about it sweetie.

JENNY: *(Starting to cry.)* Charlie.

CHARLIE: It's OK, sweetie.

(He goes to her. To Eugene.)

You want to help, go see if you can get those paintings back.

EUGENE: I don't think I can.

CHARLIE: Mine looks like a duck.

(They both look at him, miserable.)

EUGENE: *(Beat; defeated.)* I'll see what I can do.

(Blackout.)

SCENE THIRTEEN

Lillian's office. She is on the phone. Eugene sits before her.

LILLIAN: *(To Eugene.)* Is she insane?

(On the phone.)

No, not you, Ivan. I know, that's — yes, I'll be there, I'LL BE THERE I just have to take care of this. Do not let the *Times* go, I need to talk to that guy.

(Another line rings.)

Just a minute.

(She beeps it.)

Hello. Hi, Sy. Yes, it's stunning, it's really an astonishing show and it's such a tragedy what happened, the timing was just hideous, not that there's ever a good time to die, God, I sound so, but how can you ever talk about death without sounding like an idiot? I just, he was a personal friend and I really feel wretched. Yes, I know, Fred came by last week, and — I wish I could — yes, of course there are, he's been painting for years in obscurity, his loft is — I don't know, the daughter is desolate and it's just not clear what her plans are, much too soon, but as soon as I know I'll call you. Yes. This week. I'll —

(Three lines beep at once.)

Sy, I've got to go, the place is a zoo. Yes, this week.

(She hangs up, interjects to Eugene.)

Fuck him. I told him two weeks ago this was going to happen, it's not my fault he didn't — hello.

(She picks up another line.)

Ivan, I'll be there. Just give me three minutes. Look, we know it's a rave; that's not going to change if I make him wait for three minutes.

(She hangs up, grabs the other line.)

Ivan, I'll be there!

(She hangs up, continuing her rant to Eugene.)

Vanity Fair wants to do a major profile, they're talking to Dominick Dunne. Every major art critic is raving, the value of those fucking paintings tripled overnight, and she wants them BACK? That is not a realistic position, and I know she's in pain, God knows we're all devastated, but this is no time for sentimentality! Neal Costello is on the verge of offering him a retrospective at MOMA, which is astonishing given that the damn show hasn't even been reviewed yet, and in case you didn't notice, the fucking *New York Times* gave him a picture with an obit written by Robert Hughes himself, hasn't it even occurred to anybody that that didn't just happen? Mac isn't here to see this, well, he's going to get his moment in the sun just the same and it's not like I'm just doing this for myself by the way, so you just stop glowering at me like —

EUGENE: *(Overlap.)* If I'm glowering, it's because you haven't given me a moment to get a word in edgewise!

(The phone suddenly rings again.)

(Angry.)

Do you think you could put that thing on hold and talk to me for just one minute?

(She does. She looks at him.)

LILLIAN: I'm sorry. But as you can see, a lot is happening, very quickly, and if I don't take care of this, now, someone truly hideous is going to step in and exploit the whole thing.

EUGENE: That's hardly a reason for you to exploit it.

(Beat.)

LILLIAN: You find this grotesque.

EUGENE: Yes, I find it grotesque! You need to slow down. That poor girl is devastated —

LILLIAN: Well, that "poor girl" might try thinking about her father for once —

EUGENE: Don't start on her.

LILLIAN: Don't you start. I've been very patient about her, Eugene. After all. She's a cater-waiter who didn't even finish high school, and you tried to pick her up at our engagement party. And it's ridiculous, you thinking I didn't know.

(Beat.)

EUGENE: Nothing happened.

LILLIAN: I know nothing happened. I know.

(Upset, she reaches into her purse, searching for something, drops a prescription bottle.)

I have such a migraine. I'm only saying, this is exactly what he was eating himself up about all those years; this is it. This is what he wanted, and I'm the one who got it for him. And she is not going to fuck it up!

EUGENE: She just doesn't understand —

LILLIAN: Don't explain her to me. Please. I will take it from here. I will let her know that she's not getting her paintings back; the paintings that are here in the gallery are off the table. What is now in negotiation is the rest of the collection. She's sitting on millions, for God's sake, and I'm not talking a few millions. I'm talking many, many millions.

(Eugene starts to hand the bottle to her, then stops and looks at it.)

EUGENE: You just had this filled last week.

LILLIAN: And things have been a little tense since then, and now I have to have it filled again.

(She takes it back from him and shoves it into her purse. She kisses him.)

LILLIAN: *(Continuing.)* Now please, can you please go out and keep Ivan calm for just a few more minutes? That call is still holding.

(Eugene nods, considers her for a beat, and goes. She picks up the phone.)

LILLIAN: *(Continuing.)* Hello? Yes, hi, hi, I meant to call you back, but things are just crazy. I know. It's not clear what's going to happen, the daughter is very confused right now. No, I know, but I truly don't think it's going to be a problem. There's also a son.

(Blackout.)

SCENE FOURTEEN

Jenny's apartment. The light is on. Mac sits at the table, reading the newspaper and eating a donut. Jenny enters the room and sees him. He looks up.

KIDMAN: Did you see this? This guy compares me to Van Gogh. I'm an abstract expressionist, you fucking moron! Van Gogh painted flowers!

JENNY: Daddy.

KIDMAN: *(Reading.)* Christ, this stuff is unbelievable. I mean, it's like all of a sudden I invented painting. Schnabel's just shitting, you know he is. Trust me, he's eating his own liver out. Oh yeah here we go, Basquiat. Yeah, our work is so similar.

JENNY: Daddy!

KIDMAN: What?

JENNY: I can't believe you came back from the dead to read your reviews.

KIDMAN: *(Of course.)* Good reviews?

JENNY: Am I the only person in this whole city who doesn't care about those things?

KIDMAN: I think you are, babe.

JENNY: Great.

KIDMAN: Hey, come on. Somebody writes about you in the newspaper — for instance let's say maybe The Biggest Newspaper in the World — it's a temptation to at least check it out. Christ, this stuff is tedious as shit. How come the most boring people on the planet get to write for the newspapers? I mean, I sat in this apartment for years making one pithy fucking brilliant observation after another, no one put that in the newspaper. Listen to this —

JENNY: *(Cutting him off.)* Do you mind? I'm really not interested.

(Kidman sets the newspapers down, considers her.)

KIDMAN: So how's your lovely brother?

JENNY: Willie? He's fine. Busy. I haven't seen much of him since the funeral.

KIDMAN: Want to know why? He's out there, selling my paintings.

JENNY: *(Confused and surprised by this.)* He can't — he can't sell them without me.

KIDMAN: Hey, he's out there doing it! It's done. And I don't want him to get the money. I want you to get the money. You're the one who stuck it out. He doesn't get shit out of this. I don't care if he is your brother.

JENNY: Would you stop calling him "your brother" like I created him? He's your son.

KIDMAN: Don't remind me, he's a total piece of shit.

JENNY: He is not! He's, what do you expect, anyway, you were such a lousy father, what do you expect?

KIDMAN: *(A gentle rebuke.)* Jenny. Sell the paintings.

JENNY: No.

KIDMAN: I want you too.

JENNY: Well, I don't want to.

KIDMAN: Goddamn it! That's my life in there —

JENNY: It's my life too, Dad. I am the only person, I kept you going, all those years everyone told you it was shit, and now it's like oh big deal, that's your problem Jenny, none of it was true, that it didn't matter what they all said, it mattered, it's the only thing that did. And now everyone just wants, but that's what I did, with my life, and I know it was stupid, everyone keeps telling me how stupid I've been, but what was I SUP-POSED TO DO, let you die? I told you not to drink, I told you so many times and I know, I'm too good, well, I'm the one who bought the damn — it's my fau — I bought that, you were drinking, that night, if I didn't have that here.

(Beat.)

KIDMAN: Oh, Jenny.

JENNY: *(Immediately defensive.)* No. It's not my fault. You killed yourself, you son of a bitch. You couldn't be bothered to try and live, for me, because I needed you, that didn't even occur to you. You just went right ahead and killed yourself. Well, you're dead now so you don't get everything you want anymore! I'm not selling those paintings.

KIDMAN: Whoa, wait a minute. You're trying to punish me?

JENNY: Why not? It's a good reason. Maybe it's the best. You want to be famous after you're dead? Well, guess what, that's not gonna happen unless I feel like it, and I'm in a bad mood these days.

KIDMAN: You sell those paintings.

JENNY: No.

KIDMAN: You little bitch.

JENNY: Yeah, and you're an asshole.

KIDMAN: It won't make you happy.

JENNY: You don't care if I'm happy! You never cared. You just did what you wanted. You didn't give a shit about me.

KIDMAN: *(Simple.)* That is not true.

JENNY: Why don't you go away? Just go away. You're not here anyway. Are you?

(Beat.)

KIDMAN: No.

JENNY: Then go away.

(She starts to sob. He leaves. As he goes, he picks up the newspapers. She sits alone at the table sobbing. She falls asleep. The lights change; it is morning. Charlie enters. He brings the bird, and a coffee pot.)

CHARLIE: Rise and shine, sweet pea. Jenny, sweetie. Brung you breakfast.

(He touches her on the shoulder. She sits up and looks around. After a moment, she looks at Charlie.)

JENNY: Charlie.

CHARLIE: You sleep out here? You hurt your neck, doing that.

JENNY: *(Sleepy, curious.)* You brought your bird.

CHARLIE: Thought you might like the company. Yeah, she's a real good bird.

JENNY: You can't give me your bird.

CHARLIE: Not to keep, just for a little while. I come up here, I can visit her, watch some TV with you, that's what I thought. Brought you some coffee, too.

(He turns on a light and bustles about. He offers her a bagel from a bag.)

JENNY: *(Taking it.)* Did something happen to your new TV?

CHARLIE: Oh no, it's fine. Real nice. Here you go.

JENNY: Then why do you want to come up here, our TV is terrible.

CHARLIE: Just for the company, sweetheart, that's what I meant.

JENNY: Charlie.

(He hesitates. She waits for his answer.)

CHARLIE: Ray took it, I guess.

JENNY: *(Disappointed.)* He sold your TV?

CHARLIE: Got the microwave, too.

(A joke.)

Now's he lookin' at Swee'pea funny, I didn't want to take any chances.

JENNY: Look, we have some money around here somewhere, they gave me that big check. Let's go buy you a TV set.

CHARLIE: No no.

(She finds the check.)

JENNY: Yeah, why not. I don't have anything to do with this, now that Mac's not here. Let's buy you another TV set. It would make me feel better.

CHARLIE: We could buy you a TV set.

JENNY: I don't watch TV

CHARLIE: Everybody watches TV

JENNY: I don't want a TV I want you to have a TV

CHARLIE: Well, let's just wait, then. You buy me another TV, Ray's just gonna sell that one, too.

(She sighs, sets the check down, and checks the bagel.)

JENNY: What is this, lox spread?

CHARLIE: Yeah, I know that's your favorite.

JENNY: *(Starting to eat.)* This is excellent.

CHARLIE: Only the best for you, honey.

JENNY: You shouldn't be spending your money on me. And you should kick Ray out. Selling your TV It's not right.

CHARLIE: He's my sister's boy, Charlotte. She's a nice person, worked hard her whole life trying to keep him out of trouble. I hate to give up on him on account she's his mama. When I come back from the war, she used to just sit with me for days. Everybody else acting like you gotta get over this now, and here's this nine-year-old girl just willing to sit. It meant something, you know. I don't like to talk about the war now, but afterwards, you feel so beat down, like every one of us, not even that you don't have a soul, but if you do, it's a evil thing, and this world needs to spit us out. All that killing teaches you what a man's worth and that's the sad truth. Then there's this little girl, just sitting there, waiting for me to say something, day after day. Sometimes we'd take a walk. And I started thinking, there's another side to things. Can't put a price on a life. We're worth more than killing alone. That's what she give me. And now, she got so much hope sunk into that boy, I just hate to give up.

(He joins her, eating the bagel.)

JENNY: Well maybe if he got a job. That would help.

CHARLIE: It's hard, black man with a record. Least if he's gonna steal, he's only stealing from me, that's the way I look at it, 'cause honestly, he is not a very good thief. You know how they caught him? He's breaking and entering this dry cleaning operation after hours, climbs down a empty chimney they had there. Then he breaks open the cash register, takes what's there, which ain't much, looks around, can't find the safe, 'cause it's not even on the property, realizes this is all he's gonna get, $72.50, something like that, so he gets mad. Finds a crowbar and trashes the place for kicks, just 'cause he's in a bad mood now, right? So then he goes to the back door, looking to take off? It's locked. Front door's locked too! He can't get out! Tries to climb back out the chimney, get's stuck. All night! He's in there so long he pees his pants! They find him in there, the next day, yelling "Help me, help me!" Four years, breaking and entering. That boy is not bright.

(Jenny laughs. Charlie smiles at her.)

CHARLIE: *(Continuing.)* Four years. For a robbery he didn't even finish? I don't mind he took my television. I'm just back where I started, that's the way I figure it. Serves me right, selling Mac's painting like that. Sure wish I still had that.

(Jenny reaches over and takes his hand, grateful.)

JENNY: You want one? I'll give you one.

CHARLIE: Oh no, sweetie.

JENNY: He would want you to have one.

CHARLIE: He already give me one, and I sold it to that woman, and if I didn't, he maybe would still be here. I know it's stupid to think things like that, but sometimes you can't help it.

(He smiles at her, a sad acknowledgement.)

JENNY: Take a painting. Please.

CHARLIE: Those things are worth something. You can't just be giving 'em away.

JENNY: Why not?

CHARLIE: Well, because it'd be nice to have a little money for once! All those years, you working so hard, keeping things together for Mac. Wouldn't you like a little rest?

JENNY: You just told me your only regret was selling Mac's painting, and now you're telling me that's what I should do? Charlie.

CHARLIE: Yeah, that don't make much sense, do it?

(They smile at each other. The door opens; Willie enters.)

WILLIE: Hey.

JENNY: Willie!

CHARLIE: Hey Willie.

(She hugs him.)

JENNY: Where have you been? You're never here.

WILLIE: So, come live with me, you'll see me more. He's dead now. Come live with me.

JENNY: Do you want some coffee?

WILLIE: Yeah, OK. How have you been? Are you all right?

JENNY: I don't know, Willie, it's all been so — I think I'm making myself a little nuts, stuck in here. I'm so glad you came by. Can you stay? There's bagels, too. Here, you can have some of mine. Lox spread.

WILLIE: Jenny, we have to talk about the paintings.

(She stops at this, looks at him.)

JENNY: What about them?

WILLIE: We have to talk about who is the best person to handle them.

JENNY: What do you mean, "handle?"

WILLIE: Sell. Who we want to sell them for us.

(She looks away.)

WILLIE: *(Continuing.)* I've been down to the gallery, several times, and I've talked to a lot of different people, and I really think we should let Lillian continue to take care of this. She's clearly, she's absolutely as professional as anyone out there; she knew Mac, she loves the paintings —

JENNY: *(Bitter.)* None of this would have happened if she hadn't come along in the first place.

WILLIE: Look, Mac did what he wanted to do. This was what he wanted.

JENNY: *(Angry now.)* Yeah, I know. I know, OK? But I don't care. Nobody's gonna "handle" anything, because I'm not selling anything.

(Beat.)

WILLIE: Do you know how much they're worth now? Millions. Many millions.

CHARLIE: How much?

WILLIE: That's right. This is a good thing, and I'm not going to let you pretend that it's not. Our whole lives have changed. You can move out of this shithole, finish your GED and go to college. You can take a trip if you want. Mac wanted to take you to Italy? Go to Italy. He would want you to go to Italy!

JENNY: He doesn't get what he wants anymore. He's dead.

WILLIE: But you're not. And neither am I. I'm telling you, honestly, when all this started to happen, I admit I was not immediately thrilled. I mean, there's no point in my lying about it; I wasn't Mac's biggest fan. But you know what? All this hoo-ha, Mac's suddenly a genius, you know what I decided? I can live with it. You always wanted me to forgive him, I can do that. You want me to be his son? I'll be his son. I'll tell everybody whacky stories about what a crazy nut he was. What a whacky genius.

And you know what? They'll pay me for the stories. They'll pay you for the stories. And they'll pay us both for those Goddamn paintings.

JENNY: I'm not selling the paintings, Willie! Are you listening to me? I'm not selling them! We are not selling them!

(They stare at each other.)

CHARLIE: Well, I guess I better . . .

JENNY: Charlie, no, stay here, this isn't anything. This discussion is over. Please. Go, take a painting. I want you to have one.

WILLIE: What?

JENNY: I told Charlie he could have a painting! Is that all right with you?

WILLIE: I'm standing here begging you to let go of the damn things and he gets to just walk off with one?

JENNY: You want to sell them!

WILLIE: Yes, I do! They're mine now, I —

JENNY: They're not yours!

WILLIE: They're half mine. I'll take half.

JENNY: You're not taking any.

WILLIE: So he gets one and I don't get any.

CHARLIE: I don't —

JENNY: Yes. Yes! He loved Mac. He loves those paintings. You don't.

WILLIE: I love you! Doesn't that count?

(There is a terrible pause at this. Jenny cannot answer for a moment. Willie turns away, shaking his head.)

JENNY: Of course it does. Of course. I'm sorry, I'm so confused. I don't mean to be like this. I'm sorry.

(He goes to her. Jenny embraces him.)

JENNY: *(Continuing.)* I'm sorry. It's so hard. It's so hard, to know how to be, and you haven't been here —

WILLIE: I'm sorry. I thought I was doing the right thing; I knew you wouldn't want to deal with all this — it's chaos; it is chaos, and I was trying to take care of it so you didn't —

JENNY: *(Overlap.)* I know. I know, you're right, it's just — maybe if you took one, Willie, just for now, just one.

WILLIE: *(Gentle.)* Jenny, one is not going to be enough. They want all of them —

JENNY: Well, they can't have all of them, they — . OK, look. I'll give you one, and you can sell it, and it'll be worth a lot, Willie, they'll give you a lot for that, and, and —

WILLIE: You have to give me more than one, Jenny.

JENNY: *(Suddenly losing it.)* I don't have to give you any! You're just gonna sell it, it's just money to you, it's just MONEY.
(She turns away from him, at a loss. Both Charlie and Willie are stunned into silence at her outburst.)

CHARLIE: Willie, maybe now is not the best time.

WILLIE: Don't you tell me what to do here. This is not your business.

JENNY: It is his business. He is as much a part of this —

WILLIE: No, he's not! You and I were the ones who lived through it, every sorry, miserable sordid fucking moment of that man's misery, Mom's death, you and I were the end result —

JENNY: And the paintings.

WILLIE: They're not a person! They're nothing! He sat in that room and scribbled self-indulgent bullshit for thirty years, while he was also, by the way, ruining our lives, and now all of a sudden, people are saying that scribble is worth a zillion dollars, well, I want the money! Now, I'm sorry Mac's dead, not because I'm really sorry, but I'm sorry for you. OK? I'm sorry because I know you loved him, and I know you're in pain, but I didn't get what you got from him. We all know that. He loved you, and he didn't love me, and he owes me now. And I'm taking those paintings.
(She doesn't answer. They stare at each other, immovable.)

CHARLIE: *(Trying to mediate.)* It's too soon, maybe. Hey, Willie? Maybe it's just too soon.

WILLIE: *(Near tears.)* Jenny. Let me have the paintings.
(She shakes her head. Charlie stands there, awkward.)

CHARLIE: Maybe in a little while. Hey Willie. It's just too soon.
(After a moment, Willie turns and goes. Blackout.)

SCENE FIFTEEN

Sylvia's apartment. Another dinner party. Eugene, Lillian, Lucas, and Philip are there. Lillian and Eugene are arguing.

LILLIAN: *(Heated.)* It's just that this situation with MOMA could not be more out of hand, and if you honestly think —

EUGENE: *(Overlap.)* I realize that, Lillian, but I have been as clear as I know how to be about this —

LILLIAN: *(Overlap.)* That I would be asking, although why I am not, in this situation, permitted to ask for a little bit of help.

EUGENE: *(Overlap.)* That I do not want to be involved. I simply do not want any part of this!

LILLIAN: *(Overlap.)* If not for me, then for Mac. You were fond of him. I just don't understand why you can't do this for Mac.

(This finally silences him. The others look back and forth, a little alarmed.)

SYLVIA: My goodness, a battle royale!

LILLIAN: I'm sorry. I'm sorry, Sylvia.

(She leaves the table momentarily, to collect herself. Philip and Lucas take this in.)

SYLVIA: Oh don't apologize, that was very exciting. And I have to say, I'm on your side. I think Eugene is being a cad about this.

EUGENE: A cad?

SYLVIA: Well, not very nice then. Why shouldn't you pitch in a little. She's working so hard, and all she's asking is that you make a few phone calls. Isn't that it?

LILLIAN: It's all right, Sylvia.

SYLVIA: It's not, oh. Look how unhappy she is. Your bride-to-be. Why won't you help her?

PHILLIP: It's money again.

EUGENE: It's not money.

SYLVIA: Well, what is it?

EUGENE: I don't know, mother, I don't —

SYLVIA: Well, she doesn't have time for you to be confused. She needs your help now.

LILLIAN: Eugene. Just because —

EUGENE: Could we not discuss this here?

LILLIAN: Just because people are now willing to pay for those paintings doesn't mean they've been corrupted. All it means is that people with money have come to recognize what I recognized months ago: The paintings are good. And I just don't think it's wise to get sucked into some impossibly romantic position, that they were somehow "better" when no one was willing to buy them. It's a ridiculous idea, Eugene. It just is. Mac would have tossed it back in your face.

EUGENE: I know he would have.

SYLVIA: Now wait a minute. Is he arguing that those paintings are worth more if no one will pay for them?

EUGENE: I'm not arguing anything.

LUCAS: Sooo . . . you're helping?

(They all stare at him.)

EUGENE: I will talk to her.

LILLIAN: That's all I ask.

SYLVIA: Oh good, we're all friends again. Although I have a confession to make about those paintings. I still don't like them! Well, I'm not saying I don't like them. I don't like them, but it's not that I don't like them a lot. It's just that I don't love them. I like them a little. I just don't know what to think now. All right, I'm just going to say it. I don't care that everyone likes them so much. I still don't like them.

LUCAS: You just don't understand them, Sylvia. That's different.

SYLVIA: Are you sure? Because I think I don't like them.

PHILLIP: Abstract Expressionism is a very intellectual taste. It's not for everybody.

SYLVIA: I'm intellectual. I hope you're not saying I'm not intellectual.

PHILLIP: No no, of course —

LUCAS: *(Overlap.)* No, that's not at all — I think you actually like them, you just don't know it.

EUGENE: Oh, for God's sake —

SYLVIA: Stay out of this, Eugene, please! I'm trying to understand, I want to share in everyone's — everyone's so excited, and I just, I'm sorry but he was so — you didn't really like him, did you?

LUCAS: Who, Kidman? Well, he was difficult —

PHILLIP: He was a homophobe. There, I said it.

SYLVIA: Precisely. He insulted people.

LILLIAN: He had his demons, no one is denying that.

PHILLIP: Oh please, demons. If anyone else had acted like that you would just come out and call him a bigot.

LILLIAN: Yes, and Picasso was a misogynist, and Eliot was an anti-Semite and D. W. Griffiths was a racist. But they were also gifted, and so we look the other way.

(Lillian's cell phone rings. She answers it.)

LILLIAN: *(Continuing; annoyed.)* Ivan —

(To the others.)

Sorry, I'm so sorry, really, I'll be right —

(She leaves the group as they continue their debate. Eugene watches her, worried.)

LUCAS: Well, I suppose the only thing to conclude is, you can enjoy an artist and appreciate his work and still not want to have dinner with him.

SYLVIA: There. That's what I mean. I mean, I feel terrible even, the man is dead after all —

PHILLIP: Sylvia, he was rude to you; he was, and no one expects you to forget that. But the paintings are a different matter.

SYLVIA: *(To Lucas.)* So you actually like them?

LUCAS: They're magnificent.

PHILLIP: They are, Sylvia. We both need to put our feelings about the man aside and just appreciate them apart.

SYLVIA: Apart from the painter, as if someone else painted them.

PHILLIP: Yes. Someone you like. Lucas. What if Lucas painted them?

SYLVIA: Well, if Lucas painted them I would like them because he painted them and he's my friend and I would think oh how wonderful, that I have such talented friends, and I'd throw a big party to celebrate your grand success.

LUCAS: Thank you.

SYLVIA: I wish Lucas had painted them, it would be so much easier on me. Or Eugene, if Eugene had painted them, I'd be the mother of the artist, wouldn't that be fun.

EUGENE: Oh my God.

SYLVIA: Well, why shouldn't I think that would be fun? All you do is sit around and mope about having so much money. At least if you were an artist, I'd have something to be proud of.

(There is an uncomfortable beat while everyone tries not to notice what she just said.)

LILLIAN: *(Snapping.)* Ivan, I cannot deal with this now!

(Beat; to the others.)

I'm sorry, really. I'm so sorry.

(To phone.)

Tell him he'll get it, and I'll call him in the morning.

(She hangs up.)

LILLIAN: *(Continuing.)* Sorry. Where were we?

EUGENE: We were talking about art.

LILLIAN: Of course we were. Sylvia, you do like those paintings. I won't let you not like them.

(She takes her hand, firm. Blackout.)

SCENE SIXTEEN

Kidman's apartment, night. Eugene is there with Jenny.

EUGENE: Thanks for seeing me.

JENNY: No, I was glad to get your note.

EUGENE: I tried calling.

JENNY: I unplugged the phone. People keep calling, newspapers . . . I just unplugged it.

EUGENE: I don't blame you.

JENNY: *(A little awkward.)* So, I was glad to get your note, and I'm glad you came. I've been meaning to thank you.

EUGENE: Thank me?

JENNY: For trying to get the paintings back. I mean, I know that was a crazy thing to ask for. And I never heard back from you. Well, of course, I did unplug the phone. But, thank you for trying.

EUGENE: I didn't —

JENNY: I know, but —

EUGENE: *(Abrupt, suddenly bitter.)* Look, don't thank me, OK? I mean, we all know, I haven't been — look. It wasn't exactly your lucky day when you met me. I know that. I came onto you at my own — and I'm not apologizing for that, that was — and everything else, let's face it. I hunted you down. They probably would have found you anyway, but I was the one, I brought Lillian here, you knew that, I brought her here because I wanted to see you, and then that night, we were drinking, he was, and I knew it was too much and I knew it was a problem and I didn't stop it because I was thinking about you, and how I wanted to see you, and be his friend so I could come home with him, and see you. So don't thank me. Just don't thank me.

(Beat.)

JENNY: It wasn't your fault.

EUGENE: *(Erupting.)* I'm not asking for absolution!

(Beat.)

I'm sorry, but this is — do you know what you're doing? Do you have any idea?

JENNY: *(Confused now.)* No.

EUGENE: I told you, things were going to happen. I told you.

JENNY: What's happened?

EUGENE: They will not stop, do you understand that? You're being a fool! Just sitting here, like some sort of — if you rot in here with them, what will it prove? What will it prove?

(Beat. He looks at her.)

I'm sorry. I don't know what I'm . . .

JENNY: It's OK. It's not your fault.

(He shakes his head, at a loss, and prowls the apartment, looking about. She watches him, confused. He turns on her.)

EUGENE: *(Sudden.)* Would you have dinner with me?

JENNY: Dinner?

EUGENE: Yes, I would like to do something for you. I haven't been able to do anything, and I keep thinking about that first night, when we met — you were so sad, and we were so hideous — and you were waiting on us. Like a servant.

JENNY: I was a servant.

EUGENE: Yes, you were, and you behaved better than anyone else in the room, and I would like to take you to dinner. There are so many beautiful restaurants in this city, beautiful, where the food is like nothing you've ever tasted before, not even in your dreams —

JENNY: *(Smiling slightly.)* Mac said the best food in the world is in Italy.

EUGENE: Oh, no no. I promise you, at this moment in history, food is taken very seriously in New York City, and Italy has been left in the dust. And I would like to take you to a restaurant, with chandeliers, flowers everywhere, staggeringly beautiful bouquets of — six people to wait on you alone. At your place setting, there will be twelve forks, and no one will know what any of them are good for — and there will be champagne, and sorbet, in between courses — to cleanse the palate, the flavors, one stranger than the next. Once, I had sorbet made out of parsley —

JENNY: *(Laughing.)* That sounds terrible.

EUGENE: It was delicious. We will have it between the appetizer and the fish course.

JENNY: What will the appetizer be?

EUGENE: *(Thinking.)* Oysters in a sauerkraut cream sauce topped with Beluga caviar.

(She laughs at this, delighted.)

JENNY: And dessert?

EUGENE: Chocolate crusted coconut sherbet, swimming in a lemongrass citrus soup. And that's just one of them. We'll order four. The other ones, I can't even begin to describe. If I tried, you would never believe another word out of my mouth.

(They smile at each other. He reaches out for her. They kiss. The kiss becomes passionate. She pulls away.)

JENNY: This isn't right.

EUGENE: Jenny, maybe it's time you faced the fact that doing what's right hasn't gotten you anything that you wanted.

(He kisses her again. It starts to get quite heated. She pulls away.)
JENNY: We still have to make it through dinner.
EUGENE: Let's go.
(They do. Blackout.)

SCENE SEVENTEEN

Lillian's gallery. Lillian sits alone, by her desk, smoking a cigarette. She waits for a long moment. The phone rings. It rings again, and then again, and then again, as she considers it. Finally, she reaches forward and picks it up.

LILLIAN: Hello?
(Blackout.)

SCENE EIGHTEEN

Jenny's apartment. The lights are out. Willie sits there, alone, for a long moment. The door swings open. Jenny and Eugene enter, kissing. They do not see him at first.

WILLIE: Jenny.
(She turns, startled.)
JENNY: Willie — oh, man, what? You scared me.
WILLIE: We have to talk.
JENNY: What are you doing here?
WILLIE: We have to talk. He should go.
(He looks at Eugene. There is a terrible pause.)
JENNY: What happened? Something happened.
(She looks around, uneasy. She looks at the door of the studio.)
WILLIE: Jenny —
JENNY: What did you do, Willie?
WILLIE: I took the paintings. OK? I took the paintings.
(She looks at him in horror, then goes to the studio. Willie looks at Eugene.)
EUGENE: You piece of shit.
WILLIE: Look, I'm not going to say anything about whatever it is you're doing here, but this is also none of your business, so —
JENNY: They're all gone. All of them, not one of them is —

(To Eugene.)

Did you know he was doing this?

WILLIE: I did it, Jenny. I did it myself.

JENNY: You couldn't, there were too many of them, you had to — they're all gone, not one, you couldn't leave me one?

WILLIE: I did it for your own good —

JENNY: *(Losing it.)* That is a FUCKING LIE, Willie, would you just — you took the paintings.

(A breath.)

You took the paintings.

(She looks down, trying to stay somewhat on top of this.)

EUGENE: I'm calling the police.

WILLIE: That's not gonna do her any good, and you know it.

EUGENE: *(Pissed.)* Yeah, I don't know anything of the kind, asshole, so —

WILLIE: *(Overlap.)* I already talked to a lawyer, all right, and you know as well as I do, him dying intestate gives me a ton of rights in this situation. I mean, I didn't want to handle it like this. Jenny. You know I didn't. But you didn't leave me much choice.

JENNY: *(Trying to figure this out, upset.)* How did you know? How did you know I was going out tonight, even I didn't — he just came over, and said dinner, I — you couldn't have known. And moving them all, they're all — where are they — he's gone. He's gone.

(She sobs for a moment, turns away. Willie goes to her, touches her shoulder.)

WILLIE: Jenny —

JENNY: Do not touch me! You are not allowed to touch me, Willie. No more. Don't ever try to touch me again.

(He looks at her, shattered.)

WILLIE: I did it for your own good.

JENNY: You did it because you're greedy.

WILLIE: Hanging onto those pictures is not going to bring him back.

JENNY: Don't talk to me about what I'm going through —

WILLIE: *(Overlap.)* He died. He's gone. He maimed your life, he maimed mine, and he's dead now, and you need to try and figure out how to live.

JENNY: *(Overlap.)* This isn't about me — you didn't do this for me!

WILLIE: Yeah, OK, fine, I did it for me. I admit it. I did it to get something back for me. I asked you, I begged you to come live with me. He got Mom, and then he got you, and you have done nothing with your life. You're a cater-waiter for God's sake! And you're sitting here like this is some fucking holy sepulchre, some tomb, some — you're my family too!

I mean, what was it supposed to be, forever, I get nothing? He gets everything, and I —

(He stops himself. She shakes her head.)

WILLIE: *(Continuing.)* I had every right to do what I did.

JENNY: I just needed more time. Why couldn't you —

WILLIE: We did not have time. It was happening now. Time was the one thing
I couldn't give you.

JENNY: You didn't even try. You took them all, all of them — that's not —
that's mean, Willie. That's revenge.

WILLIE: That's not — I tried. God, I did nothing but — I begged you, and
you wouldn't give me any, you wouldn't give me — why didn't I matter?
Why — this is on you, Jenny. This is on you.

(He turns away, furious. She looks at his back, suddenly defeated.)

JENNY: I just couldn't do it. When it was just me and Mac, and the paintings,
I just thought that was better. All those years, watching him paint, he
was so — big. While he was painting? It was a sight to see. And they
were so beautiful. I used to wonder where they came from; the color, and
the light, it was such . . . a gift. From, I didn't know where, but they were
a gift. And I was a part of them. Then when he left, I just wanted to hang
onto that sense that I did something, I — my life wasn't about money.
It was a gift. That's all I was trying to do.

WILLIE: A gift to him, but not to me.

(A beat. She closes down.)

JENNY: You need to get out of here. You got what you wanted. Take the paintings, and take the money, and get out of here, and don't ever come back.

EUGENE: Jenny —

JENNY: Both of you. Leave me alone.

(She goes to her bedroom. Blackout.)

SCENE NINETEEN

Charlie's apartment. It is dark. Ray and Jordy are counting money.

JORDY: No, come on, this ain't right.

RAY: That's right.

JORDY: You think I'm stupid?

RAY: I don't know you're some kind of genius, but that's not saying that ain't
right.

JORDY: Hey Ray, you know what? You talk bullshit. And I'm six hundred short here.

RAY: Hey you want to count my split? 'Cause —

JORDY: Five thousand dollars, you said —

RAY: I said four —

JORDY: Fuck you, man. Don't you fuckin' talk to me like I'm a fuckin' moron!

RAY: It was my gig, I cut you in.

JORDY: I did all the fuckin' work.

RAY: Yeah, how you figure that? 'Cause my memory is I arranged the job, I got the truck —

JORDY: *(Overlap.)* I figure that 'cause you and the skinny guy stood around chatting up old times while I was movin' that shit —

RAY: Bullshit, you a half-brain crackhead, your fuckin' problem —

JORDY: Fuck you —

(He pulls a knife. Ray looks at him, shocked. Charlie enters.)

CHARLIE: Hey, how's it goin' — hey. Whoa. Shit.

(The two younger men look over, startled.)

RAY: Hey, Uncle Charlie.

CHARLIE: What's goin' on?

JORDY: I want my six hundred dollars.

(To Charlie.)

He took six hundred dollars off me.

RAY: I never did.

CHARLIE: Put that thing away. I'm telling you, we are not having any sort of conversation here, till you put that thing away.

(Jordy pockets the knife. Charlie considers them both.)

CHARLIE: *(Continuing.)* OK, Ray. Now why don't you tell me what you did.

RAY: I didn't do nothin'.

CHARLIE: *(To Jordy.)* That right?

RAY: *(Reacting.)* You gonna believe him, over me? Your own nephew, that's real nice. Mama gonna be real happy to hear about that —

CHARLIE: Don't you talk to me about your mama.

(Beat, to Jordy.)

Now, you tell me what this is about.

JORDY: We did this job.

RAY: Whoa — that is not —

JORDY: Yeah, and you're a fuckin' liar, 'cause I heard you talking to that guy, agreement was five thousand dollars, and you stiffed me, man. I am six hundred short. Six hundred bucks. Short.

RAY: That is not —

JORDY: Yeah it is —

CHARLIE: Tell your friend to shut up because I'm talkin' to you now, you little piece of shit.

(Charlie suddenly grabs Ray, shoves him against the couch, reaches into Ray's pocket and takes out a wad of cash.)

CHARLIE: *(Continuing.)* Not enough you stealing from me, you doin' jobs now? You gonna break your mama's heart one more time, that what you're doing?

(He hurls him to the floor. Ray tries to crawl away.)

RAY: No way! It was a legit job! We moved those paintings! No stealing about it!

(Charlie stops, looks at him.)

CHARLIE: You stole Mac's paintings?

(They face off.)

RAY: I moved 'em. Willie told me about his sister goin' crazy, he needs to get them out of there. So that's what we did. I'm on the lookout, see when she takes off, give him a call, and we move 'em.

CHARLIE: *(Taking this in.)* You stole Mac's paintings.

RAY: *(Protesting.)* They ain't called the cops yet, and they ain't goin' to, Charlie. Them things half Willie's to begin with, and she ain't gonna want the trouble.

(Ray starts to pick up the money.)

CHARLIE: 'Cording to Willie.

RAY: That's right. Aside which, he gonna keep us out of it. Cops get involved, he did the whole thing himself. Better for him, better for us that way. I'm telling you, there is no downside here. Till this fool starts up with all his money negotiations.

CHARLIE: They catch you, how many years you back in for?

RAY: I told you, that ain't coming into it.

CHARLIE: Long as you can trust Willie. A white man. Any of it goes wrong, you really think he'll keep you out of it? 'Cause the way I see it, you put your freedom on the line for five thousand dollars.

RAY: Hey, don't you talk to me about money. A black man wants respect in this community, he got to have money, and I'm not talking minimum wage. You go get yourself shot up in Vietnam, how much they give you for that, Charlie? Nine hundred dollars? Nine-thirty-two a month? You can't even buy yourself a TV set! Only way a black man earns respect, he got to have the cash. Then they listen. And now they gonna start listening to me.

CHARLIE: That's fine, Ray. That's a fine way to think about it. 'Cause way it looks to me? White man bought and sold you like a slave.

RAY: *(Stung by this.)* Yeah, listen to you, tired old black man spends all his time running after some white girl. I mean, she's a nice piece of ass, but you honestly think she gonna be dishin' that honey your way? Then again, maybe you'll get lucky. 'Cording to Willie, she's a complete fuckin' nut job.

(Beat.)

CHARLIE: You get out of my house. You get out of this neighborhood. I ever see you again, I'm sending you away.

RAY: You mean I don't get to sleep on your shitty little couch no more? That really breaks my heart.

(Beat.)

See ya 'round.

(He goes. Blackout.)

SCENE TWENTY

Sylvia's apartment. Another dinner party, with Lucas, Willie, Lillian, Eugene, and Sylvia. Mac's painting is there.

LUCAS: You just — took the paintings? You took them! Is that legal?

SYLVIA: Oh, who cares if it was legal? It was bold, and daring, and we applaud you!

WILLIE: *(Answering the question.)* It was no more or less legal than her refusal to give them up. I had to do something.

PHILLIP: Is she going to sue?

WILLIE: I don't know. It's unlikely.

SYLVIA: Well, that's too bad, because if you ask me, the only thing further that we need, is a trial. Wouldn't that be fun?

WILLIE: Really, what I did, I did it for her own good. I think, with time, she'll realize that. I think she may know it already.

(But he doesn't seem too sure. Lillian pats his hand.)

LILLIAN: You didn't just do it for her. You did it for Mac.

WILLIE: Oh —

LILLIAN: Don't be modest. We had many many talks about this, and Willie realized that time was of the essence and his father's legacy, to the world, was the most important consideration. It's true, Willie. What you did was very brave.

SYLVIA: Well, I'm happy things have finally settled down, because you seem like a very nice young man, but I feel that I must be forthright. I was not your father's biggest fan.

WILLIE: No?

SYLVIA: Oh, I love the paintings, of course I love the paintings, but frankly, I found him — difficult.

WILLIE: *(Confiding.)* So did I.

SYLVIA: *(Relieved.)* You didn't like him either. Thank God. But we mustn't judge an artist by the way he behaves. Phillip taught me that.

LUCAS: Well, when your sister feels better about the whole thing, I think we should invite her to dinner. To make the picture complete.

SYLVIA: What? Invite her? But she waited on us!

PHILLIP: Oh my God, I just put it together. That's the girl? The girl who was here, who went on and on about being poor?

SYLVIA: Yes and she's not poor anymore, and you'd think she'd be grateful, instead of just giving everyone so much trouble.

EUGENE: Maybe she just decided some things were worse than poverty.

LUCAS: *(Good-natured.)* Here we go again.

SYLVIA: Change the subject!

LILLIAN: Not at all. I'd like to hear what Eugene has to say.

EUGENE: Would you?

(There is a pause while they face each other from across the table. Their attitude toward each other is distinctly frosty.)

LILLIAN: Yes. Mac's retrospective opens in two weeks, advance word is stunning, his work will be seen alongside every major Expressionist in every major museum in the world in the years to come, and if you think things could have worked out better, I think we'd all be interested in hearing how.

EUGENE: Do you really want me to answer that?

LILLIAN: Why don't you just tell us what's bothering you.

EUGENE: I just think there are loose ends.

LILLIAN: What kind of loose ends?

EUGENE: Questions. You know, after something terrible has happened, a death, everyone sits around and wonders, if I had only done something a little different, maybe this wouldn't have happened. We all blame ourselves.

SYLVIA: It's no one's fault.

EUGENE: I was drinking with him. Someone gave him those pills.

LILLIAN: It wasn't the pills that killed him. It was the pills and the alcohol and the years of sheer, pointless excess that killed him.

(To Willie.)

Forgive me.

WILLIE: It's true. One way or another he was going to do himself in.

EUGENE: Other questions, then. You know, ever since that night, I've been wondering why, when you moved the paintings to the gallery, why'd you take all of them? I understand you were in a difficult situation, but it did seem pretty harsh. Why didn't you leave her just one?

WILLIE: *(Nervous now.)* Well, actually I didn't — I wanted to. But Lillian — she said she needed to see them all.

EUGENE: Really? Why?

LILLIAN: They're important work. They had to be catalogued. She doesn't have proper security in that apartment, not to mention the dust, the heat, the humidity, it's a disastrous environment for fine art. There were many reasons.

EUGENE: Objective reasons.

LILLIAN: What other kind of reasons would there be?

EUGENE: I'm just asking questions, Lillian. It's my nature. Actually, both of us, that may be the reason we first fell in love. We're both the kind of people who look for answers. We sit, we watch, we think. Somehow, we always know what the other is doing.

SYLVIA: *(Joking.)* Well, I don't know if that's such a good thing.

LILLIAN: It's neither bad nor good. It all depends on how one acts. Or doesn't.

EUGENE: On the basis of that knowledge.

LILLIAN: Yes.

SYLVIA: Well, now I don't understand what you two are talking about.

EUGENE: It's all right, mother, we understand each other.

(Standing.)

I've got to go.

SYLVIA: Oh Eugene, you can't! We haven't had the savory yet.

EUGENE: I'm full, Mother. Lillian, you and I — this clearly isn't working out.

LILLIAN: *(Cool as a cucumber.)* No, clearly not.

EUGENE: So that's it then.

LILLIAN: Yes.

(The others look around, surprised.)

LUCAS: What?

WILLIE: *(Sudden, to Eugene.)* Take the painting.

(Eugene stops; looks at him.)

WILLIE: *(Continuing.)* Take it.

(Eugene picks up the painting. The others react.)

SYLVIA: Eugene, what on — sit down. Sit — My Kidman! You can't!

EUGENE: It's not yours, Mother.

(He heads for the door.)

SYLVIA: Eugene, stop it! Stop it, thief! Thief!

(But before anyone can move, he goes. Blackout.)

SCENE TWENTY-ONE

Jenny's apartment. Jenny and Charlie are watching television. Jenny fools with the rabbit ears.

JENNY: There . . . there . . .

(She backs up.)

CHARLIE: Oh.

JENNY: I hate that.

(She gets close again.)

CHARLIE: There it is!

JENNY: Yeah, but I can't stand here all night.

CHARLIE: Try a different thing with the antenna. Like, get it so the picture's not really right, and then when you back up, maybe it'll clear out.

JENNY: Does that work?

CHARLIE: Yeah, it works. Mac used to do it all the time. Here, let me.

(He goes to work on the rabbit ears. She goes back to the table.)

JENNY: I think we're gonna have to break down and buy another TV, Charlie.

CHARLIE: No, this is fine.

(Jenny picks up a pile of envelopes off the table.)

JENNY: No, we should just do it. Willie keeps sending these checks. I should just cash one of them, buy the both of us a nice dinner, and get a decent television set.

CHARLIE: Cable?

JENNY: Yeah, cable. Why not, cable.

CHARLIE: Whoa, whoa whoa, got it.

(He backs away from the set. The two of them watch, entranced.)

JENNY: That's beautiful.

CHARLIE: OK. You want to cash one of those things, that's up to you. I'm just sayin', in terms of entertainment, our needs are taken care of. Ain't that right, Swee'pea.

(He turns to the bird and notices Eugene, standing in the door.)

EUGENE: The door was open.

JENNY: *(Startled.)* I know, I . . . Come in.

(She turns the television off.)

EUGENE: I tried to call. Your phone is still unplugged.

JENNY: I know. I'm crazy.

EUGENE: No, it's totally understandable. I brought you this.

(He brings forward the painting.)

JENNY: Oh.

EUGENE: I'm sorry I couldn't do more.

CHARLIE: *(Seeing the painting, stopping.)* Good Lord, you found my duck.

JENNY: This is the duck?

CHARLIE: That's the duck!

JENNY: It's not a duck.

(Happy, she takes it to a chair and sets it on it, so they can all look at it.)

CHARLIE: What do you mean, that's not a duck. That is a duck.

EUGENE: It's abstract, it can be anything.

CHARLIE: People say that, but I don't know.

JENNY: It's not a duck. It's me.

EUGENE: It is?

JENNY: Yes, of course it's me. Mac wasn't painting abstracts, all those years. He was painting me.

CHARLIE: Oh.

(They look at it for a long moment.)

CHARLIE: *(Continuing.)* Well girl, you look like a damn duck.

JENNY: I do, don't I? I do.

(They continue to look at the painting. Fade out.)

END OF PLAY

THE BUTTERFLY
COLLECTION

ORIGINAL PRODUCTION

The Butterfly Collection was originally produced at Playwrights Horizons during the 2000–2001 season. It was directed by Bartlett Sher and had the following cast (in order of appearance):

SOPHIE	Maggie Lacey
FRANK	Reed Birney
MARGARET	Marian Seldes
LAURIE	Betsy Aidem
ETHAN	James Colby
PAUL	Brian Murray
Scenic Design	Andrew Jackness
Costume Design	Ann Hould-Ward
Lighting Design	Christopher Akerlind
Sound Design	Kurt B. Kellenberger
Director of Development	Jill Garland
Production Manager	Christopher Boll
Production Stage Manager	Roy Harris
Artistic Director	Tim Sanford
Managing Director	Leslie Marcus
General Manager	William Russo

Prior to Playwrights Horizons' production *The Butterfly Collection* was seen in readings at the South Coast Repertory's Pacific Playwrights Festival and at New York Stage and Film Company in association with the Powerhouse Theatre at Vassar, Summer 2000

CHARACTERS

SOPHIE: 28
PAUL: early 60s, a novelist
MARGARET: early 60s, Paul's wife
FRANK: 40, Paul and Margaret's son, an antique dealer
ETHAN: 42, Paul and Margaret's son, an actor
LAURIE: mid-30s, Ethan's girlfriend

SET

The comfortable library/living room of Paul and Margaret's home in upstate Connecticut. A stairway goes up to the second floor, where Paul's office is located. Off left leads to the kitchen and dining room; a doorway to the back porch and yard opens directly onto the living room as well.

ACT I

A woman, Sophie, stands alone and speaks to the audience. She tells her story simply, with matter-of-fact good humor.

SOPHIE: My father's father collected butterflies. This was years ago, in the thirties, and he was quite poor, so he had few resources with which to pursue this elegant hobby, but apparently there was some kind of a network, a network of butterfly collectors, that spread all over the world. These butterfly collectors would write to each other, and trade butterflies through the mail, from exotic locations, Guatemala, South Africa, New Guinea. I don't know more than that, about how it worked, but the fact is, over the years this man collected and preserved many plates of butterflies, beautiful square plates in which he lined the insects up with tiny slips of paper identifying the genus and the species. There were at least a hundred and thirty of these plates; it was an astonishing and exhaustive labor of love. But he died, young, thirty, thirty-two, he caught pneumonia and apparently went very quickly, and as I said, they were poor. So after he died my grandmother took the three children back to her brother's farm in Ohio, where they were equally poor, but at least had family — this brother, and my grandmother's mother, a woman whose legendary meanness is still spoken of, by people who never even met her. The butterflies went with them, but my grandmother had no real idea what to do with them. Huge piles, plates of butterflies, cluttering the barn, or the garage, it must have seemed a strange madness to her. Finally, a neighbor suggested she donate them to the local state university, and one day, someone drove over and picked them up. Years later, when I was fourteen, my mother said to my father, we should go see them, so we drove for hours, to the University of Stubenville, to visit the butterflies. When we got there, no one had any idea what we were talking about, until they found someone who had been there a long time, who said Oh yes, those butterflies. He explained that they had been stored in a poorly insulated closet for years, where they were finally badly damaged by water, and tossed.
(Blackout.)

SCENE ONE

The lights shift to reveal the living room of a large, rambling New England country home. Margaret, Ethan, Laurie, and Frank are examining a small piece of sculpture.

FRANK: Isn't it amazing?

MARGARET: Oh, Frank, it's absolutely stunning.

LAURIE: What is it doing? That's a snake.

FRANK: Yes, the snake is strangling Laocoön, and eating his children. The original is spectacularly gruesome.

ETHAN: What period is it from?

MARGARET: It's just magnificent, Frank.

FRANK: *(Answering Ethan.)* Which, the original or the copy? Because this, I think this is a copy of the copy.

ETHAN: I don't understand what you just said.

FRANK: There's a copy of the original in the Uffizi, and the original, which nobody knows exactly, it's Roman, maybe sixth century, is in the Vatican museum somewhere, no one will ever let you see it. Anyway, the story is it was dug up in the middle of the fourteenth century, they found it in somebody's garden near Florence, in Florence, Rome maybe, I don't remember, and Michelangelo saw it and was just electrified, it changed his entire — this is why, he realized, it spoke to him. It spoke. And he saw what could be done. What sculpture could be. That painting was not, that he was not, in fact, in his soul, he was a sculptor. That's what the Laocoön taught him.

LAURIE: Oh.

(She reconsiders it with new respect.)

FRANK: Yes. Which is why, I think, this piece is probably a copy of the copy. Semi-antique, nineteen ten, eleven, Cabrian marble, hand-carved. Whoever did it was a master. Look at the detailing.

ETHAN: And where did you find this? Somebody in the neighborhood had it just hanging around the house?

FRANK: No, I don't, an estate sale over in Barrington. Some old lady died and the kids were just — it was on the lawn, for crying out loud. In there with framed pictures of cats, and you know, bad jewelry. Who she was, where she got it, it's a mystery. Twelve dollars.

MARGARET: It's exquisite. Congratulations.

FRANK: *(Pleased.)* Thank you.

MARGARET: Your father has to —
(Calling offstage.)
PAUL! Come see what —
(To Frank.)
If you ever decide to sell it, you must let me know first.

FRANK: Oh, no, I'm not —

MARGARET: PAUL! Come see what Frank found! Where did he — wasn't he out back?

ETHAN: I don't know.

MARGARET: He can't be writing, that girl isn't here yet.

ETHAN: There's a new assistant?

MARGARET: She's coming up this afternoon. Well, I don't know where he is.

LAURIE: Does he live? Does he save his children?
(She looks up from the figurine, hopeful.)

FRANK: Laocoön? No. The snake is too powerful. His children die, he dies. It's a terrible story. Ovid, I think. Virgil? Heroditus?

MARGARET: *(Looking up stairs.)* I think he's writing. Oh dear. Well, she's late, isn't she? She's late and he started without her, that's not good.

LAURIE: Does Paul always work with assistants?

MARGARET: Well, the past, what is it now, twenty some odd — at the beginning of course no. He didn't work with anyone.

ETHAN: He worked with you at the beginning, Mom.

MARGARET: Yes, I know, but it wasn't the same. I typed for him, mostly. A little bit of spelling and grammar.

LAURIE: So what do these assistants do?

MARGARET: *(Shrugging, a little smile.)* Typing mostly. A little spelling and grammar.

ETHAN: But he has a Nobel now, so it's much more important typing and spelling and grammar.
(A tortured act.)
More elusive, more luminous spelling and grammar. More evocative and rigorous typing and spelling and grammar.

MARGARET: If you think I like it when you make fun of your father you're wrong, you know.

ETHAN: I don't think that.

FRANK: *(To Laurie.)* How long are you are you here for?

LAURIE: We haven't decided yet. It's so lovely, I can't imagine ever going back to the city. I can't believe how lovely it is here.

FRANK: Well, because I was thinking you should come down to the shop.

Because if you don't get out of the city, often, it's what people do here. Of course people do a lot of things, but antique stores is one of — because there are so many things, like this little Laocoön, just treasures, that people have hung onto for so long. And it's a treat, really, to see them. If you wanted to come down.

LAURIE: Of course I want to see your shop. There should be time for that.

MARGARET: Of course there's time. You're staying for at least a week.

ETHAN: Mom.

MARGARET: Ethan, I insist this time. I've only been hounding you for years. How long have you two been, five —

LAURIE: Two —

MARGARET: Two years. I've been hounding you for two years. Two years.

ETHAN: We've been busy.

MARGARET: For two years?

ETHAN: It's been a very active two years.

MARGARET: (Ignoring him, to Laurie.) And let me just say right now the guest-house is yours. If you wanted to stay all summer, you'd be more than welcome. I wouldn't make that offer if you were here in the house because I think Paul would — well let's face it, we'd all drive each other a bit mad, but the guesthouse gives us just enough distance. Such a wonderful invention: The guesthouse. I do like having money.

ETHAN: Laurie works, Mom.

LAURIE: I can take some time. Really, I intended to take some time, I thought we might —

ETHAN: Well, I have auditions.

LAURIE: Yes, but you could run in for those, couldn't you? It's not that far. I'm not saying the whole summer, but —

MARGARET: Why not? You should stay. The guesthouse is yours. And you have to at least stay for Frank's birthday, that's why you came!

ETHAN: You know very well that even with the guesthouse, I can't possibly stay for more than three days. Last time we tried, it was a bloodbath. Duchess of Malfi, without the laughs. I think it's very brave, verging on foolhardy, that I've agreed to come at all.

MARGARET: Well, if you would be respectful of your father, and you should, after all, he has a Nobel —

ETHAN: I know about the Nobel, Mom!

MARGARET: Well, you don't act like it, that's all I'm saying.

FRANK: He's been asking about you.

(This more or less stops the conversation cold as Ethan considers this.)

ETHAN: He has not.

MARGARET: Yes, he has. Just, out of nowhere. What you're doing. If you're in a show.

ETHAN: You are both pathetic liars.

FRANK: No, it's true. Last week, he asked Mom where your reviews were.

ETHAN: He read my reviews?

FRANK: Yes!

ETHAN: The good ones or the bad ones?

MARGARET: Oh, please. You know I only save the good ones.

ETHAN: Well, if he did read them, it was largely so he could make fun of the writing style.

MARGARET: Oh Ethan —

(Paul enters. He carries with him a handful of pages from a yellow legal pad. They are covered with a loose scrawl.)

PAUL: Where is she, is she here yet?

(He goes to the back door to look.)

MARGARET: There you are, Paul. We were just having some iced tea, would you like a glass?

PAUL: She was supposed to be here this morning, right? Am I wrong about that? Roger said he told her the morning.

MARGARET: I didn't speak to him.

PAUL: I spoke to him. That's what he said. This morning. Hours ago.

ETHAN: Hi Dad, great to see you.

MARGARET: Ethan and Laurie are here for the weekend, but I think they should stay longer, don't you? You remember Laurie. You've met, haven't you?

LAURIE: Yes, several times. In the city.

MARGARET: That's right, at that brunch. And at the theater one night, I'm sure.

PAUL: *(Distracted.)* Yes. Hi. Glad to see you. Ethan. You're staying just the weekend?

ETHAN: We don't know yet. Maybe a while. Frank's birthday is coming up. Maybe we'll stay till then.

PAUL: Oh. Good.

(He looks out the window. Ethan rolls his eyes, but Margaret is clearly encouraged.)

MARGARET: I'm glad you came down, Paul, you'll get to see Frank's little treasure. Frank, show your father the Laocoön.

PAUL: The what?

FRANK: It's not . . .

MARGARET: Look, isn't it fantastic. He found it at an estate sale.

(She indicates the figurine, which Paul considers briefly.)

PAUL: What is it?

FRANK: Its . . . you know, the Laocoön. Michelangelo . . .

PAUL: Michelangelo didn't do this.

FRANK: No. No. He saw it. At an estate sale . . .

PAUL: *(Impatient.)* What?

FRANK: *(Fighting to stay on top of this.)* He saw it, when he was young. It was, it influenced him, he realized what sculpture . . .

(He starts to disintegrate.)

MARGARET: *(Helping out.)* He liked it. It made him want to be a sculptor.

PAUL: And what a terrific career choice that was. Couldn't finish anything except a statue of Moses with horns growing out of his head. If it had been up to Michelangelo, there would have been no Sistine Chapel.

FRANK: Well . . .

PAUL: Artists should never be allowed to make their own decisions.

ETHAN: Oh, my God.

MARGARET: Ethan.

ETHAN: What?

(Trying to be nice.)

I'm sorry, I just, uh — artists should never make their own decisions? That's —

PAUL: Yes?

ETHAN: I don't know. It just sounded a little nuts, to me.

PAUL: "Nuts."

ETHAN: Never mind. Sorry.

(He is trying. Margaret jumps in.)

MARGARET: *(To Laurie.)* He's been writing all morning, with no help. It puts him in a mood.

PAUL: Don't apologize for me. I'm not in a mood, and I'm hardly "nuts." I'm just saying, Michelangelo was no sculptor.

ETHAN: *(Laughing.)* No — What do you call the Pietà?

PAUL: A sentimental homosexual's mother fixation. What do you call it?

ETHAN: A masterpiece.

PAUL: Really? How original.

ETHAN: You just said "I like the Sistine Chapel!" That's not exactly earth-shattering.

PAUL: I wasn't trying to be earth-shattering, and that's not what I said.

MARGARET: *(Mediating.)* So what are we arguing about now, whether or not the Sistine Chapel is any good?

PAUL: Actually, I think we're arguing about Ethan's manhood, but that's nothing new. How long has it been since you made any money, Ethan? Maybe if you got a job once in a while, you wouldn't have to come up here and take issue with every word I say.

(There is a sudden silence at this.)

PAUL: *(Continuing; knowing he crossed a line.)* Sorry. I'm sorry. I'm . . . this is . . . Christ. Where's that girl? Why isn't that girl here? She was supposed to be here by now.

MARGARET: I'll call Roger, see if he knows anything.

FRANK: I have to go, Mom.

(He collects his statuette and stands to go.)

PAUL: Oh God, please! There's no need for everyone to start fleeing like frightened rabbits. The monster will go back into his lair. When that girl gets here, just tell her — . You know what to tell her.

(Beat.)

It's good to see you, Ethan.

(He hands Margaret the Yellow Pages and goes back upstairs. The others sit in silence for a moment.)

MARGARET: He's much better. He really is. If that girl weren't late —

FRANK: He's been writing about death for twenty years, that would put anyone in a mood.

ETHAN: Why are you defending him? He makes you, you can't even complete a sentence when he's in the room!

MARGARET: Ethan.

FRANK: *(Defending himself.)* I'm, I'm not defending him. I'm just saying, it's not so bad anymore. You don't see him much, really. You know, he's sort of like a nasty old pet, this psychotic cat who comes out once in a while and howls at the moon. Mostly he stays in his den.

(Beat.)

He really did ask to read your reviews.

ETHAN: *(Curt.)* It's fine! I'm not here to see him anyway, and it's a good thing because you know he's just going to hole up there for our entire visit. He's finally finishing the new one, is that the story this time?

(To Laurie.)

These are the reasons one does not have to behave like an actual human being. One: One is started a novel. Two: One is in the middle of a novel. Three: One is finishing a novel.

FRANK: I don't, it's not clear, actually. Finishing, no. That's not, no.

ETHAN: No? Really? Because I thought —

(Frank shrugs, embarrassed, looks away. Margaret doesn't notice.)

MARGARET: There's just some pressure. Because he's rather late, this time.

ETHAN: How late?

MARGARET: Writers are always late. Dostoevsky, they were pounding on the door, while he slipped the finished pages under it. That happens sometimes.

ETHAN: So Roger's been coming up, has he, pounding on the door?

MARGARET: He's given him a deadline.

(There is an awkward pause at this. She is clearly embarrassed to admit it. Ethan looks at Frank.)

ETHAN: A "deadline"? I don't even know what that means.

FRANK: *(Embarrassed.)* He's, it's, there's been some concern, the advance.

ETHAN: What about it?

(Beat, laughing.)

Oh come on. He's not being asked to give it back?

MARGARET: Exactly. It's preposterous. Sometimes it just doesn't come, you'd think they'd know that by now, the whole lot of them. He'll have it when he's done, I don't know what else anyone expects.

ETHAN: They did? Wait, you mean, they really did, they did?

LAURIE: How much is it?

MARGARET: Nothing! One-fifty, something like that, complete pocket change to them. Less than pocket change, the whole house got bought up whenever that was, and now they're owned by Rupert Murdoch or someone, you know that if you go through all the channels of this one owning that one, and that one being owned by someone else Rupert Murdoch is behind it all! And you're going to tell me Rupert Murdoch really needs a hundred and fifty thousand dollars? He doesn't even know it's gone!

ETHAN: Is it? Gone?

MARGARET: That's not the point!

LAURIE: Is he going to give the money back?

(There is a terrible pause at this.)

LAURIE: *(Continuing; alarmed.)* What? Did I say something wrong?

MARGARET: It is absurd for them to ask for it. It is an insult to a man of Paul's stature. A complete insult. None of them, everyone he worked with for years is gone, and they've all been replaced by twelve-year-old idiots, and they're all obsessed with the Internet and not one of them has a shred of manners anymore.

Marcuse was right, capitalism will be the death of all of us, it just sucks the life out of every culture it touches. I blame this whole thing on the fall of the Berlin Wall. They all think it's only money, it's profits and losses and dollars and cents and that damned — fucking — Internet, well, that's not all there is to life! There is art, and culture, and — dignity. Harold Brodkey took eighteen years to write *The Runaway Soul,* and no one ever asked him for the advance back. And needless to say, he did NOT have a Nobel.

(Snapping.)

Where is that girl? He's going to lose an entire day. I'm going to call Roger right now and tell him what I think — this is ridiculous.

(She heads off. Frank, Laurie, and Ethan sit, a little stunned.)

FRANK: She's out of her mind. She's so, I don't know, I've never — That's why, I had to, I didn't know what else —

ETHAN: Frank, it's OK. I'm glad you called. She needs me here, of course I want to be here.

FRANK: Him too. I mean, it's true. When they asked for the money back. It shook him up.

LAURIE: How late is he?

FRANK: I don't know. Nine years, ten years.

LAURIE: Whoa. Really?

FRANK: Harold Brodkey took eighteen —

LAURIE: I heard.

ETHAN: Do you think he's lost it, finally?

FRANK: I don't know.

SOPHIE: *(Offstage.)* Hello?

(All turn toward the door. Through the window, Sophie appears.)

FRANK: I just don't know.

(Blackout.)

SCENE TWO

Sophie sits on the couch, going through the pages, and yellow sheets. Paul comes down the stairs. She jumps, stands, nervous. He looks at her.

PAUL: Hello.

SOPHIE: Hi. I'm, hi, I'm Sophie Marks.

PAUL: *(Matter-of-fact.)* I know who you are.

(He holds out his hand. She gives him the pages. He sits to read them with a pencil in his hand.)

SOPHIE: I didn't, uh, your son gave me the pages you left and said you needed me to type them up and put some shape on them. I wasn't sure, since I hadn't spoken to you directly, I mean, there are places, obviously, where I had to improvise . . .

(Paul starts to mark on the pages. She watches him, silent, for a moment.)

SOPHIE: *(Continuing.)* I wasn't sure how far to go. What you've done is so — I didn't —

PAUL: I'm sorry, but could you try and finish your sentences? I have a son who does that. It's hard to follow.

SOPHIE: I'm sorry. *(Then.)* Actually, I'm not sorry, I'm nervous. You're making me nervous, a little. That's why I keep interrupting myself.

PAUL: You're doing just fine now.

SOPHIE: Oh good.

(There is the faintest edge to her response. He raises his eyebrow at her, noting her tone, and goes back to working on the pages. She watches him.)

SOPHIE: *(Continuing.)* It's all right then, what I did?

PAUL: I'll let you know if it's not right.

SOPHIE: *(Laughing a little at this.)* Yeah, yes, of course. Sorry.

(She smiles and sits, not quite knowing what to do now.)

PAUL: Did you like it?

(He looks up from the pages and indicates them.)

SOPHIE: Di — oh. Yes. I did.

(Beat. He looks at her.)

What? You want me to tell you what I thought of it?

(He looks at her, waiting.)

I like it's . . . tone. The coolness of the surface. There are places where I was having trouble holding onto it, because that glide can, in places, get a little too facile for my taste but overall I liked the elegance. My stuff always seems so, tied, almost, by a chain to the emotional reality that I'm trying to travel, and I know that's a strength, but it's also too earthbound, whereas there's something you do, where it lifts, the language takes it to someplace otherworldly almost and yet connected to the emotion. So the, there is compassion there, I think, and wisdom, without a loss of aesthetics. It's quite . . .

(He is staring at her.)

I'm sorry.

PAUL: No no, you're doing very well. Did you learn that in graduate school?

SOPHIE: No, I've always talked like that.

(She raises an eyebrow a little, wondering if he will smile at this. He doesn't.)

PAUL: "Facile."

SOPHIE: Facile, I mean, facile in the academic sense. Uh, fluid, easy.

PAUL: I know what facile means.

SOPHIE: *(Rattled.)* No, I'm sure you do, I just, uh . . .

(She stops, unsure.)

PAUL: Don't stop. Please. What else did you think?

SOPHIE: *(Good-natured, direct, but backing off.)* You know, I don't believe you really want to hear what I think.

PAUL: Why not?

SOPHIE: Well, because I'm a little nobody, and you're — not.

PAUL: How old are you?

SOPHIE: Twenty-eight.

PAUL: Mailer was twenty-five when he wrote *The Naked and the Dead.*

SOPHIE: But he didn't win the Pulitzer until he was in his forties.

(He starts to read again.)

SOPHIE: *(Continuing.)* Um, would you like to read something I've written?

PAUL: What?

SOPHIE: I just thought, we're going to be working together, and clearly you're going to be relying on my sensibilities, as a writer. So I was thinking you should maybe . . . read something I've written.

PAUL: *(Cold.)* Thank you, but right now, I would like to read something I've written. If it's not too much trouble. Since I've already lost an entire day because you were late.

SOPHIE: *(Embarrassed.)* I had trouble getting out of the city.

PAUL: How fascinating.

(He goes back to the pages. Sophie sits, now miserable.)

SOPHIE: Look, could we start over?

(He looks at her.)

I'm sorry. This just started so badly. I'm sure it's my fault. I'm sure it seems that I'm not humble enough. And please believe me, I don't mean for that to come across. I feel humble. I'm so grateful to be here, I know, believe me, what a tremendous thing this is. And Norman Mailer's probably a friend of yours; I'm sorry, I didn't mean to be flip about his Pulitzer.

PAUL: His first Pulitzer.

SOPHIE: Yes, his . . . yes. I see. I do see. I just, I get a little, when I'm nervous,

I just . . . But, I want your good opinion. I want to be of service to you. Please let me start again.
(Beat.)
What you've written here is brilliant, it's just brilliant. To be able to work with you, even to be around while you're working is truly a privilege. I'm so grateful. You're such a genius.
(He considers her. Blackout.)

SCENE THREE

Several days later. Ethan is on the phone.

ETHAN: No, absolutely not. He's seen my work — well, then fuck him if he hasn't seen me in something over the last six years, where the hell has he been, running around the regionals? Oh, London. Of course, London, that's so much more impressive, he's probably been over their directing *Joseph and the Amazing Technicolor Dreamcoat,* and he thinks that makes him the God of Theater. Oh Caryl Churchill, big — whose agent are you?
(Beat. He listens, briefly.)
Fine, that's fine, I understand your point but you need to understand, I'm forty years old and I've done the work that one is supposed to do to get one's self to the point that one is supposed to get to, where one doesn't have to audition anymore. I've gotten the reviews, I've gotten the awards, and not only that, I have the pedigree, my father has a fucking Nobel Prize, I'm a leading man now, I look fantastic, I'm funny, I'm the guy everybody supposedly wants and I still have to audition? For the opportunity to play a part that's going to pay me three hundred dollars a week? Are you joking? No really, are you joking?
(There is a longer pause while he listens to his agent lecture him. Laurie enters, hands him a cup of coffee. He rolls his eyes at her.)
ETHAN: *(Continuing.)* Oh, Sam, God, I understand, on a financial level, why I should have taken that sitcom; God knows the money part makes complete sense. But legitimacy? It would have made me more legitimate? Could you — I don't — I have to go now. No. Good-bye.
(He hangs up. Laurie looks at him.)
ETHAN: *(Continuing.)* Apparently, I am not yet "A" list. This from my agent,

a person who works for me, and who I pay. What time is it? Would it be bad for me to have a drink at nine in the morning?

LAURIE: They won't even let you read?

ETHAN: No, they want me to read. They want me to read!

LAURIE: Oh.

ETHAN: Yes, according to Sam, if I agree to humiliate myself one last time, and if the director doesn't find me too OLD, and if I get cast, and if he doesn't botch the production, and if the playwright does some work on the script, and if the critics don't annihilate it, or me, I will finally and irrevocably have made the "A" list. And that's why I should go in and grovel.

LAURIE: It's not groveling.

ETHAN: It's positively, groveling! And I don't care that everyone does it. It doesn't make any sense. Could someone explain to me when groveling became such an attractive quality in a man?

LAURIE: I'm not saying you should grovel. I just, I thought you wanted that part.

ETHAN: I am going to have a drink.

(He goes to the sideboard and pours himself a scotch.)

LAURIE: Ethan! It's nine in the morning!

ETHAN: Yes. It is.

LAURIE: OK. I thought we were leaving today. Are we not leaving today?

ETHAN: No. We are not leaving today.

(He downs it.)

LAURIE: Well, OK. Maybe we should take a drive. I mean, if you don't want to go back to the city, maybe we should take the day and drive over to the mountains, and find some lovely B and B, you know, some place just completely romantic —

ETHAN: There's a great idea. Because if we leave, it will break my mother's heart. You know that. She's only been looking forward to this visit her entire life.

LAURIE: *(Bringing him back.)* Hey, hey — HEY.

ETHAN: Sorry. I'm sorry.

LAURIE: *(A beat, then.)* What is it? Is it your father?

ETHAN: My father? What father? I come up for the first time in two years and don't see him for the entire time I'm here. Why would that bother me? He read my reviews, what more could I possibly want?

LAURIE: We should go.

ETHAN: I am not going back to the city.

LAURIE: We can go anywhere —

ETHAN: *(On a roll now.)* All that crap about making money — you know I didn't, as you know, I did not take that fucking sitcom job because he implied that it was beneath me. More than implied, it was a huge, God, I had to listen ad infinitum to him going on about the death of culture, television being the psychic ruin of us all, and God knows, it is shit. We all know that. Spiritual shit. So I'm not saying he was wrong. But to throw it at me. Within minutes, I hadn't even — how long had we been here? Five minutes?

LAURIE: Ethan, the sitcom, that whole offer, that was years ago —

ETHAN: That's what I'm saying! And then he throws it at me, within instants of our arrival, that I can't make a decent living! I had the chance to make a decent living, and I opted for art instead, so he can just fuck off!
(He turns his back on her, angry. There is a long beat where he sets down the empty glass, and sits at the table, paws restlessly through a pile of magazines and review books.)

LAURIE: *(Simple.)* If it makes you so unhappy to be here, we should go. We only meant to stay the weekend anyway.

ETHAN: I don't want to go back to the city, because then I will have no legitimate excuse not to read, is that impossible for you to understand?
(Beat.)
I'm just disappointed, they asked me to read for that part, and I thought it was going to be offered to me. I'm forty years old. I have an Obie, for God's sake, well now I feel stupid even mentioning that, obviously, who gives a shit about an Obie. I'm disappointed. And afraid I won't be able to do it anymore. If I take one more humiliation? All I have to work with is myself. This is the instrument, me, I'm the instrument. If they take that, if I let them take that? I won't be able to act.
(Beat.)
This isn't a speech from *Long Day's Journey*. This is the truth.

LAURIE: Thanks for the clarification.
(She goes to him, climbs on him, and kisses him.)

LAURIE: *(Continuing.)* You are a wonderful actor. You don't have to read for that fucking part. Fuck 'em. They can just offer it to you. They don't deserve you. They should be so lucky. And you are a big hunk.

ETHAN: And my penis?

LAURIE: Yes, it's huge.

ETHAN: Thank you.

LAURIE: Actors. You guys are sooo easy.

ETHAN: You know what we should do today? We should go down to Frank's shop. He's desperate to show it to you, and it really is fantastic.

LAURIE: That sounds great.

ETHAN: Absolutely, it's the kind of thing you love. All cluttered and interesting, there is nothing not worth looking at down there. That little statue he had, everything is that fantastic, and he can go on, like that, about all of it.

Little icons and artifacts and just pure junk, it's quite spectacular. And he has a little kitchen in back, where he makes sandwiches for anyone who stops by.

LAURIE: *(Laughing.)* Sandwiches.

ETHAN: Yes, little cucumber and egg things. He even trims off the crusts. What can I say, he's a complete fruit, but it's charming. We can spend the whole day there. Go have lunch on the pier.

LAURIE: I'll get my purse.

(They kiss. She goes, passing Sophie in the door, as she does. Sophie carries a stack of papers and books.)

LAURIE: *(Continuing.)* Good morning.

SOPHIE: Hi.

LAURIE: How's it going?

SOPHIE: Excellent. Just, it's so . . .

(She can't even say, she's so excited. She disappears up the steps. Laurie goes. Ethan turns, after Laurie's left, and looks after Sophie up the stairs. He goes back to paging through a literary magazine. After a moment, she comes back down.)

SOPHIE: *(Continuing.)* Have you seen Paul?

ETHAN: No. Oh wait, it's Monday. I think Mom said he'd be going into the city today. Lunch with his agent or something.

SOPHIE: Oh.

ETHAN: He didn't tell you?

SOPHIE: It must've slipped his mind.

ETHAN: That's the advantage of being a genius. You don't have to bother with being polite.

SOPHIE: Did he say when he'd be coming back?

ETHAN: Probably not till late afternoon.

(She is clearly disappointed and not certain where to go now.)

ETHAN: *(Continuing.)* So it's going well, then. The work. You're enjoying it?

SOPHIE: It's amazing. He's — amazing.

ETHAN: Nobel Prize winner.

SOPHIE: It's not that. It's just such a privilege to be, even, near someone who has such a profound understanding of — everything, he's so —

ETHAN: Oh, everything.

SOPHIE: He has so much at his fingertips. His mind, the way he can just move between Borges and the Bible, Emily Dickinson, Montaigne, Mark Twain, Dante —

ETHAN: Dante. Let me guess. Not the *Inferno,* that would be much too commonplace. He quoted — the *Purgatorio.*

SOPHIE: The *Paradiso.*

ETHAN: The *Paradiso!* Of course. Even better. That's perfect.

(He laughs. She bristles, a little embarrassed. Awkward now, she turns to go.)

SOPHIE: I'm sorry. I must sound like an idiot.

ETHAN: No no, don't go. Please. I'm always complaining about how rude Paul is and I'm no better, it's disgraceful the way I behave, it really is.

SOPHIE: No.

ETHAN: Yes, it is and I, truly, I can do better. Surprisingly enough, wallowing in an informed and gifted bitterness yields interesting nuggets of wisdom. And I promise to stay off the subject of the great man. Or, if you like, I can regale you with hilarious anecdotes that are simultaneously quite respectful of his genius.

SOPHIE: It must be hard, to be his son.

ETHAN: Are you kidding? It's a delight, a complete delight. So much fun. As is, I'm sure, your relationship with your father.

(This makes her laugh.)

SOPHIE: Oh yes.

ETHAN: What's he like?

SOPHIE: You know . . . I should work.

ETHAN: I completely understand. Very well put. You're writing a novel, is that it? A novella? Short stories? What is it you write?

SOPHIE: I don't know what it is yet. It's fiction. Actually, it's not even pure fiction. It's based on a . . . family story.

ETHAN: Family again.

SOPHIE: No, not actually. It's not about family.

ETHAN: What is it about?

SOPHIE: Butterflies.

(Blackout.)

SCENE FOUR

Paul and Sophie, in light. She scribbles as he speaks.

PAUL: He stands, there's a quality of light, at the window, that he, not peach, or sand —

SOPHIE: The color, or the quality?

PAUL: The quality, the scent —

SOPHIE: The scent? The smell of the light?

PAUL: *(Impatient.)* The texture of something fleet, a hovering sense of loss, just this side of, well of course it's death, but that carries such a — you want just the tip of it, the taint without the weariness, the taste of it in the light —

SOPHIE: In the light?

PAUL: Light, change, peach, apricot, it's too heavy — are you writing this down?

SOPHIE: Light, change, peach —

PAUL: Christ, I hate the English language, it's so fucking inadequate — the taste of grief that hovers like a memory, the memory of Venice at dawn appearing like a melody, sorrow, grace, in the smell of the light, not peach —

SOPHIE: Rose?

PAUL: Oh God help us, rose, go back to the taste of grief —

SOPHIE: *(Reading.)* The taste of grief that hovers in the shifting light —

PAUL: That's bullshit —

SOPHIE: No, it's —

PAUL: Facile, huh?

SOPHIE: No, no —

(Paul grabs the pages and looks at them shakes his head. He scribbles on them.)

PAUL: This is complete — what is this —

SOPHIE: Night —

PAUL: Night, night, evening, night is better, evening is so bad Victorian but it does — Venice, what's — fuck, get Venice out of here — Christ, every time someone tries to talk about light Venice comes up —

(He pushes the pages back, she scribbles.)

SOPHIE: I like the grace.

PAUL: What?

SOPHIE: *(Pointing.)* Melody, sorrow, grace. Grace.

PAUL: You don't think it's too facile?

SOPHIE: No, no, I — there's something subtle about it, grace, something holy without the weight of, the thing we yearn for —

PAUL: Yearning, Christ, God help me, everybody's always yearning, we're always fucking yearning —

SOPHIE: Well, we are!

PAUL: *(Ignoring her.)* Fucking yearning for what, to live forever, I wish I was young again, I wish the human race wasn't so pathetic, I wish sex was not ultimately humiliating — all that fucking yearning. What do you yearn for?

SOPHIE: *(Simple.)* I yearn for grace.
(Beat.)

PAUL: Christ. Read, read what we got. He stood at the window —

SOPHIE: *(Reading.)* He stood at the window and worried the light. What was it, what is it? Not, peach, or apricot, the words drifted through the night, clumsy, missing entirely; it wasn't a scent, but the taste of grief, the yearning for grace, hovering in the shifting light.
(Blackout.)

SCENE FIVE

A few days later. Margaret is watering the plants as Laurie watches her.

LAURIE: I mean, I'm glad, I really am, I've been trying to get him to take a break for I don't know how long. So I'm relieved, he's finally decided to take some time.

MARGARET: Well, we're delighted. You're more than welcome, weeks and weeks, the whole summer. It's absolutely wonderful to have someone to talk to, when Paul gets writing he's . . . oh dear. Is this a fungus or dust? I hope this isn't some sort of horrible fungus.
(Laurie looks.)

LAURIE: It's dust.

MARGARET: It is dust? Are you sure? Are you one of those plant people?

LAURIE: Oh God no.

MARGARET: Frank will know. He's a complete genius with this sort of thing.
(She carries the plant to the back door and places it outside.)

MARGARET: *(Continuing.)* There, I don't want it infecting things. You don't think it's infected anything, do you?

LAURIE: I think it's dust.

MARGARET: There, that's a very positive thing to say. You're a very positive person.

LAURIE: I just hope that he and Paul can maintain this truce.

MARGARET: Oh no no. That's really, most of it is in Ethan's head.

LAURIE: Then you do think it will be all right?

MARGARET: Absolutely.

LAURIE: I mean, being here, the whole point would be to take a break, not get involved in something else that's going to make him feel terrible about himself. I mean a real break, out of the city, when we're there he can go for weeks or even months God forbid between jobs, but there's all the auditioning and readings and reading the *Times* and fretting over who's more famous than he is, or who got that part that he wanted — it's hard, I don't have to tell you about it. I just watch it wear on him. And I don't blame him. He's really such a wonderful actor, and I don't think I only think that because I love him, do you?

MARGARET: I always thought he was gifted. Of course I'm his mother.

LAURIE: And now of course he's turned forty, which hardly helps. He's forty years old, you know, you wonder, you turn forty and you have to wonder what your life is adding up to.

MARGARET: He's what?

LAURIE: I know, it's just a number, and the fact is, you're only one day older than you were the day before, all that, but forty, it's symbolic, it is.

MARGARET: Ethan's not forty. Oh dear, no. He's forty-two.

LAURIE: What?

MARGARET: Oh, actors.

LAURIE: Are you sure?

MARGARET: Am I sure? I'm his mother. Ethan is forty-two, and Frank is forty. I think Frank is forty.

LAURIE: Then you're not sure.

MARGARET: About Ethan I am. The first-born, you remember everything. It's a curse for everybody. He's forty-two and Frank will be forty.

LAURIE: *(Chagrined.)* I threw a big party for him. Rented a room in a restaurant. It cost a fortune.

MARGARET: Oh, yes, I remember, we couldn't make it down. But you had a good time?

LAURIE: Wonderful. We had a wonderful fortieth birthday party for a man who had just turned forty-two.

MARGARET: Well, that's what's important, isn't it? That you all had fun. And don't worry so much about Ethan. He'll be all right, now that he's got you.

LAURIE: Oh.

MARGARET: No, it's true, it really is. When I see him with you, I know he's going to be just fine.

(Sophie enters from the stairs.)

MARGARET: *(Continuing.)* Ah, someone emerges from the crypt! How's it going up there?

SOPHIE: Wonderful, thank you.

(She heads for the kitchen.)

MARGARET: Can I help you with anything?

SOPHIE: Thanks, I've got it.

MARGARET: Got what?

SOPHIE: Oh, no, I was just — Paul asked me to get him some iced tea.

MARGARET: Well, I can do that.

(She heads for the kitchen herself.)

SOPHIE: I don't want to bother you.

MARGARET: Don't be ridiculous. I've been getting my husband iced tea for forty-some odd years. It's hardly a bother.

SOPHIE: Yes, but —

(She is uncomfortable. Margaret stops.)

MARGARET: Yes?

SOPHIE: It's just, I made it for him yesterday and he said something about, he'd never had it, that way before, and that's why he asked me . . .

(Beat.)

MARGARET: Surely there are not that many ways to make a glass of iced tea. One goes to the refrigerator. One takes the pitcher out. One pours it into a glass with ice.

SOPHIE: I put lemonade in it.

MARGARET: Well, that would be relevant if Paul liked lemonade.

SOPHIE: No, he did. He liked it very much. So he asked me if I'd make it for him again.

(Beat.)

MARGARET: *(Short.)* Well, who knew. Forty years of making iced tea, who knew it could be so complicated, so worthy of an extended debate.

SOPHIE: No, I just — well, anyway. It's my job, isn't it? I'm happy to do it.

MARGARET: By all means.

(She gestures to the kitchen. Sophie goes.)

MARGARET: *(Continuing.)* Well, now I feel ridiculous.

LAURIE: No.

MARGARET: Don't patronize me, Laurie. I know when I'm behaving like an idiot.

LAURIE: It can't be easy, having a total stranger living in your house.

MARGARET: No. It isn't, is it? It just never is.

(After a moment, Sophie reenters, carrying iced tea.)

MARGARET: *(Continuing.)* Well, and there we have it. Iced tea and lemonade, all mixed together. That looks just delicious.

SOPHIE: Would you like me to make one for you?

MARGARET: *(Dry.)* No, I wouldn't, thank you.

(Sophie heads for the stairs.)

MARGARET: *(Continuing.)* So what are you two working on up there?

SOPHIE: Well, um — his novel.

MARGARET: Yes, dear. Which novel?

SOPHIE: Oh — I — there's only one, isn't there?

MARGARET: God, no, he's got six or seven in drawers, half-finished, barely begun, in all states, really. There was one he worked on for four years, he had something upward of six hundred pages, and he finally abandoned it in sheer terror.

SOPHIE: That's terrible.

MARGARET: You have no idea. There were a few years in there, my God, he hadn't a clue what he was doing anymore. It was after his third novel, which was not well-received, really some of the critics were quite cruel and he's never been what you'd call a populist writer, so when the critics abandoned him he did not have the luxury of turning to his audience for comfort. Which made it just that much easier for Dartmouth to deny him tenure. Well, with that temper he's never been exactly embraced by the academy, so we had no money, two small children and he develops what might be called the opposite of writer's block — starting a new project every other week, each one more promising than the last, but none of them growing quite, being given the time to grow before he was onto the next. And heaven forbid I go back to work to support us, not that he has issues with that but he was not going to help out with the boys, besides which he needed me around just to keep him sane, I suppose. As sane as he ever gets. We finally got through, he finished his fourth novel and won the National Book Award for his fifth. Smooth sailing ever since. More or less.

(Beat.)

SOPHIE: I had no idea.

MARGARET: It wasn't that bad.

> *(Beat.)*

> The iced tea? He doesn't like to be kept waiting.

SOPHIE: No, of course. Thank you.

> *(Beat.)*

> Thank you.

> *(She goes. Margaret watches until she is out of earshot, then.)*

MARGARET: I don't like her.

LAURIE: Why did you tell her all that?

MARGARET: Oh please. All that youth and beauty, naïve eagerness, everything ahead of her. What does she think is ahead of her? Ask yourself, what does she think?

> *(Imitating her.)*

> "Thank you. Thank you." It's enough to make you sick. And you know he's up there just drinking it in, with all that lemonade in his iced tea —

> *(Sudden, off another plant.)*

> Where is Frank? Wasn't he supposed to be here by now? This is not dust. This is mildew, this is some disease. Where is he?

LAURIE: He and Ethan were going on some antique hunt. Ethan had something in his head he wanted Frank to find for him.

MARGARET: *(Astonished.)* Ethan?

LAURIE: Yes.

> *(Almost laughing, in her confusion.)*

> What is it?

MARGARET: Nothing. I'm sorry. I'm being ridiculous. It's nothing.

> *(Blackout.)*

SCENE SIX

> *Paul and Sophie, in light, in argument.*

SOPHIE: I just don't think it's — I mean, have we not seen this, nine thousand —

PAUL: Of course, it's "facile" —

SOPHIE: Oh my God. Are you ever going to —

PAUL: No, I don't think I am —

SOPHIE: Well, then it is facile. It's facile. He's afraid of dying —

PAUL: We're all afraid of dying —

SOPHIE: I'm not.

PAUL: Oh, yes you are.

SOPHIE: All right. Of course I am. But she is a twit. Does he have to fall in love with such a complete — it's just contempt —

PAUL: Contempt?

SOPHIE: For both of them! Isn't it? She's just such —

PAUL: She's beautiful.

SOPHIE: That's not enough!

PAUL: It is for him.

SOPHIE: It's not! My God, this is someone who can stand with his hand on a doorknob for forty pages, thinking about the nature of time and she has no interior life whatsoever —

PAUL: She's young, she hasn't amassed the kind of experience that taints the imagination —

SOPHIE: Oh, "tainting" again, what is wrong with being tainted? All of us are tainted —

PAUL: She's not.

SOPHIE: Then maybe she should be. She's just, if that's it, if this thinly drawn — *(Paul looks at her.)*

PAUL: Yes?

SOPHIE: *(Beat.)* I think the less of him. He's just projecting onto her. It makes him a narcissist.

PAUL: We are all narcissists, my dear. We are all tainted narcissists.

SOPHIE: Then she is, too. My God, I'm not suggesting anything that hasn't been achieved time and again by the Victorians. Henry James and Edith Wharton, for heaven's sake, after Archer and Isabel Lily Bart the fact that male writers now don't even attempt —

PAUL: *(Angrily amused now.)* Excuse me?

SOPHIE: Oh, come on! You know what I'm talking about! John Updike has never written a believable woman in his life. Thomas Woolf? Hardly. Saul Bellow, Brodkey, your friend Mr. Mailer, let's face it, the whole twentieth century —

PAUL: Oh really?

SOPHIE: Chock full of misogynistic creeps. Conrad, Lawrence, even Fitzgerald, Daisy notwithstanding, surprisingly Hemingway actually does better than he's given credit for, when he takes a shot at it — but overall — not to say they're not geniuses, but really. Half the human race. Don't you think it should be considered a limitation if you can't imagine what it means to be human for half the human race?

PAUL: You who know so much about men.

SOPHIE: But it's not about me, is it, Paul? Let's face it, most of you guys positively brag about the fact you think women are subhuman. It's the last form of bigotry that's still considered hip.

PAUL: I find your mind interesting, Sophie, but in this instance you are full of shit. This has nothing to do with gender studies 101. My novel is about an older man in love with a younger woman, with all the joy and grief that that implies.

SOPHIE: So that's it. You don't have to imagine her life as richly as —

PAUL: *(Cold.)* What? Am I being too facile?

SOPHIE: *(Backing down.)* No. I'm sorry.

PAUL: *(Turning on her.)* Would you like to try it?

SOPHIE: What?

PAUL: Go ahead. You're so fucking sure. Show me what you mean.

(He holds the pages out to her. She takes them. Blackout.)

SCENE SEVEN

Ethan is on the phone. Margaret moves in and out of the room, setting up for a party.

ETHAN: Absolutely not. No. I told you two weeks ago, two weeks ago, Sam — I am not sabotaging anything! If they want to offer me the part, I will happily accept it, it's a wonderful part even for three hundred fucking dollars a week — No, I'm not going to meet with him, that's ridiculous, either he wants me to do the part, or he doesn't, having a cup of coffee with the man isn't going to convince him that I can act! All he can learn from a meeting is whether or not I look like my headshot, and I'm not driving three hours into the city for that. Yes, it is, three solid hours; they're doing construction on the Cross Bronx. Yes, they are!

What am I — I am relaxing, Sam. That is what I am doing here. I am relaxing in the country with my family.

(Paul appears on the stairs. Ethan sees Paul, goes back to the phone.)

ETHAN: *(Continuing.)* Look, it's my brother's birthday and my mother is making a big thing of it, and she disapproves of people who do business on the phone after six, so I've got to go. Yes, I will but I'm not going to change my mind. Seriously, I find it ridiculous that the instant I insist on being treated with the barest pretense of respect, everyone acts like I'm crazy. It's a very sick business we're in. Good-bye.

(He hangs up. Paul stands at the foot of the stairs, uncomfortable.)

MARGARET: There you are. How's it going up there?

PAUL: Ahhhh.

MARGARET: Well, then it's time you took a break. Here's Ethan, he's been here two weeks already, and you two have barely spoken. Ethan, tell your father about your play.

ETHAN: *(Annoyed.)* There is no play, Mom.

MARGARET: Yes, the one they want you for. Would you like a glass of wine, Paul?

(She goes. Paul and Ethan consider each other for a moment.)

ETHAN: Hello, Dad.

PAUL: Yeah, hi.

(He goes to the table of food and looks at it, clearly unsure about what to do. Ethan watches.)

ETHAN: They're hors d'oeuvres. You eat them.

PAUL: I guess I'm not hungry.

(He moves away from the table, and he looks out the back door.)

PAUL: *(Continuing.)* So, what was that about? You doing another play?

ETHAN: *(Encouraged by his interest.)* Actually, I'm not, this time.

PAUL: It's not any good, huh?

ETHAN: It's fine. It's just not the right circumstance, for me, at the present time.

(Paul nods, shrugs.)

PAUL: Why not?

ETHAN: Well — the producers — it's hard to explain. It's a matter of pride, I guess. Not in a bad way. At least I hope not.

PAUL: Sounds kind of — tough.

ETHAN: Yeah, it is, kind of.

(Beat.)

PAUL: I've never fully understood the appeal of theater.

ETHAN: *(Beat.)* That's an interesting thought, Dad. Thank you for mentioning it.

PAUL: No, I mean it. It's just — such an emotionally indulgent form. No wonder Henry James couldn't make any sense of it.

ETHAN: Henry James couldn't make sense of it because he was boring, and while one can get away with writing boring novels, it is considerably more difficult to get away with writing boring plays.

PAUL: Henry James couldn't make sense of it because the form doesn't support complexity of language and thought.

ETHAN: Shakespeare notwithstanding.

PAUL: You can't bring in Shakespeare. He was a poet.

ETHAN: *(Irritated now.)* He was a playwright.

PAUL: The genius was in the poetry.

ETHAN: *(Growing anger.)* You can't dissect it! This part of it is genius, that part —

PAUL: I'm not talking about Shakespeare. I was just making an observation about the theater. As a form.

ETHAN: What about it? As a form.

PAUL: Well, it's never really produced a first-rate writer, has it?
(Laurie enters, with a bottle of wine.)

LAURIE: Hello, Paul, how good to see you out of your lair.

ETHAN: *(Losing it.)* WHAT DID YOU SAY?

PAUL: OK, here we go.

LAURIE: Oh. I interrupted something.

ETHAN: He just called the theater a second-rate art form!

LAURIE: Oh, Paul. What a thing to say.

PAUL: I didn't say that.

ETHAN: Oh, come on —

PAUL: What I said was, it's never produced a first-rate writer. There is a profound difference.

ETHAN: Not to you!

LAURIE: So Shakespeare —

ETHAN: Doesn't count.

LAURIE: *(Surprised.)* Doesn't count?

PAUL: *(Dismissive.)* Shakespeare, again. You might as well bring up Hitler.

ETHAN: Shakespeare and Hitler, yes, I always talk about them in the same sentence —

PAUL: *(Clarifying.)* People toss around Shakespeare, Einstein, Hitler, fucking Mozart as if they weren't complete anomalies, well guess what? Twenty thousand years of human history, you're going to get the occasional freak of nature.
(Margaret enters, carrying glasses.)

MARGARET: Did you open the wine, Laurie?

LAURIE: Uh, no, I got a little distracted.

ETHAN: Shakespeare was a freak of nature.

MARGARET: Really? Is that Frank?
(She looks out the door.)

PAUL: Yes, a freak of nature, obviously genius is a freak of nature or history or we would see a little more of it, wouldn't we? But instead we're still out here crawling in the mud.

(Frank enters, carrying a package.)

MARGARET: Here's the birthday boy! Happy birthday, sweetheart.

FRANK: Thank you.

ETHAN: That's fascinating, Dad, and as far as I can tell, it has nothing to do with the power of the theater to change men's hearts and minds.

MARGARET: Really, Ethan, Paul, do we have to talk about Art? It won't end well, it never does.

PAUL: Nothing changes men's hearts and minds! If we could change men's hearts and minds don't you think we would have done it by now?

LAURIE: You brought your own present.

FRANK: No, actually, it's for — Ethan, did you tell her? He didn't tell you, did he?

ETHAN: Then art is what, frivolity? Narcissism? Scribbling nonsense on the walls of a cave?

PAUL: We're not talking about art, we're talking about theater.

ETHAN: *(Angry, direct.)* All right then Dad, what is it? What is it, now, about theater that is so fallen, so corrupt, that no one working in the theater can ever achieve the heights of genius available to, oh, say, a novelist?

FRANK: *(Alarmed.)* He didn't say that.

LAURIE: He kind of did.

PAUL: You want to know what's wrong with the theater? All those people, all those fucking people everywhere, on the stage, in the audience. Wrinkling their candy wrappers. Turning on their hearing aids, talking on their cell phones. You sit there going, where the fuck are the words, you're so drowning in people you can't find the damn words. They're there, they're gone, and no one even notices! Half the actors can't speak, but that's fine, because half the audience can't hear. Or think for that matter. All that emotion. Bad one-liners. Every other word is fuck. Every character's a victim, some battered woman or unhappy homosexual. Don't talk to me about Shakespeare, we're talking about the theater. And remember, you asked.

(Sophie comes down the steps, overhears the whole thing. Paul stops her as she tries to sneak behind him and into the kitchen.)

PAUL: *(Continuing; to Sophie.)* Where are you going?

SOPHIE: I'm sorry, I didn't want to interrupt.

PAUL: No, stay, it's a party. Somebody give her something to drink.

(Laurie does.)

FRANK: I disagree. I think theater is — . I've had evenings in the theater that I will, I carry them with me, performances, moments, the way someone looks in the, stage light is so pretty, sometimes I just remember, or or . . .

PAUL: Finish your damn sentence.

MARGARET: Paul.

FRANK: *(Sudden.)* "Your name is a golden bell hung in my heart, and when I think of you, I tremble, and the bell swings and rings along my veins, Roxanne, Roxanne, along my veins. Yes, that is love. That fire, that music."

(A beat.)

PAUL: *(Ironic.)* A golden bell hung in my heart, swinging and ringing, that's good.

FRANK: *(Not backing down.)* It was, just beautiful. I saw it twenty years ago, more than that, and I think about it still.

LAURIE: Cyrano? That's from Cyrano, isn't it?

FRANK: Ethan did it. In high school.

MARGARET: Yes, he was very good in that.

FRANK: I saw it four times. Theater is, theater is —

PAUL: *(Impatient.)* Is what?

ETHAN: It is a form that seeks transcendence.

PAUL: Rostand was a melodramatic hack. Molière was a comic. Come on, who are the writers? O'Neill, too many Catholic hang-ups, Shaw had his moments, but all that endless droning, who cares. Ibsen, too much moralizing. Strindberg, too much sperm. Who else? Mamet? He's just watered down Pinter, Pinter is watered down Beckett, and Beckett, OK, he could write, but he was a novelist.

ETHAN: Samuel Beckett could write. What a brilliant observation. And for this they award the Nobel Prize.

PAUL: Actually, they award the Nobel for achievement in Literature, Ethan. Not for the quality of debate one has over drinks with one's dissatisfied and disappointed middle-aged children.

ETHAN: That would actually wound me, Dad, if I hadn't already heard you dismiss Shakespeare's plays this evening.

PAUL: *(Snapping suddenly.)* That's not what I said! Good God, what I say is outrageous enough, you don't have to twist my words!

MARGARET: *(Sighing.)* Oh really, both of you. We haven't even had dinner yet! How are we ever supposed to make it through dinner?

ETHAN: Fine, let's talk about something else then. How's the book coming, Dad? I heard there was some trouble about the advance.

(Beat.)

PAUL: You're right. I don't know why I even attempt this bullshit. I'm going back to work.

LAURIE: Oh, no —

MARGARET: Paul, please —

ETHAN: Oh, let him go —

PAUL: Sophie, are you coming?

(He stops on the stairs and looks at her. Sophie stands, embarrassed. All look at her.)

SOPHIE: *(To the others.)* I'm sorry.

(She starts to go, then stops. She looks at Paul.)

SOPHIE: *(Continuing.)* But maybe if we just — thought about all of this, a different way. Because Paul and I, were talking, the other day, about the inadequacies of, of, language, and language, spoken language — maybe — out of context —

PAUL: For God's sake, Sophie, would you finish your Goddamn sentence?

SOPHIE: *(Cowed.)* I just meant, the movement of language, it's inability —

PAUL: *(Snapping.)* Finish the damn sentence!

SOPHIE: *(Suddenly snapping back.)* What is the matter with you? You come down here, and tell your son that his life's work is foolish —

PAUL: That is not what I —

SOPHIE: It's close enough. How could he hear something like that from you, from his father, without feeling demeaned, and unloved —

MARGARET: No no no.

ETHAN: That is not what this is about.

MARGARET: They just do this. It's a debate, that's all. A family full of artists, what else do we have to talk about?

SOPHIE: But you're not arguing about — I mean —

(Beat. They all stare at her.)

SOPHIE: *(Continuing; embarrassed.)* I'm sorry. You're right, I don't seem to be able to finish my sentences. I'm, forgive me. You're having a party. I must go.

FRANK: No, you're right, you . . . It's all right.

ETHAN: Yes, absolutely, we must seem completely insane, there really is no point to arguing with him about anything. He just delights in saying outrageous things. You should hear him on the subject of Michelangelo.

MARGARET: Let's not go back to that, please.

SOPHIE: *(To Paul, very contrite.)* I'm sorry.

PAUL: *(Quiet, kind.)* It's all right, Sophie.

THE BUTTERFLY COLLECTION 93

(There is something quite intimate about their exchange. After a moment, Ethan steps forward.)

ETHAN: So, no running off. It's Frank's birthday, there's presents and everything. Look, there's even one for you.

(She looks over, startled at this.)

SOPHIE: There is?

(Ethan picks up the package that Frank has brought with him. This surprises Frank.)

FRANK: Oh. I thought —

(He looks at Laurie, briefly, as Ethan hands it to Sophie.)

ETHAN: We looked for days. This wasn't easy. Go ahead, open it.

(Now abashed, Sophie looks around, and obediently opens the present. It is framed plate glass, upon which butterflies have been pressed and labeled. She stares at it, speechless.)

MARGARET: Well, isn't that lovely.

LAURIE: What is it?

FRANK: *(Miserable, confused.)* It's a plate of butterflies. Circa Nineteen Thirty, private collectors, there was actually quite a worldwide subculture of amateur lepidopterists. Nabokov, with his work with the South American blues obviously would be the most famous of these enthusiasts, but there were many, many — who went to extraordinary lengths, apparently, some of the collections are massive. All in private hands, and no one wants to break them up, naturally. Just finding one, it was prohibitive.

ETHAN: Frank finally found a dealer in Ashton, he drove eighty some odd miles —

FRANK: You can get knockoffs on the Internet, now, but they're cobbled together, obviously, just for people to hang on the wall. Not scientifically accurate. Ethan said it had to be the real thing.

ETHAN: Do you like it?

SOPHIE: *(Overwhelmed.)* It's beautiful, I don't — I — I'm sorry.

(To the others, an explanation.)

My grandfather was a butterfly collector. I'm writing about it.

(To Ethan.)

Thank you.

(To Frank.)

Thank you.

(He nods, uncomfortable. Laurie finally steps forward.)

LAURIE: May I?

(Sophie shows it to her.)

Oh, look, all the little white ones. Like a flock. Is that what butterflies fly in? Flocks?

SOPHIE: I don't know. I still know so little.

ETHAN: That's not true. You should read what she's written. It's fantastic.

LAURIE: Oh. You've read it.

SOPHIE: It's in very rough form.

ETHAN: It's brilliant.

PAUL: *(Dry.)* Maybe you'll let me look at it, sometime.

SOPHIE: Yes, of course, when it's ready, I — I —

PAUL: Well, it's lovely that we're all being civil, but I hope that doesn't mean I have to stand around and wait for her to finish a sentence. Are we ready to eat?
(Blackout.)

SCENE EIGHT

Late that same night. Sophie sits alone on the couch. A single light is on. After a moment, the back door opens. Ethan enters.

ETHAN: I saw the light.

SOPHIE: I couldn't sleep.

ETHAN: Are you all right?

SOPHIE: Yes, I was, I was trying to write, but that room is so small, sometimes. Lovely, but small. Sometimes it's hard to think in there.

ETHAN: It's hard to think everywhere in this house.

SOPHIE: No.

ETHAN: Don't be polite.

SOPHIE: I wasn't.

ETHAN: Yes, you were, and there's no one here but me. You can say whatever you want.

SOPHIE: That's not exactly true.

ETHAN: *(Laughing a little.)* You're very tortured, aren't you?
(He sits next to her. She moves.)

SOPHIE: I'm not. Maybe I am. I don't know.

ETHAN: That was fantastic, what you did. Standing up for me like that.

SOPHIE: It was horrifying.

ETHAN: That's what made it so fantastic.

SOPHIE: Oh, God.

ETHAN: Please don't regret it. It was wonderful.

SOPHIE: No, my God, he was so — and when he heard, that I let you —

ETHAN: Let me what?

SOPHIE: You know what. You all, all of you act like you're not aware of what you're doing, and —

ETHAN: Now I don't know what you're talking about, Sophie. You need to be clear.

(He looks at her, uncompromising.)

SOPHIE: *(Direct.)* Why did you give me that?

(She points to the butterflies.)

ETHAN: You're so aware of everything, you tell me.

SOPHIE: *(Persistent.)* In front of everyone. Why did it have to be in front of everyone? It was your brother's birthday —

ETHAN: Frank and I have been scouring the entire eastern seaboard for that thing. Was I supposed to wait? Well, I couldn't wait.

(He moves in, takes her hand. She tries to back away. He won't let her.)

ETHAN: *(Continuing.)* What do you think, why do you think I gave you the butterflies?

SOPHIE: Don't play games with me.

ETHAN: I'm not playing games. I've been watching you coming and going, in and out of his lair, you're like a light —

SOPHIE: *(Rebuffing him.)* Please.

ETHAN: I'm sorry. I don't know what I'm saying. I'm at a loss for words.

SOPHIE: No one in this house is ever at a loss for words.

(Beat.)

ETHAN: Do you want me to take them back? The butterflies?

SOPHIE: *(Beat.)* No. They're the most beautiful things I've ever seen.

(He kisses her. The kiss becomes rather passionate. He leans over and turns out the light. At the window, a figure can be seen, watching.)

(Blackout.)

END OF ACT I

ACT II
SCENE NINE

Laurie and Frank. Frank has set two enamel angels on the coffee table. Laurie is distracted.

FRANK: They're Venetian. I, it's not clear what period, probably late eighteenth century. Enamel on silver. I found them at an auction in Bennington six months ago, and I was convinced that one of my regulars, she's, but she didn't want them.

LAURIE: No? Why not?

(She looks off, toward the kitchen.)

FRANK: I don't know. Because I thought they were — clearly, because the cast is silver, instead of pewter, they were probably poured for some, well some prince or duke, could've been a bishop perhaps although the enamel suggests a more decorative, private chapel, probably, in one of the palazzos . . .

LAURIE: A palazzo? Where?

(She looks at him fully now.)

FRANK: Well, they're Venetian. So, a palazzo. On one of the canals.

LAURIE: Have you ever been to Venice?

FRANK: Yes, several times.

LAURIE: I haven't.

(Beat.)

I've wanted to. They say it's so beautiful. But there's never the right time, you know. I'm working, or Ethan's in a show, or has an audition he doesn't want to, you know, it's just the way things happen. You mean to go to Venice, and you never, it never . . .

(Really looking at the angels, almost surprised, suddenly.)

They have wings.

FRANK: Yes, they're angels.

LAURIE: Well, Frank. They are so beautiful. They're exquisite.

(She sits, overwhelmed.)

FRANK: I thought so.

LAURIE: Is that a lute, she's playing?

FRANK: Yes.

LAURIE: What kind of horn is that? It looks like a clarinet.

FRANK: I don't know, actually. Maybe it is a clarinet.

(Laurie wipes her eyes.)

LAURIE: Well, look at me, I'm ridiculous. They're so beautiful, they made me cry.

FRANK: I'm glad you like them. They're for you. I want you to have them.

LAURIE: Oh, Frank, I could never afford to buy something like this.

FRANK: No, it's a gift.

LAURIE: Well, but — they must be worth a fortune. Look at them. They're the most beautiful things I've ever seen.

FRANK: I thought so. I thought you would think so. And I felt so stupid, I must apologize, not that, these are not an apology, I, just, I misunderstood. Ethan can be so charming. I don't get to spend time with him. When we were little, I used to follow him around, like a young god, he was . . . well, you can imagine.

LAURIE: Yes.

FRANK: I thought they were for you. The butterflies. But these fly too, you see. Well, they don't literally fly. You know that. Of course, the butterflies don't either. They're dead.

LAURIE: Yes, this is a much better gift because angels don't die, do they? They are never dead. That's important.

FRANK: Well . . .

LAURIE: *(Chattering, brave.)* No, it is. I know about this. Just before Ethan and I met, I'd been with someone for a long time, six years, and he was, he worked at the Brooklyn Museum, and then he went over to the Public Library, he was one of those people who's a curator or something, I could never quite get it completely straight, but it was all quite important, scholarly, knowledgeable. And he was a wonderful, decent person, kind, and interesting, he knew everything about everything, but the fact is, he was just obsessed with death. Literally. It was all we talked about.

FRANK: For six years?

LAURIE: Yes! He knew so much about it. You know, historically how different cultures defined death, what it meant to people, different religions and how they define the afterlife. Anytime we'd go on holiday, wherever we were, we had have to stop at the graveyards and study the aesthetics of the local headstones. Because of the Brooklyn Museum, obviously, he knew so much about the Egyptians, so we would have, oh my God, endless, I know so much about mummification, I could do it. I could actually mummify somebody.

FRANK: Really.

(They are both starting to laugh.)

LAURIE: Yes, but that wasn't even — the field-trip aspect of it all was actually kind of entertaining. But the rest of it was just so relentlessly dreary. And I did come to realize, finally, that he may have been fascinating, and honest, and a good person, but he was also completely nuts. I mean, just because you're embracing death does not mean that you're not running away from life. And then I met Ethan, with all that anger and bitterness, and he seemed such a life-force, he . . .

(Catching herself.)

Do you think angels really fly? I mean, you don't ever really see it, in art, paintings and sculpture, and you know, those things in church, the only ones who seem to fly, ever, are those disgusting little fat babies.

FRANK: Putti.

LAURIE: That's such a good word for them, isn't it? Putti. Fat flying babies. But the angels, you know, the titans, they just seem to stand around with those majestic wings and deliver messages, or wield swords or play instruments. Why is that, do you think? Maybe the wings don't work. That would be just like God, wouldn't it, to make something that beautiful that simply doesn't work. Like Ethan. Not like Ethan, not — I don't know what I'm saying. I'm sorry. What's Venice like?

(Frank shifts, uncomfortable, feeling for her.)

FRANK: One morning, the first time I went there, I couldn't sleep, because of the time difference, so I got up at I think four or four thirty in the morning, and walked around and everything, the piazzas were utterly deserted, and I stood outside Saint Mark's Basilica and there was a nun, sweeping the sidewalk while the sun rose. And then I got lost and found a tiny square, walls and windows rising so simply, archways, children, Marco Polo was born there, this plaque on the wall. It's like that. It's like them.

(He indicates the angels. She looks up at him, simple.)

LAURIE: What should I do, Frank?

(Frank looks at her, shakes his head, inarticulate. Ethan enters, from outside.)

ETHAN: There you are. I've been looking all over for you.

LAURIE: Really? Because I've been looking for you.

ETHAN: Yes, I was afraid you'd be worried.

(To Frank, blithe.)

I couldn't sleep last night so I got up and walked into town. I don't know what's the matter with me. Maybe Paul's right, maybe I am having some sort of midlife crisis, although I would hate to give him credit for any sort of insight about me whatsoever. These are nice. Good god, they weigh a ton. What is this, solid lead?

(He looks at the bottom of one of the angels.)

FRANK: Silver.

ETHAN: *(Impressed.)* No, really?

(To Laurie, lying easily.)

I should've left a note, I know, but I honestly didn't think it would turn into an all night jaunt. It truly did not even occur to me until I was six miles down the road that you might wake up and worry.

LAURIE: I did wake up.

ETHAN: I'm so sorry. You must have been frantic.

LAURIE: No. I did, actually, I saw a light on, up here, so I thought it might be you. So I came up to see.

ETHAN: You did.

LAURIE: Yes. I stood at the window. The light was on, and then it went out. But it wasn't you, I guess, because you were walking.

ETHAN: Yes. It was quite nostalgic. Frank and I, when we were kids, we used to spend summers with our grandparents over in East Hampton. Sneak out and spend the night howling at the moon. You'll have to come with me, next time. It's fantastic, the moon, stars, smell of dew and wet leaves. *(He is idly playing with one of the angels. Frank steps forward and takes it from him.)*

FRANK: Please.

ETHAN: Oh, sorry. It's so solid, you forget, don't you, that it's some sort of unbelievable treasure.

FRANK: I don't.

(He sets it down, not looking at Ethan. Sophie enters from the kitchen. She stops. They all look at each other.)

SOPHIE: Good morning.

ETHAN: Yes, hello. Off to work?

SOPHIE: Yes.

(Beat, to Frank.)

Thank you. For the butterflies. They mean so much to me.

FRANK: You're welcome.

(She goes. Blackout.)

SCENE TEN

Sophie and Paul, in light.

PAUL: *(Off pages, vaguely surprised.)* Some of this is good.
   (He hands it to her.)
SOPHIE: Thank you.
PAUL: The one phrase, where the sister says "some three years ago," that has a
   nice sound to it.
SOPHIE: Oh.
   (Beat.)
   "Some three years ago?"
PAUL: Yes.
SOPHIE: Well, knock yourself out, Paul.
   (He doesn't crack a smile.)
SOPHIE: *(Continuing; cautious.)* I mean, that's all you liked? I wrote ten pages
   about, well, what you asked. You asked me to write that, I would never,
   otherwise. I'm sorry. I just — I — I — I know it's ridiculous for me to
   try and write about one of your characters, but you proposed it, and
   I — I tried — and — this is as important to me as it is to you. I know
   I'm a complete neophyte. I know that. But I'm a writer, too.
PAUL: Did you think what you wrote was good?
   (Beat.)
SOPHIE: Yes, I did, actually. I thought some of it was good.
PAUL: Well, that's what I said. Some of it is good. Some of it's facile.
SOPHIE: Yeah, OK.
PAUL: I mean that in the good sense. The academic sense.
SOPHIE: OK. I said OK.
   (She starts to put it away.)
PAUL: Some of it's good, I said.
   (He holds his hand out. She hands him the pages back, confused.)
SOPHIE: So . . .
PAUL: Some of it's useful.
SOPHIE: *(Surprised.)* You're going to use it?
PAUL: What's this butterfly thing Ethan was talking about?
SOPHIE: *(Reacting, startled at the change of subject.)* Oh. It's nothing. I, it's
   something I've been working on, based on a family story.
PAUL: What's the story?

SOPHIE: It's not a story, actually; it's just what happened. My father's father collected butterflies, and the butterflies were lost.

PAUL: How were they lost?

SOPHIE: By accident. Someone didn't take care of them, and then . . . they were thrown away.

PAUL: What are you writing about it?

(She struggles to articulate this. It is the most open she has ever been with him.)

SOPHIE: I'm not sure yet. I'm haunted by it. That someone could spend so much time on something beautiful, that someone else just couldn't see. That someone else would treat so carelessly.

PAUL: What was he like? The butterfly collector.

SOPHIE: I never knew him. He died when my father was very young.

PAUL: What does your father say about him?

(Sophie shakes her head, at a loss. After a moment, she gets it together.)

SOPHIE: My father actually doesn't speak of him at all.

PAUL: Why not?

SOPHIE: It's not his nature.

PAUL: What is his nature?

SOPHIE: *(Beat.)* I'm not writing about him.

PAUL: Maybe you should be.

SOPHIE: You haven't even read it.

PAUL: Why are you so defensive?

SOPHIE: Why am I — I'm sorry.

(Beat.)

I don't want to talk about this.

PAUL: Why not?

SOPHIE: *(Definitive.)* Because I don't.

PAUL: Why not?

SOPHIE: Paul — you know, Paul — why do you do this? I mean, what are we like bugs to you? We are, you know, you put us in a jar, you shake it up and see what happens. Well, you know, you're — your family may find it amusing, actually, I don't know what they find it, but you're not my father. I don't have to do this.

(She stands, to go.)

PAUL: I don't want to be your father.

(She looks at him.)

SOPHIE: I'm going, now. I, I don't know —

PAUL: Sentences.

SOPHIE: *(Suddenly really unnerved.)* Would you stop that? Please?

PAUL: Don't go, Sophie. Don't go. Show me what you've written about the butterflies.

SOPHIE: It's terrible. I don't want you to see it. You'll think it's terrible.

PAUL: No.

(He goes to her. She is miserable. After a moment, he reaches over, takes her face and kisses her. She goes along with it for a moment, then pulls away, sudden.)

SOPHIE: No, no, I can't do this. I'm sorry. Oh. I'm sorry. I can't do this.

PAUL: Yes, you can.

SOPHIE: No. I can't.

(Paul reaches for her again, but she absolutely pushes him away.)

SOPHIE: *(Continuing.)* I'm sorry. I have so much respect for you. And I'm so flattered.

(This was the wrong thing to say.)

PAUL: Oh, you're flattered.

SOPHIE: Please, don't — .

PAUL: Don't?

(Beat.)

No, please, tell me how to feel.

SOPHIE: I'm sorry.

PAUL: Stop apologizing.

(She looks around, helpless, caught.)

PAUL: *(Continuing.)* Those pages? The butterflies? Or would that make you uncomfortable, too? Do I have to beg for that, too?

(She shakes her head. After a moment, she reaches into her folder, takes out a slender manuscript, and hands it to him. Blackout.)

SCENE ELEVEN

Several days later. Margaret is looking through cookbooks. Ethan prowls behind her, alert, looking for Sophie.

MARGARET: How does this sound? "Braised Quail in a Pinot Noir Sauce."

ETHAN: No one really eats quail.

MARGARET: Well, you wouldn't use quail, of course, you'd get those little cornish game hens.

ETHAN: Then why don't they call it Cornish Game Hens in a Pinot Noir Sauce?

MARGARET: Because it doesn't sound as good, I should think. Braised Duck in Pinot Noir . . . no, that doesn't work either. Oh, how about this? Poached Salmon in a Lime Cilantro Dressing. That sounds very good, but maybe it's too fishy. Do you think it sounds fishy?

ETHAN: Well, "salmon"?

MARGARET: Yes, I see your point. Then again, it could be Orange Roughy, which does not sound a bit fishy, but in fact always is. Salmon isn't always terribly fishy, in fact I find salmon the least fishy of all fish. If only your father would give me some leeway on this fish issue. Fish issue, well, that does not sound good, does it? That's the problem, being married to a writer, you think about things like this.

ETHAN: I think salmon sounds terrific. I vote for the salmon.

MARGARET: You just want it because I reminded you that your father doesn't like it. Really, Ethan, you're ridiculous.

ETHAN: That is a terrible thing for a mother to say to her favorite son.

MARGARET: Who said you were my favorite? You come up here and annoy your father, you're not my favorite at all. Oh, listen to this: Oysters in Heavy Cream with Sauerkraut, Lemon and Caviar.

ETHAN: That's impossible.

MARGARET: Do you think that sounds good?

ETHAN: It sounds like it will kill you.

MARGARET: It's an appetizer, of course, it's not the sort of thing you could make a whole meal of.

ETHAN: Thank God.

MARGARET: Oysters, heavy cream, sauerkraut, lemon and caviar. I'm trying to figure out what that would taste like.

ETHAN: Russia, before the revolution.

MARGARET: Exactly. I think we have to do it. I could run up to Mystic and get them right off the pier, I haven't done that in years, there's no point, really, since Paul won't eat fish, but oysters. If you and Laurie came with me, we could have lunch. Now this is a plan.

ETHAN: He's gone all day then?

MARGARET: Yes, he had a meeting with Roger to discuss his progress with the book.

ETHAN: Has there been progress?

MARGARET: I guess we'll find out, won't we? If it goes well, I think we might be able to relax, finally. If it doesn't, well then I don't know, I can't think about that. He'll meet with Roger and then lunch with the book review, I think, they want him to do a piece on someone . . . Thomas Mann? Did he already do that?

ETHAN: Somebody did. Somebody always does.

MARGARET: Yes, and I never liked his books. So boring.

ETHAN: Puts Henry James to shame.

MARGARET: Exactly. Books are just like people, aren't they? Some of them are just so worthy, and wonderful and filled with — worthiness, but you just don't like them. And then some of them are just frivolous and entertaining and — I'm not saying romance novels, not like that, but Charles Dickens, for instance. I know he's not as refined as Henry James, but he makes me cry, and laugh, and all those strange sentences. It's life, isn't it? Some books make you feel alive.

ETHAN: Like people.

MARGARET: Some people, yes. For all their faults, you can't help but love them.

(She goes to him, kisses him with real affection. .)

MARGARET: *(Continuing.)* You should take that play, you know.

ETHAN: "That play" has not been offered to me, Mom.

MARGARET: Please. Your agent calls about it every day. I know a few things about agents. They don't call like that unless they know you're going to get it.

ETHAN: You may know about agents, but you know nothing about the theater.

MARGARET: I may not know anything about the theater, but I know plenty about you, young man. You should go back to the city, do that terrible audition, meet with those horrible play people and charm them, Ethan, I've seen you be charming. Just do whatever you have to do to get that part. And then once you have it, you'll feel better, and you can take Laurie out to a nice dinner in a very nice restaurant and treat her like a queen, because that's what she is, you know.

ETHAN: *(Beat.)* I know. I know, that's what I should do.

MARGARET: *(Gentle.)* I know you know that.

(He kisses her hand, admitting she's right. Sophie comes down the stairs. He looks at her, guilty. She looks away, quickly.)

SOPHIE: Excuse me.

ETHAN: There she is, the elusive Sophie. We've barely caught a glimpse of you all week.

SOPHIE: I'm sorry. I've been so busy.

(She heads for the kitchen.)

ETHAN: That's no excuse today. I happen to know that Paul is up and gone.

MARGARET: Don't bother her, Ethan. She said she's working.

ETHAN: You just said he was going to be gone all day.

MARGARET: I'm sure she has plenty to do nonetheless. Thank you, Sophie.

(Sophie turns to go.)

ETHAN: She's not a slave.

MARGARET: I didn't say she was.

SOPHIE: I'm fine.

ETHAN: I don't think you are. Look at you, running away like a scared little girl. You are running away, is that right?

SOPHIE: *(Beat, polite.)* I'm afraid I have to.

ETHAN: Well, I won't let you. The ogre is gone for now, and we're just his nice relatives. Come sit and have a coffee with us. All this running away, you can't possibly keep it up forever, it's making all of us extremely tense.

(Sophie does not know how to respond to this. Laurie enters. There is a sudden chill.)

MARGARET: Oh, there you are, Laurie. We have such a wonderful plan for the afternoon, we're going into Mystic to buy oysters and have lunch. You, me and Ethan.

LAURIE: We are?

MARGARET: Yes, but we have to leave now, I think, because it's a forty-five minute drive, oh, and we can stop and pick up Frank, that will be fun. Let me just find the car keys.

(She goes into the kitchen. Laurie, Sophie, and Ethan are alone for a moment.)

SOPHIE: Excuse me.

(She goes. After a beat.)

ETHAN: I think that Paul may have already ruined that nice girl. Remember when she showed up, how charming she was?

LAURIE: We need to go back to the city, Ethan.

(Beat.)

ETHAN: Do we? Why?

LAURIE: Please don't do that. Please. The past five days have been hideous, every time I try to talk to you, this — being — is there, you're like a different person and I've been so stunned, I guess, that I've just waited, and hoped that you'd come back. But I can't keep trying and just getting — this. This. I've been trying to understand and I can see how it happened —

I can. He's so hard on you, he barely speaks to you, and she's up there, with him, all the time —

ETHAN: Yes, yes. OK. Yes.

(*Beat.*)

LAURIE: Yes?

ETHAN: (*Ashamed.*) Yes.

LAURIE: Then you admit it. That —

ETHAN: (*Simple.*) Laurie. Don't. You're right. I'm saying you're right, we should go back. We'll go back. To the city. Today.

LAURIE: Good.

(*There is a sad moment. She starts to cry, a bit.*)

ETHAN: Oh, don't — please — I feel terrible enough as it is —

LAURIE: I'm sorry. It's just, I've been so frightened. It's just been terrible, not being able to talk to you, you've been so —

ETHAN: I know. I know, I know, there's no excuse, I'm not trying to make one, but you're right, this place works on me, it's him, obviously, you're right about that, too, not to make excuses, but it's just deeply confusing for me to be here. I tried to tell you. Before we came.

LAURIE: You did, I just thought you were finally at a place where you could make your peace with it, and him, you've been so well, so much happier, lately —

ETHAN: Yes, because of you. You've brought so much sanity into my life, everything seems possible and you were coming with me, so I thought I could handle it or I never would have come. You know that, don't you? If I knew, before, what it would be like, what would happen, I would never have put us in this situation.

LAURIE: You haven't before? Have you?

ETHAN: What do you mean?

LAURIE: Have you, Ethan? Before.

(*Beat.*)

Have you cheated on me before.

(*Beat.*)

ETHAN: No. No, absolutely not, and God knows I've had the opportunity, but I — you've brought meaning into my life, Laurie, just simple meaning, you know that, I haven't ever needed anyone the way I need you, I couldn't put that in danger, please tell me I haven't —

LAURIE: I don't want to lose you, Ethan —

ETHAN: Tell me I haven't lost you.

(There is a terrible, sad moment. She reaches over and takes his hand. He hugs her, holds her for a long moment, kisses her.)

LAURIE: Can we go now? Can we just go home right now?

ETHAN: Absolutely. Lunch with Mom, then we go.

LAURIE: No, now. Just now, please.

ETHAN: Laurie. It's fine. We'll be out of the house, we'll be away from it, and then we'll go. Come on, Mom is on pins and needles about Paul's book, we can't just let her suffer all day.

LAURIE: I know, but I just need to heal, now, we need to —

ETHAN: This is what we should do. You go have lunch with Mom. Let me spend the afternoon packing us up —

LAURIE: Ethan —

ETHAN: And then she's got this terrific dinner planned, some kind of oyster extravaganza. Not to be missed, it sounds like. So. We'll say a proper good-bye. And never look back.

(He kisses her hand. She looks at him, devastated.)

LAURIE: Are you acting?

ETHAN: *(Startled.)* What?

LAURIE: *(Devastated.)* Oh, God. You're acting, aren't you?

ETHAN: No. No!

(He looks at her, beseeching. Laurie looks away. Margaret enters.)

MARGARET: Here we go, I'm sorry that took a minute, but I needed to make a list. Are we ready? Oh, we should stop, shouldn't we, and bring Frank his angels, it makes me much too nervous. All week, I can't believe he just left them here.

(She starts to pick up the angels.)

LAURIE: *(Upset, covering.)* No, he gave them to me.

MARGARET: What?

LAURIE: He brought them, they're for me. They were a gift.

MARGARET: Oh, he couldn't.

LAURIE: Why not?

MARGARET: Well, I — . I suppose he could. I just — did he tell you how much they were worth?

LAURIE: No.

MARGARET: They're worth eighteen thousand dollars, at least. That's what he paid for them. I'm sure he could, in this market — well. You're sure he meant to give them to you?

LAURIE: *(Beat.)* Yes.

MARGARET: Well, then we'll just leave them here, won't we? Shall we go?

ETHAN: Laurie and I are taking off tonight, Mom.

MARGARET: *(Pleased.)* Are you?

ETHAN: Yes, I'm going to bow down to the gods of theater, kiss some ass and see if I can resurrect my career.

MARGARET: I think that's wise.

ETHAN: So, she's going to have lunch with you while I take the afternoon to pack.

LAURIE: *(Still.)* You're not coming with us, then.

ETHAN: *(Quiet.)* We just decided, Laurie, to take off right after dinner. You said you wanted to get on the road.

LAURIE: Yes, that's what we decided.

ETHAN: So . . . I just think I should skip lunch.

(A slight, sad pause.)

MARGARET: Oh, Ethan.

LAURIE: It's fine, Margaret. You and I will have a lovely time, just the two of us.

(She goes to Ethan, decides at the last moment not to kiss him, and goes. Margaret looks after her, then turns back to Ethan.)

MARGARET: Ethan —

ETHAN: Yes.

(Margaret shakes her head, and goes. Ethan sprawls on the couch for a long moment, thinking. Sophie enters, carrying the plate of butterflies. She sees him on the couch and turns to go back immediately.)

ETHAN: *(Continuing.)* Hello.

(Beat. Sophie stops, speaks with a polite innocence.)

SOPHIE: I'm sorry. I thought you had gone. Margaret said you, all of you, were going to lunch.

ETHAN: No, I decided not to go.

SOPHIE: Well. I'm glad you're here. I didn't mean to disturb you. But I wanted to return the butterflies. I didn't realize how valuable they were. I simply can't accept them.

ETHAN: You can't?

SOPHIE: No.

ETHAN: But you thought I was gone. So why bring the butterflies?

SOPHIE: I was going to leave them here. With a note.

ETHAN: Look. I'm sorry I put you in this position. It wasn't my intention. I —

SOPHIE: No, it's fine, I put myself there, I don't blame anyone, I just, it can't happen again.

ETHAN: No.

SOPHIE: No.

ETHAN: I'm going back to the city tonight.

SOPHIE: Good. So, here are the butterflies and and — that's all.

ETHAN: Please, keep them.

SOPHIE: I can't keep them.

ETHAN: If you're worried about my girlfriend —

SOPHIE: I'm not worried about your girlfriend. Perhaps you should worry about your girlfriend; I don't know your girlfriend. The person I am worried about is . . .

(She stops herself.)

ETHAN: What?

SOPHIE: Nothing. Please. Just take them back. I need to go.

(She starts to go.)

ETHAN: He hit on you.

(She turns and looks at him.)

SOPHIE: What?

ETHAN: My father. Hit on you. Didn't he?

SOPHIE: *(A beat; surprised.)* Yes. He did.

ETHAN: What did you do?

SOPHIE: What did I do?

ETHAN: It's a fair enough question, Sophie. You're not as innocent as you pretend to be, and I suspect you've been hit on before.

SOPHIE: Never with such exquisite complication.

ETHAN: *(Angry.)* Are you going to tell me what happened or not?

SOPHIE: What do you think happened? He kissed me, and — it was — I, I am very confused right now, all right? So —

ETHAN: Did you enjoy it?

SOPHIE: Enjoyed it? I don't — I was overwhelmed —

ETHAN: *(Over.)* Oh, overwhelmed. That's good. He overwhelmed you. So you had nothing to do with it. It was rape, huh, you didn't enjoy it at all, you fought but you know, a sixty-four-year-old guy, he can be pretty overwhelming —

SOPHIE: *(Angry.)* OK, "overwhelmed" was the wrong word. I was thrilled. It was thrilling —

ETHAN: *(Enraged.)* Thrilling. Which part, the kiss or the rest of it, was it thrilling to have my father feel you up?

(She stares at him in shock. He backs down, turns away, knowing he's gone too far.)

SOPHIE: Look. I am here to work. This is — I am here to write. I am here to learn.

ETHAN: An aging Nobel laureate and his demonic son have both fallen for you, simultaneously. If you can't learn from that, you're no writer.

SOPHIE: Yes, that's very amusing. Thank you.

ETHAN: Did you sleep with him?

SOPHIE: *(Biting.)* No! I didn't sleep with him!

ETHAN: Are you going to sleep with him?

(She looks at him, enraged by this.)

It's a fair question, Sophie. You came here —

SOPHIE: I came here to work —

ETHAN: Well, other things happened, didn't they? What, am I just his son? Is that all I am to you, "his son," you made a mistake, you slept with the son when you could have had the man himself! Sold yourself short, didn't you? Got to get rid of the son now, 'cause Dad's the real prize!

SOPHIE: That is not what I am doing!

ETHAN: It is exactly what you're doing!

SOPHIE: You're leaving anyway, you just said —

ETHAN: Well, that explains your relief. I'm taking off, so you and Dad have a clear playing field.

SOPHIE: This is impossible. You see? You must see how impossible this is, already — this entire week has been a nightmare, going in there ten hours a day after I turned him down, believe me, is no fucking picnic, but I do it! And I intend to continue doing it, so I cannot do this!

(She starts for the door.)

ETHAN: So you're doing this for your art, that's why you've been dodging me all week?

SOPHIE: I'm trying to survive here!

ETHAN: It's going to save you, isn't it? Make you whole. Make you wise. A really great sentence, shows you a corner of insight into the human condition, you think you've seen the face of God. That's why Paul has you. Got to get close to that, he's the lodestone, the magic, you have to touch it, like the hem of Christ's robe —

(Beat.)

It's OK. He's got me, too. All that art, all that approval, all that love, just out of reach. That big hole inside you, he's the only thing that can plug that up. And he's a complete shit head.

SOPHIE: I should have done it. Is that what you're saying?

ETHAN: Quite the opposite, Sophie. I think you know that.

(Beat.)

SOPHIE: I am drowning here.

ETHAN: I have to know this. If it were just me. If it were you, and me, and nothing else. No one else. What would you be saying to me now?

SOPHIE: *(Lost.)* It's not possible to do that.

ETHAN: It is. He is not here. I am the only one here.

(He is close to her. They kiss. The kiss begins to get involved, but she pulls away.)

SOPHIE: We can't do this here.

(She takes him out. Blackout.)

SCENE TWELVE

Later that day. Dusk. It is raining. The phone is ringing.

Frank and Laurie enter the house, on a run, carrying grocery bags. Margaret runs for the phone.

MARGARET: Ethan, pick up the phone! Ethan, where — oh —

(Getting the phone.)

Hello? Oh, Roger —

(Beat.)

Well, that's wonderful, Roger. I know, we all slow down a bit with age, I'm afraid, so — yes, except for you, it seems, you're a speed-reader, calling so quickly. Paul isn't even back yet, he's still en route. I will, I'll tell him. All right. Bye bye.

(She hangs up.)

Well, Roger loves it!

FRANK: Dad finished? He finished it?

MARGARET: No, he compromised. He gave him half of it. So the advance is off the table, the twelve-year-olds are sated, and the writing is very good, that's what Roger says. Apparently there's some section about a girl, he thinks it's the first time Paul has actually cracked the female psyche. I'm not going to tell him that, of course.

FRANK: That's great, Mom.

MARGARET: Yes, I couldn't be more — just, relieved.

(Laurie picks a book of the shelf.)

LAURIE: This is the first one?

MARGARET: Yes, but you can't read that, you'll never make it through. It's very beautiful, but a little boring. This one is my favorite. Oh, and this is good.

(She takes the books off the shelves, gives them to Laurie, and goes to the door, looking.)

MARGARET: *(Continuing.)* What time is it? I should start in on those oysters, but I don't see the point of it if no one's going to show up.

FRANK: We're here.

MARGARET: Yes, but there's oysters for six, and they're rather rich. If the three of us ate them all I think it might be a deadly catastrophe.

LAURIE: *(To Frank.)* Which ones do you like?

FRANK: They're all good.

MARGARET: Don't listen to him, what does he know. He hasn't read any of them.

LAURIE: *(Surprised.)* Frank. You don't read your father's books?

FRANK: *(Vaguely embarrassed.)* I grew up with it. For a long time I thought that everyone had a father who wrote books. Then when I realized it was something special, I found that I preferred not to know. Sort of like seeing an island off in the distance. If you've never been there, you can pretend there are pirates on it. If you have been there, you know that there are no pirates, there's only a McDonald's.

MARGARET: Well, what a charming image, Frank. I'll be sure to tell Paul, you don't read his books because you don't want to know where the McDonald's is.

FRANK: He doesn't care if I read his books, Mom.

LAURIE: Still, aren't you curious? Not everyone's father has a Nobel.

MARGARET: Oh, dear, yes, but you know they give those things out for all sorts of reasons. Paul's year, apparently the committee was angry because the academics kept shouting about Third World writers and literary racism, things like that, so they were determined that it would go to a First World White Man. Three cheers for the patriarchy, that was the rumor.

LAURIE: That can't be why they gave it to him.

MARGARET: Of course not only that, but you'd be surprised, how things factor in. He's a wonderful stylist, it's true, but some of them slip. When he gets cocky, the surface — frankly, there's nothing underneath.

LAURIE: What should be underneath?

MARGARET: That's an excellent question. You could be a critic.

FRANK: Show her the one you wrote.

LAURIE: What?

MARGARET: Oh Frank, I didn't write it. You've got to stop saying that.

FRANK: You wrote a lot of it. Here it is —

(Laurie looks at them, amazed, as Margaret and Frank fight over the book.)

MARGARET: I drafted a few sections for him. He was having a hard time, I told you about that —

LAURIE: You wrote some of his books?

MARGARET: I contributed to one or two. He reworks everything so many times it doesn't finally amount to more than an idea or two.

FRANK: You wrote big chunks —

MARGARET: I drafted. Drafting is different from writing, and it happens much more than you know. Brecht? It doesn't take away from his genius, mind you, but he didn't write all those plays. No indeed. He slept with some very smart women, that one.

(Beat.)

This is nice, isn't it? Just the three of us. Screw the oysters, we'll have a party just ourselves. Would you like some cheese and crackers? Oo, brie —

FRANK: Yes. Thank you.

MARGARET: I'm not taking anything away. Truly. I didn't need any ridiculous Nobel committee to tell me how good he is. And it doesn't matter, the ones that slip. I've lived with the man, and I know what genius is. Three or four of those really, really stand up.

(Off the book in Laurie's hand.)

And that one is unbelievably good.

(Margaret exits. Laurie turns to Frank.)

LAURIE: I can't believe you've never read them.

FRANK: Well, neither have you.

LAURIE: Well, he's not my father, and yes I have.

FRANK: You have?

LAURIE: Yes, of course. When I started seeing Ethan I read them all.

(She puts the books back on the shelves.)

FRANK: But you —

LAURIE: I didn't anything. You both just assumed. You have a very strange family, Frank.

FRANK: (A concession.) All families are strange, I think.

LAURIE: Mine wasn't.

FRANK: No?

LAURIE: It was just me, and my dad, and my mom. Both of them worked. Sometimes we didn't have enough money, but it always came out all right. And we were all so happy with each other.

FRANK: That sounds — wonderful.

LAURIE: I think it was! Although, maybe it was a little too cozy, is that possible? Clearly, I haven't rushed into marriage, and the men I get involved with. Maybe we weren't really happy. Or maybe I had too much happiness, as a child. Maybe now, I'm looking for unhappiness.

FRANK: Do you really think that?

LAURIE: Well, I spent six years talking about death in what may have been the most ludicrous relationship ever tolerated. And now I've spent an entire week lying next to a man, to a man who the entire time, has been thinking about another woman. The evidence is not in my favor.

(It pains her to admit it. Frank thinks, trying to be positive.)

FRANK: A week, that's not so long, to be unhappy.

LAURIE: *(Brave.)* It is long enough for me. Here, Frank, I hate to do it, but I'm going to have to give these back to you.

FRANK: No, please.

LAURIE: They're much too valuable. I would just worry about them all the time. You keep them. Save them for me. Then come see me, in the city, and tell me how they're doing.

FRANK: *(A brief surprise and disappointment.)* Are you going?

LAURIE: Oh. Yes. I most certainly am.

FRANK: Don't go. Come —

(Struggling.)

There's an extra room. In my apartment. I have the entire building, you know. Above the shop, there's, it's almost like a guesthouse.

LAURIE: I've had quite my fill of guesthouses.

FRANK: Then, it's a room. It has it's own bathroom. And the kitchen, it's right there.

(He stops. She looks at him.)

LAURIE: I don't think I can, Frank.

FRANK: No, of course not. It's foolish. I just hate, after — what, if I hadn't, my God —

LAURIE: Frank, it's not in any way your fault. How could it be?

FRANK: I know, that's not — .

LAURIE: What then?

FRANK: It just makes me sad. To think of you alone.

LAURIE: You're alone.

FRANK: Oh. Well. No, it actually, I'm surrounded by so much beauty. The things of culture, the treasures — it's my life's work. People destroy each other. Cultures die. And I'm left with the angels. So. It doesn't seem so bad, really, at all.

(He shrugs, embarrassed.)

LAURIE: *(After a moment, a statement.)* You're not gay, are you?

FRANK: Me? Oh. No. Why?

LAURIE: Ethan told me you were.

FRANK: Oh. No.

(He laughs a little at the thought.)

LAURIE: Why does he think that?

FRANK: Oh, Ethan, he — I don't know.

(Beat.)

Listen. I, I wanted to — . If you had met me. First. If you had met me, first, do you think —

(He can't finish. Beat.)

LAURIE: Oh. I don't know, Frank. There's just no way to know.

FRANK: No, it's fine.

LAURIE: Frank —

FRANK: It's fine. Of course it's fine. Oh, and here he is.

LAURIE: Ethan?

FRANK: My father. Paul.

(Paul appears through the back door, as Margaret returns with the wine.)

MARGARET: Is that Paul? There you are, we've been so worried.

PAUL: Fucking traffic.

MARGARET: Roger called, sweetheart.

PAUL: He called? Already? What did he say?

MARGARET: He loved it. He put everything aside, spent the morning and afternoon reading it, and he loves every word. You have to call him back and hear him, he was raving. You're still a genius, his favorite writer, of course none of us are surprised to hear it.

PAUL: No, that's . . . good news.

(He sits, relieved.)

MARGARET: *(To Laurie.)* He always worries. And he's always wrong.

PAUL: *(Half to himself.)* Well, you never . . . it shouldn't be a surprise, I suppose, after all this time, but you just never get used to it. There's always that terror, maybe it's not good, maybe you've lost it. Hemingway, Christ, what a fate. He liked it?

MARGARET: Loved it. It's good you let him see some of it. It was a very smart thing to do.

(Paul shakes his head and moves around, restless.)

PAUL: I have to get back to work.

MARGARET: Paul, no. It's past six, and I have oysters.

PAUL: Oysters? I don't eat fish.

MARGARET: And oysters are not fish. You like them, you know you do.

PAUL: I have to work.

MARGARET: Really, Paul, I've been looking forward all day to making this strange and wonderful dish —

PAUL: Sophie! Where is she, is she in her room? Go back and get her.
(He heads for the steps.)

MARGARET: Paul, please. We'll have champagne, it's such good news about the book, Roger says it's really good, as good as anything you've ever done —

PAUL: Then I'd better finish it, hadn't I? Somebody find that girl and send her up.

LAURIE: She's not here.
(Beat. Paul turns.)

PAUL: Well, where is she?

LAURIE: She went off, with Ethan.

PAUL: Where'd they go?

LAURIE: *(Deliberate.)* She's with Ethan, Paul. She's with Ethan.
(Frank looks down. All of them stand for a moment, while Paul figures this out. Blackout.)

SCENE THIRTEEN

Paul, in light. Sophie enters, flustered.

SOPHIE: Hello. Good morning. I'm sorry I'm late.

PAUL: Overslept.

SOPHIE: Yes, I got in late. I was out late, so, I'm sorry. How did it go, yesterday?

PAUL: Sit down. I read your pages.

SOPHIE: You did. I didn't want to ask, I know you've been worried about — how did it go, with Roger?

PAUL: Sophie, I finally read your butterfly story. Do you want to know what I think of it or not?

SOPHIE: *(Beat.)* Yes.
(But she doesn't. Paul looks at the pages, then nods.)

PAUL: They're good. It's good.

SOPHIE: *(Deeply relieved.)* It is.

PAUL: The way you build the internal structure, deepening the tone as the writing goes on, is sophisticated. Beautiful opening sentence, "My father's father collected butterflies," elegaic, evocative — the coldness of the storytelling is maybe a bit off-putting, but it develops into something quite moving. Technique is good overall. There's a warmth at the center of the piece that's terrific, the sort of thing you can't teach, it's either there or it isn't. Kind of old-fashioned, even. Gardner would've liked your stuff.

SOPHIE: Thank you.

PAUL: I have a few reservations about some choices. Images collapse in places, sentences run on a bit. A piece of fiction is like a creating a record, does your generation remember records?

SOPHIE: You mean like a phonograph record?

PAUL: God, now I really feel old. Yes, an old phonograph record, the line of the narrative is like a groove on a record and your job as a writer, is to make sure the needle — the needle, right, the reader — doesn't skip out of the groove. So every word is essential. Right? Every image, every comma, exactly in place. Understand?

SOPHIE: Yes.

PAUL: You have an agent?

SOPHIE: No, I —

PAUL: Good. Agents will ruin you; they put young writers on the market years before they're ready and they never develop, or grow into anything. It all becomes hype. Who else have you shown this to?

SOPHIE: No one.

PAUL: *(Correcting her.)* My son.

SOPHIE: Yes. Your, your son, but other than that —

PAUL: No. No one. If it's not ready to be seen, you don't let it out of your hands. When you're young, you get one shot. That's it. No one wants to hear from you. They are not hungrily reading every manuscript looking for the next girl genius. No agents, no editors, no friends of friends who work at *The New Yorker*, none of that nonsense until every sentence lifts off the page.

SOPHIE: OK.

PAUL: You understand? I'm saying this is good. This is good enough to work on for as many years as it takes. But as it stands, a starting place, you and I need to look at the particulars that are missing as yet. Who is the butterfly collector? What are the facts of his life? All this stuff about you and your family — the writing as I said is a bit plain, good but the larger question is, does it belong there at all.

SOPHIE: Take it out? Altogether?

PAUL: *(Thoughtful.)* He's the center. This paragraph here, that's where the meat of it is. The rest won't get you anywhere, is my bet.

SOPHIE: One paragraph?

PAUL: This paragraph, yes.

SOPHIE: Yes, but it — it's not merely — about — him —

PAUL: Then it should be.

SOPHIE: Why? Why is it always about the man —

PAUL: It's not always about the man, but this time it is. It's your writing, Sophie. You've given him the drive. Everyone else is a mere fact. Including you. This this this — goes —

(Tossing pages aside, he circles one paragraph.)

This is where you start over.

(He shows her. She doesn't reach for it.)

I've lost you.

SOPHIE: No.

PAUL: Don't tell me no, Sophie, for the past three weeks I've spent every waking minute with you sitting two inches away from me. What I've just told you is your dream come true. You're good, you're the real deal, so what's the problem?

SOPHIE: *(Quiet.)* You know I am serious about this.

PAUL: I said, it was good.

SOPHIE: And then you took it away.

PAUL: I merely pointed out that there are six hundred thousand people out there who think they're fiction writers. If you can't do better than this, you're just one of them. I think you can do better than this. That's actually what I said.

(A beat; he sighs.)

What did you think I was going to tell you? That it's perfect, I'm sending it to Roger tomorrow, we're going to make you a star?

SOPHIE: No, of course not —

PAUL: What I told you is better than that. You're an artist. You're the real thing, and you respond to that with some sort of peevish display of disappointment, what is it you want? You're young, you're pretty, and you're hoping to be the next literary pinup girl, is that all you want?

SOPHIE: I have to go.

(She stands.)

PAUL: You respond to criticism the way you respond to life. You run. This impulse will not serve you in the years to come.

(She turns, looks at him, suddenly flaring.)

SOPHIE: This is not about my character.

PAUL: Isn't it?

SOPHIE: No, Paul, it isn't. This is about the fact that you're angry because I turned you down.

PAUL: I can barely remember the girls I slept with. The ones I didn't don't give me a lot of reasons to think about them.

SOPHIE: Oh, you're not angry? Because that is like only the most hostile thing I have ever heard in my life —

PAUL: Well, you're young.

SOPHIE: And you're mad because I slept with your son, and not you.

(Beat.)

PAUL: Sex is sex, and writing is writing, and if you can't tell the difference, I can't help you with that. At the end of the summer, you can go back to New York and write a memoir about the three months you spent turning me down. You and Joyce Maynard can tour the country, give a lecture series.

SOPHIE: You're forty years older than me, how was I supposed to — is that what you would have wanted? For me to just sleep with you because — you're old?

(She grabs her manuscript and starts to go.)

PAUL: Sit down, Sophie. We have work to do.

SOPHIE: You —

PAUL: I don't give a shit who you sleep with. I have a novel to finish.

(He hands her a sheaf of yellow pages.)

We left off, she's in the garden.

(Blackout.)

SCENE FOURTEEN

Later the same day. Frank and Margaret are considering a plant.

FRANK: OK, Mom: I've studied it, I've worried it, I've considered it, I've tasted it. It's dust.

MARGARET: You're sure.

FRANK: I work with antiques sixteen hours a day, Mom. Dust, I know.

(Ethan appears in the doorway.)

ETHAN: Ask me what's happened today.

MARGARET: Oh, Ethan, really, I'm angry with you.

ETHAN: Ask me, Mom.

MARGARET: I won't ask. If you've been up to anything worse than what you've done already, I most certainly don't want to know about it.

ETHAN: Frank, ask me.

FRANK: I don't want to know either.

ETHAN: I got the part.

(This gets Margaret's attention.)

MARGARET: They made you that offer. Oh, Ethan.

(She kisses him.)

See, you should listen to your mother. I told you you would get that.

ETHAN: Apparently they were trying for somebody famous, but everyone's off doing sitcoms. *(Laughing.)* And then I was so absolutely uninterested, they began to panic, they were going to lose me as well. I mean, you always hear that, as soon as you decide you don't want something, or at least give up on getting it, that's when it comes back to you, but I thought that was some sort of idiotic metaphor about love, releasing a bird or something. Who knew it was literally true?

(Margaret is finally laughing with him.)

MARGARET: Where's Laurie? Has she heard?

(She looks out the back door. There's an awkward pause.)

ETHAN: I haven't told her yet. Sam just called, just this minute. Have you seen her?

FRANK: *(Startled.)* She went back to the city yesterday.

(Ethan picks up on this, hopeful.)

ETHAN: Oh, she did. That's right, we were going to. I was — so she went ahead?

FRANK: Yes. She did.

ETHAN: Did you talk to her, before she left?

FRANK: *(Chilly.)* Yes, as a matter of fact I did.

(The two brothers consider each other. Ethan nods, finally.)

ETHAN: Yes, I know, I've been behaving badly. I'll make it up to her. As soon as I get home, I'll apologize, day and night. It'll be fine.

MARGARET: You're leaving too, then?

ETHAN: I have to. Rehearsals don't start for a few weeks but I have absolutely done nothing all summer and my life is a disaster. I've got to put things in order. You know, pay the bills, get the dry cleaning done.

It's all just nonsense, but I have to do it now because once the play starts, I'm not going to have time to think of anything.

FRANK: What — that, what?

ETHAN: What?

(There is a brief pause as Frank considers smacking him.)

FRANK: *(Finally angry.)* That's it? That's why? You're leaving now so you can do laundry? So you can give yourself permission to turn into even more of a complete — narcissist, two weeks from now, that's why you want to go back now, when if you had — for weeks you've just been making a ruin, a ruin of people's — and that's why you're going back now? To do laundry?

ETHAN: What are you so mad about?

FRANK: What am I so mad about? You have everything, everything and she's, you run around, taking everything else, as if it's your right, it's not your right! You're not the only person on the planet. You're little! You're as little as the rest of us. Time is going to pass you by, just the way it passes us all. Only not all of us do damage.

ETHAN: You don't live, either.

FRANK: I live.

ETHAN: You sit in your little shop all day, dusting things off, until someone comes by and buys it from you. You don't get out there and act, you don't — do anything! You're a shopkeeper. You collect. And look how happy it's made you. Well, you know what? I am not going to apologize for the damage I cause. And you are not going to make your everyday, damage-free misery my problem.

MARGARET: Ethan.

FRANK: I am the audience, you asshole. The entire human race is the audience to people like you, and you — once in a while, couldn't you try to be worth it?

MARGARET: Frank.

FRANK: Don't talk to me, Mom.

(He sits. Ethan raises an eyebrow and turns to Margaret.)

ETHAN: That was a lousy thing to say. Heaven forbid he might actually be happy for me. It's not my fault he's never done anything with his life.

(Margaret sighs, takes a beat, and puts her plants back in place.)

MARGARET: You know, sweetheart, you can be really — exhausting.

(She looks up as Paul heads down the stairs.)

PAUL: What's all the yelling? Ethan?

ETHAN: Yeah, hi Dad. I was just telling Mom. I'm taking off.

PAUL: You're going?

ETHAN: Yes, I am. I got offered that play.

PAUL: What play?

ETHAN: The play. We talked about it the other night, at Frank's party, remember? Shakespeare is no playwright, et cetera et cetera?

PAUL: That play?

ETHAN: Yes.

PAUL: I thought you weren't going to do that.

ETHAN: I changed my mind.

PAUL: Why'd you do that?

ETHAN: They offered it to me.

PAUL: So it's only worth doing if you don't have to ask for it, is that how that works?

(Beat.)

ETHAN: That's right, Dad. Go ahead and fucking demean it.

MARGARET: Oh no. I have had quite enough for one day. Before anyone says another word, I'm making us all cocktails, and we're all going to have a civilized drink.

(She heads for the kitchen, but Paul continues. She stops.)

PAUL: He's been telling everyone for weeks it was beneath him. Now he wants us to what, congratulate him on getting something he told everyone he didn't want in the first place?

MARGARET: Paul, please. I ask for so little from you. And I am exhausted right now.

ETHAN: (Overlap.) Fuck you. You think you're the only fucking person on the planet, everyone in this fucking crazy family —

MARGARET: Ethan! After what just was said between you and Frank, I really think —

FRANK: Don't drag me into this, Mom. I don't say anything, as a rule, but I am not — this is not — you can't —

MARGARET: (Overlap.) I know, I'm sorry, you're truly the one person I could ever count on to behave rationally which is why I'm putting my foot down, now. I'm asking all of you. For me.

(There is a moment of silence.)

Thank you.

ETHAN: It's fine, Mom. It's fine. For you, OK, but him — I'm not getting dragged into his destruction, anymore. Sitting up here, eating people up like some giant toad —

PAUL: Stick to acting, Ethan; simile's not your strong suit.

ETHAN: You can't do it anymore! You're the one who can't finish a sentence, you can't write a Goddamn fucking sentence without someone holding your hand! Roger keeps sending these girls to get you through it, rather than admit you've lost it —

MARGARET: *(Dry.)* Well, thank you, I certainly appreciate everyone trying, for my sake —

ETHAN: And he's still trying to fuck them! Ask her, Mom! In your house! He's hitting on her in your house, ask her!

(Sophie stands in the doorway. She is very still. No one sees her. Frank tries to protect Margaret from all this as Paul explodes.)

PAUL: Is this about a woman, Ethan? Is that what this is about? A woman? Because my understanding is that you've been fucking her. Wasn't that enough for you? What is it you want?

ETHAN: *(Shoving him away.)* Nothing. Forget it. You know, the only reason I even came here was because these two were in a complete panic, he's falling apart, he can't write anymore, he's reading your reviews! The old man actually had a half a second of thinking about somebody other than himself, he had a flash of curiosity about his first-born son, that must mean he's dying —

PAUL: Sorry to disappoint you.

ETHAN: That's all right. I'll be back to see it when it does happen, Dad. Looking forward to it.

PAUL: Wishing your father dead — oh, Ethan, it has a nice sort of Greek ring to it but wouldn't it make more sense to grapple with something a little more subtle, such as your own sense of inadequacy?

ETHAN: Actually, Dad, the only thing that makes sense anymore is leaving.

PAUL: If only you would.

ETHAN: As if I was even here to you! As if I even exist to you.

(Beat.)

Consider it done. We'll just say I sprang out of the earth, full grown, while you sat off in some room somewhere, scribbling bullshit and screwing your students. You had nothing to do with me.

PAUL: I had nothing to do with you? Do you even hear yourself? Go do your play, the theater deserves you. But don't kid yourself into thinking you're your own man. You might have been, if there were more to you. But you're just what I made you. Feels good doesn't it, going off to do your art, you're in the heat of it, I am too, it's all going better and the rest of it is suddenly gone. The self-loathing. The contempt, hating yourself so much that the rest of humanity has to bear the brunt of it, the fear of death or even worse, failure, worse than that even mediocrity, hovering out there. For half a moment, perhaps, it occurs to you to snap out of it, but change is a fleet thought, isn't it, fuck the chance to find something in yourself, so that when you die you're not just looking at the end with terror in your bones, trying to figure out why all of it, fame, awards, the luck even just to do it, every day, why that just didn't add up to more. Why the sheer beauty of just being alive never lifted your heart beyond — this.

(Pause.)

ETHAN: That's it? That's what I get after forty years? You'd be a better person if you weren't so much like me? That's your fatherly wisdom?

PAUL: If that's what you heard, that's what you get.

(To Margaret.)

Are we having those oysters?

MARGARET: *(Startled.)* Well, they're still in the refrigerator, not quite as fresh as they would have been last night but still very fresh, if you're really interested.

PAUL: You said you had some recipe.

MARGARET: Spectacularly decadent, yes.

PAUL: That sounds good. You still want that cocktail?

MARGARET: I think I could use one, frankly.

PAUL: A Rob Roy, right?

(She looks at him, even more startled.)

MARGARET: If it's not too much trouble.

PAUL: I hope I can remember how.

(He heads for the kitchen.)

ETHAN: *(Yelling after him.)* Hey, it's been great! Huh? Fun visit! Because you know, I was nowhere near scarred enough!

(Margaret sighs.)

MARGARET: Well.

ETHAN: It's OK, Mom. I'm leaving. I wish I'd never come.

(As he gets to the door, it occurs to him what he's said. He stops, frustrated with himself.)

ETHAN: *(Continuing.)* I didn't mean that. I'm sorry, Mom. It's been great to see you, at least.

(He tries to kiss her. She turns on him.)

MARGARET: There is a cost to things, Ethan. Are you even aware of that? Are you aware of what this past week has cost us all? Are you aware of what it's cost you?

(She looks away. He glances over to Sophie, who is trying to quietly sneak out of the room.)

ETHAN: *(To Sophie, awkward.)* You'll come see me, won't you? This fall. As you may have guessed, I'm doing that play after all. I'm not sure when we open, mid-September, I think. I hope you'll come.

SOPHIE: Come see your play?

ETHAN: I think it's going to be pretty good.

SOPHIE: *(Beat.)* Of course. Thank you.

(He goes. After a moment, Margaret looks up at Sophie, polite.)

MARGARET: So it's going well? The writing?

SOPHIE: *(Short.)* Yes.

MARGARET: I could tell. I think it's been twenty years since he last offered to make me a drink.

SOPHIE: The writing is going very well.

MARGARET: Good. And as for the rest of it — I hope that you don't take any of that personally. I certainly don't. Although I suspect that's a sort of trick that comes with age. Oh, dear. You know at times like this one can't help think about Tolstoy, can one? All that nonsense about happy families, and unhappy ones. He was a very good writer, but really, as if we could separate it out. This family is happy, and this one — isn't.
I hardly think it's all that simple.
(Checking her watch.)
Will you be having dinner with us? I think it's just Paul and I, tonight, I don't know if Frank's staying.

FRANK: No.

SOPHIE: No, I don't think I will join you, either.

MARGARET: All right.

(Margaret goes. After a moment, Sophie continues down the steps. She sees the butterflies, where she left them. She goes to them, looks at them for a moment, picks them up and sets them on the coffee table. She picks up one of the angels and brings it down with real force on top of the butterflies. The glass breaks. Frank jumps out of his chair, totally startled by what she's done.)

FRANK: No, please!

(She stops, looks at him.)

SOPHIE: Why, is it very valuable?

FRANK: It's not that. It's just — if you use the angel, the gesture is much too baroque.

(He takes the angel from her. She looks at the shattered frame.)

SOPHIE: It felt good, actually. It meant so much to me. But it felt quite good, to destroy it. I guess that's no surprise.

FRANK: No — no — listen. My mother is right. You shouldn't — it's not . . . personal.

SOPHIE: Yes, I understand that. I do. It's just funny. For the past three weeks, both of them have been trying to sleep with me, and I was never even in the room. That is funny, isn't it?

FRANK: Hilarious.

SOPHIE: And I went along with it. It was like someone just said, here, I'm gonna hit you in the head with a hammer, and I said, OK. And then they hit me in the head with a hammer. And now, my head hurts.

(She starts to go. Frank sees that she's left her butterfly story, which is now a bit crumpled. He picks it up, looks at it.)

FRANK: Don't you want this?

SOPHIE: No. I don't.

FRANK: This is the butterfly story?

(She doesn't answer. He looks at it, briefly.)

Ethan said it was really good.

SOPHIE: Ethan was trying to seduce me.

FRANK: If it wasn't any good, he wouldn't have tried.

SOPHIE: Well, I don't need it anymore, do I? It's poisoned, now, isn't it? Well?

FRANK: I don't . . . I can't tell you that.

(Then.)

Would you like to know, you never asked me, about the plate?

(Sophie turns, surprised, and somewhat curious at this change in subject.)

SOPHIE: What about it?

FRANK: I met the man who made it.

SOPHIE: You did?

FRANK: Yes, he's, he's very old. Ninety-six. Mean as a snake.

SOPHIE: Of course.

FRANK: His favorite part was, uh, killing the butterflies. He liked to watch them beat their wings in agony and then go limp. He's got hundreds of plates, stacked in a room in the back of his son's house. The son is seventy-two. It's just the two of them, and they don't seem to talk to each other. The old man sits in the back room, killing butterflies, and the son sits in front, watching television. They seem to live off packets of frozen food, and there was this odd moment when the son went to the freezer, took out a sort of solid wedge of something frozen, went into the garage, and cut it in half with a power saw. I don't know what that was about.

SOPHIE: Is this supposed to make me feel better?

FRANK: It's just facts. They don't take away from the plate. They're different things, life and art; you shouldn't get them confused. It's hard, because they lie right next to each other, don't they, hovering behind each other, all the time. All the dark and the light that is life. And the art that we make of it. But really. Try not to get them confused.

(Melancholy, he hands her the story, and goes. After a long moment, the lights dim down to a spot on Sophie.)

SOPHIE: In the room next to him, Katie was scolding the boys to sleep. He raised his head at the interruption, rubbing his eyes beneath the spectacles, tired tonight, some nights his eyes stung with the delicacy of the work. Through the thin walls her voice rose, shrill, with exhaustion, as the boys foolishly protested their innocence. It was their nightly ritual, her anger, their half- hearted rebellion, roles acted almost unknowingly, played out within the ether of their love for each other. He felt flushed, a cold coming on, and he knew Katie would be in soon, to scold him into bed as well, although both of them were still unaware of the pneumonia already nestled in his lungs. He was nearly finished. His final specimen, a tiny peacock pansy, fluttered anxiously in its jar, as it fought the effects of the anaesthesia which would render it finally inert. When just a child, the spectre of death in the form of a terrified insect caused him inordinate delight, but over time his response changed, as he grew by degrees unnerved, then horrified, then fascinated, then philosophical, as he proceeded year after year to murder these stunning creatures in the name of love. For what was it if not love that kept him awake night after night, humbled by his own devotion to them? There was a time, he knew, when tribal peoples had carved butterflies into stone, had reckoned them messengers from the gods. In the deepest part of him, he understood these ancient beliefs. And so as his own death bloomed within him, the butterfly collector watched as the wings went still, one more specimen of doom and beauty surrendering itself to his care.

(Blackout.)

END OF PLAY

BAD DATES

ORIGINAL PRODUCTION

Bad Dates was originally produced at Playwrights Horizons June 3, 2003. It was directed by John Benjamin Hickey and had the following cast:

HALEY . . . . Julie White

Scenic Design . . . . Derek McClane
Costume Design. . . . . Mattie Ullrich
Lighting Design . . . . Frances Aronson
Sound Design . . . . Bruce Ellman
Casting . . . . James Calleri, C.S.A.
Director of Development . . . . Jill Garland
Production Manager. . . . . Joshua Helman
Production Stage Manager . . . . Megan Schneid

Artistic Director. . . . . Tim Sanford
Managing Director. . . . . Leslie Marcus
General Manager. . . . . William Russo

CHARACTERS

HALEY: Late 30s to early 40s, a restaurant manager

SET

Haley's bedroom in a no-frills apartment in New York City. It is a friendly, warm space, not frilly. At the top of the play there are clothes thrown everywhere, and a lot of shoes, a very, very lot of shoes. Upstage right is the door to Haley's bathroom. Stage left is the door to the hall leading to another bedroom: the unseen domain of Vera, Haley's daughter.

ACT I
SCENE ONE

A woman, Haley, stands alone, in her bedroom. It is a friendly, warm space, not frilly. There are clothes thrown everywhere, and a lot of shoes, a very very lot of shoes, although the shoes are not in piles. She handles them with some care.

HALEY: Do you like these shoes? They're cute, right?
(Dissatisfied, she throws them down and goes to pick through several pairs that are on the bed. She starts to put them on.)
I can't wear shoes anymore. You know, it's not that you can't wear them, but you start to go, oh God these things hurt, they're kind of like some medieval Japanese perversion.
(She goes down the hallway, calls.)
Vera! Hey, come look at these. Come on, it's a big night for me.
(A doorway open, the sound of teen music, Haley yells over it.)
Do you think these are cute? I mean — these are cute, right? You're right, you're right. They hurt, anyway.
(The music stops as Vera's door is shut. Haley hobbles back into her bedroom.)
Listen, I haven't looked at these things in years. It's not like I have a fetish or anything. I mean, I know that it looks like I have a fetish. Well, I do have a fetish, but it's not like some crazy Imelda Marcos fetish, although I admit it might look like that.
(She looks at a pair of shoes in a box, then shows them to the audience.)
These aren't as cute as I thought. Joan and David. Remember when you thought they were cute, and now they're not, they're just not hip enough? It's 'cause the name isn't good enough, that's what I think. Jimmy Chou, much cuter name and sure enough the shoes are cute in a timelessly cute way.
(Off the dagger-like heel.)
Well, maybe not cute. They look like you could stab someone with this heel, don't they, what is that about? Anyway, I used to live six blocks from this shoe store in Austin, George's shoe store, I kid you not that was the name, not very glamorous, the name or the store, which was kind of a little dump but this guy George had some sort of a deal with all these major shoe designers and he got their leftovers, which he sold at rock-bottom prices out of this icky little hole in the wall. This place was a

miracle. Everything he sold was something like twenty or thirty bucks, I am dead serious, you could go down there at least once a week and pick up a three hundred dollar pair of Chanel pumps for a mere thirty dollars. Well, you couldn't do that every week, that only happened to me once, but it was an unforgettable day, as you may imagine. Here they are . . .

(She holds them up, jubilant.)

OK. A little conservative but still unspeakably chic. Thirty bucks. But you had to have the right size foot. Six to seven and a half, that was mostly what he sold, that's mostly what the leftovers were, your foot's bigger than that you are mostly out of luck. I took one of my friends there, she's a size nine, she had to go outside and have a good cry. Anyway, the other cool thing about this astonishing little store, there was a lady's spike heel shoe, huge, it was like size eleven or something, and someone had glued little macaronis all over this shoe, and then spray painted it brown, and it was in the window. It looked like something a kid would have done, and then to be nice, his dad put it in his store window. So I was very touched by this shoe, even though the color it was spray painted was kind of icky. If you're going to go to all the trouble with the macaroni, wouldn't you think to paint it lime green, or sparkles or something? Anyway — oh ow. Oh no. This can't be . . . oh no . . .

(She has on the Chanel pumps, which are too tight.)

Dammit, they shrank. Shoes don't shrink. My feet grew. Oh shoot. They're not that cute anyway. Yes, oh yes they are. Oh I'm going to just weep. Shoot. Maybe I'll just frame them, or something. Anyway this shoe store, you just couldn't resist —

(She opens a box and, surprised, sees a huge wad of cash.)

Oh wow, well, this does not belong with the shoes now does it?

(She packs it back up and puts the shoebox under the bed.)

Anyway, I ended up with some pretty strange shoes, I'll admit, zebra stripe half boots, gold lame spikes, you know, stuff you just think is too wild to pass up, maybe the occasion or the outfit will someday present itself. And George was nice, and I'm moved as I said by the shoe with the macaronis. So I end up with this huge collection of shoes for very little money. And I was pregnant. The two things really didn't have much to do with each other, although I'm sure I was wearing something in this mess the night Vera was conceived. Whatever. So the next thing I know I have six hundred pairs of shoes, a husband — Roger — and a kid. And then things start disappearing around the house, including the Toyota, which Roger has traded for three pounds of marijuana. I hope you don't think ill of me for admitting all this. Because I am not that person anymore, having a child makes some of us grow up. Not all of us, Roger being the relevant case in point. I'm going to weep I am just going to weep, do none of these fit? What kind of cruel universe would do that to me? So the next next thing I know I'm a divorced waitress with a five-year-old kid — see these are cute, and they fittttt.

(She looks at herself in the shoes in the mirror.)

Yeah they're cute, of course they're cute, they belong to my daughter. I look like a thirteen-year-old in them.

(She starts to take them off.)

(Yelling to door.) Hey, I found your blue buckle shoes!

(She sets them in the hallway, shuts the door.)

Anyway, we move to New York, Vera and I. Fresh start. We're in the big city, getting by, you know, I got a nice little job as a waitress. I found this amazing apartment — rent-controlled! And things are looking up, definitely, when it turns out this restaurant I'm working at is some kind of front, some Romanian mob put all their money in it as a tax shelter or money laundering, I can't even, believe me, you didn't want to know, at that point I was raising a five-year-old and the less I knew about —

(She starts in on another pair, very high heels.)

I'm mostly hoping the Feds or the police or whoever don't find out whatever illegal activity is going on, because I don't want to lose my job. Then sure enough — ow, God, ow —

(She walks around.)

OK, these hurt but they fit.

(She continues to walk, looks at herself in the mirror.)

I'm sorry this story is taking so long. Because it's just of course the police do figure out something — I think it was money laundering —

(She starts to change her clothes, into a snakey little dress.)

— Which I of course suspected, as I said, and then have to lie about when all these detectives descend and ask how much you know. I felt like such a terrible person. They had this whole complicated sting worked out, one of those things that they spent years setting up, so you know they've been working for years figuring out something you knew all along. But you can't really feel sorry for them because why the hell did it take them so long? Besides which they're being kind of pushy and snotty around the restaurant, making us all wait in the back, where there's no place to sit, and not telling anyone what's going on, my little girl is with her babysitter and I'm not even allowed to call, and all of us, we're all like great, there goes my job, and finally I say to one of them, the cops, What's going on, anyway? And he's like, some big macho, when we need to talk to you, we will let you know. And there is so much creepy attitude, I mean, this is our lives he's messing with and he's just some big old nasty cop. So I say to him, look, is this about the money-laundering thing? And he sort of looks at me, all surprised, and says Oh you know all about that, huh. And I said, well, isn't it common knowledge? At which point one of the cooks offers me a cigarette, just to get me to shut up. I mean, I admit I was being a bit stupid, they had already taken Veljko off in handcuffs. We all of course felt that it was about time somebody did — Veljko was just a big fat criminal, there was no question, big and fat and mean, he looked like Al Capone or a cardinal or something, and it was a huge relief someone finally arrested him, but my point is, this was clearly a serious matter, I had no business mouthing off to anybody.

(She looks at herself in the mirror.)

OK, that looks good. Right? This is very good. I look like a hooker. Well, maybe I can wear this with a scarf. You know, look like a hooker wearing a scarf or something.

(She starts to look for a scarf.)

So then, all the guys who are running the restaurant are completely arrested but then the family, which as it turns out not all of them, apparently, are mobbed up, you know how those things work, there's always like a couple who are not complete criminals but they can call up the complete criminals when they need a favor. So that side of the family decides to keep the place open, but they have no idea how anything works, so I'm the one ends up walking them all through it night after night 'cause I'm apparently the only one who knows anything about how the place works. Everybody else there is so concentrated on their own little piece of turf no one knows anything about the whole place, except me. So, you know, the noncriminal Romanians finally go to hell with it, and put me in charge, because apparently I'm sort of weird restaurant idiot savant. Who knew? Born to run a restaurant. Which is exciting. When you find something, some strange combination of, who you are and what you can do, to find your gift like that? How many people get that to fall on their head like that? 'Cause I started out being like just a waitress trying to support herself and her kid, I mean I was just another person who married a moron and then had a load of shit to deal with.

(Off outfit, in mirror.)

Yeah OK, this is a clear disaster but I do like the top.

(She starts to take off the skirt.)

So things are swinging. I'm allowed to do things that nobody else ever thought of, add stuff to the menu, change the layout of the place and get rid of the lousy flatware, you know, plus I went out and stole somebody's chef, not the nicest thing I've ever done, but they were abusing him over there, I mention no names, but chefs are artists. You treat them nicely. And the next thing I know — 'cause this stuff happens so fast you can't even, you would not believe and I mean that — we get reviewed in *The New York Times*, it's a rave, and Leonardo DiCaprio throws his birthday party at my restaurant and we are on Page Six! And business goes through the roof. Which could not be more fun.

So I'm feeling fantastic, because there is nothing better in life than being allowed to do a job that you're good at, so guys are asking me out all the time. I mean I am *en fuego*, and I don't actually have time to date, between the restaurant and Vera, so I'm turning them all down, which makes 'em want me even more! But I'm thinking, there's got to be a way to work this out, I miss sex, it would be fun to have someone to talk to, besides Vera, who is a great kid but let's face it she's seven by that point and I'm hitting my sexual prime. So I'm contemplating this, I'm ready, there's this guy hanging around who seems like a good possibility, you know, he's nice, and funny, and great looking in this skinny way. You know how great looking skinny guys are sometimes? So he's showing up three or four nights a week, just to have a drink and flirt. And this is very high-end flirting, you know, when he says something snappy, and you hand it right back to him only better and then float away to show some-body to their table, and then curve back around the bar for another daz-zling four-second encounter, it was sooo dreamy, and he finally asks me out, and I am yes yes yes. I mean, I like this guy, I really — He — what-ever. The thing is, right then — right then, this friend of mine, Eileen, sees this Joan Crawford marathon on some movie chanel. And she comes over the restaurant laughing her fool head off, and says have you seen Mildred Pierce? 'Cause Haley, it is you. She thinks this is this big hilarious blinding insight, cannot stop laughing, so I rent the video. You know, I go out, I rent the video, and I watch it.

(Haley looks at the audience. Beat.)

OK. Have you seen Mildred Pierce? Joan Crawford, gorgeous, competent, devoted to her kids, husband turns out to be kind of a loser, so she goes out and gets a job — as a waitress. She's got no training, does it because she has to, and turns out to be — well, you know, kind of a restaurant idiot savant, gets her own place, it's a huge hit, she doesn't have time to date but men are falling over her so she finally starts to date them and terrible terrible things happen, and everything goes to shit. I mean, I am not making this up. That is what happens in this movie I truly, I mean, oh Lord. And oh, get this. The kid's name? She has an evil daughter? Veda. My kid's name is Vera. And they are nothing alike, Vera is really a good kid, she's more like the tragic daughter who dies, but still. I mean! On top of it, this guy who's been sniffing around, asking me out, is just a dead ringer for Monty, the evil socialite who Mildred marries and who steals from her and then destroys her and seduces her daughter. I mean, I was just — OK, he didn't look exactly like him, but they were both skinny. And I just went, no, I got my restaurant, I got my kid, for the first time in my whole life I got enough money so I'm not worried about it every waking moment of every single day. I am not tempting fate.

(She is now dressing herself in much more conservative clothing, a long skirt, and a sweater.)

I mean — I'm not saying watching that movie five years ago made me realize I couldn't have a man in my life. It just made me think. So I said NO to Monty and I did without. And you know, it's all right, everybody has to do without something in their lives. A lot of people have to do without the work that they love, I know people, can't get a job, doing the thing that they love, and it's a wound that they carry. You know, really, a great sadness. I think that would be a bigger loss, frankly. 'Cause I have family, my kid is fantastic, and I have friends. My friend Eileen, she doesn't have a boyfriend or a kid, plus for the longest time she was always in and out of work, she's a, one of those, you know — she paints, or photography, or film something — she really is a genius, but she never seems to land somewhere where they'll just let her do what she does, whatever that is at the time. It's hard. And she drinks, you know. Well, why not . . .

(She goes down the hall to Vera's room.)

Vera! Come look at this!

(Over Vera's music.)

Don't just make a face. I'm real nervous. Tell me what you think, is it the skirt? Don't tell me what you think. You're thirteen, what do you know.
(The music stops. Haley comes back into her bedroom.)
She's right, this skirt is way too something, who knows what.
(She adds a belt.)
Anyway Eileen. Once things worked out for me at the restaurant I gave her a job of course, what else can you do with somebody like that, it's not what she wants to do but at least she's working for someone who loves her, and she's a pretty good bartender, no surprise there. So last week, this is what happened: Eileen gets us invited to this benefit for Tibetan Buddhist Books. I kid you not. She has a friend who said we could come to this thing for free, which seems to me like no way to run a benefit, but apparently it's more common than you would think. So this "benefit" is out on the Island, so we take the train out there. And sure enough everyone is walking around this gorgeous estate, talking about Tibetan books. Acres and acres of lawn and huge trees and this gorgeous sprawling mansion and people dressed in traditional Buddhist robes serving brie with sun-dried tomatoes, and glasses of Chardonnay to everybody. And then the celebrities start to arrive. Not a lot — Janet Leigh, of all people, shows up, and then a couple of television stars who I didn't know. And then people start to say, Richard Gere is coming, Richard Gere is coming, but he never came.
(She starts to go through her makeup, looking for lip gloss, puts it on as she continues with the story.)
So anyway, they finally seat us at tables which are scattered about this gorgeous lawn. Now the thing is, Eileen, as I said, got us into this thing for free because a friend of hers is on the committee, and they need people to fill out tables. So they basically split us up. And I get seated at this table, the kindest thing, the only thing to say about this table, is that it is the table of the weirdos. Real nuts, every one of them, and I'm like, Hi, I'm Haley Walker, I mention the restaurant, blah, blah, blah, and this old lady starts talking about how she's trying to communicate with bugs. Some famous Buddhist told her to do that, and suddenly the entire table is having a seemingly endless conversation about how when a mosquito lands on your arm you should become one with it, rather than flicking it off before it gives you encephalitis.
(She rolls her eyes.)
Then it starts to rain, just a little, and the lady who owns the house, who doesn't want to let us in her house for some reason, gets up and starts

talking about how the rain is a gift of the Buddha. So we're all sitting there, getting rained on, thinking about how it's a gift of the Buddha, and then it starts to rain really hard, and the lady who's house it is suggests we all put our napkins on our heads. So all of us are sitting there with napkins on our heads, getting rained on, including Janet Leigh.

(She stops, looks at herself. She looks very nice. She bites her lip, goes back to the piles of shoes and starts to look again, for a pair that goes with her lovely but staid outfit.)

So it's raining and raining and we're all getting rained on, but the conversation about bugs just keeps going. And there's this guy sitting next to the old lady who started the whole thing, who cannot get enough of this. He is positively fascinated by her stories about talking to bugs. And then he turns to me and says, "Have you ever tried it?" No shit. And the entire table, all the weirdos turn and are all looking at me with deep and real, serious-minded expectation. There is a hush, an absolute, definite hush. So I say, "No, I am not friendly with the insect world but there are several amphibians with whom I play golf regularly." And then they all continue to stare at me, but now there's a kind of shocked disappointment that gathers in the silence. And I confess, you know, I think I may have let a little bit of an edge creep into my voice, when I said it, so I guess I did communicate that talking to nut jobs about bugs in the middle of a thunderstorm was not especially my idea of a good time.

(She sighs, remembering her own bad behavior.)

So then the Bug Guy, you know, the one who attempted to drag me into this in the first place — he says to me, "So . . . what's a frog's handicap, these days?" And I mutter, "The ones I play with are pretty much scratch golfers," and the old lady gets huffy about not understanding golf and goes back to the damn bugs and the hope that all sentient beings might someday come to enlightenment. And then I think oh dear God, they're not talking about the bugs now, they're talking about me. It was completely mortifying. So I'm sitting there, feeling bad, and wet, and like a bug, and then I realize, in this sort of strange, hallucinatory moment, that the Bug Guy is looking kind of good, and the things he's saying about bugs are really kind of fascinating — and it is then that I realize that maybe it has been too long since I've been on a date. When the Bug Guy starts looking good, it's time to get out of the house.

(Beat.)

Tonight, I'm going on a date.

(Blackout.)

SCENE TWO

Haley is in her robe, with a towel on her head. She is eating a pretzel and on the phone, on her bed.

HALEY: No I am not wearing that. B.J. — I look like a slut in that dress. Yes, you do, you were the one who told me at Sue Jane's wedding, it was the first time I wore it and you said I was the only one who wasn't dressed like a chicken, AND I looked like a slut. *(Laughing.)* What, the one with the little sleeves? I hate those sleeves. B.J., that has polka dots. Well, now I know you're crazy, I look terrible in that purple thing. I gave it away, that's how bad I looked. Oh, good-bye, you're no help at all. Good-bye. Tell Frank I said hi. Bye.

(She hangs up the phone and starts to lay outfits out on the bed, this time trying tops and skirts and shoes together, like Barbie outfits.)

HALEY: *(Continuing; to audience.)* All right, that first date was not what you would call a success. It was a bad date. I'm obviously out of practice, and having decided to date again as a matter of necessity, I went out with the first guy who asked and it was just a matter of getting my feet wet. What's that terrible thing they used to say, about kissing, you have to kiss a lot of frogs before you find a prince. Not that I kissed this guy. OK, I did kiss him, and he was an asshole, but by that point I was just trying to get out of the entire predicament and just go home and get to bed, so one kiss seemed a small price to pay. Regardless of the fact that there was tongue involved.

(She rolls her eyes and tosses all the clothes together, shoves them into a laundry basket, and kicks it.)

Oh for heaven's sake, it's not like I don't do this every day anyway. You know, dress? But that is where things went off, right at the beginning, after all that messing around I did with my clothes, the first thing out of that guy's mouth, the very first thing he says to me was, "What are you wearing?" Can you believe that? My mother used to do that to me. And I say to him, why? What's wrong with it? And he says, "It just makes you look kind of old." That was the beginning. Now, I know I've been out of the game for a while, and I'm not in my twenties anymore but you have got to be kidding me, men are out there, running around, thinking that shit's OK. I'm not even — this guy is over forty, of course men at forty are considered the hottest thing going. And I'm like — well, it doesn't matter how old I am. The point is, I am not as old as him.

(She sighs, and starts to dress, still eating pretzels. The outfit she chooses this time is considerably sexier.)

So after that spectacular opening we go to — I picked the restaurant, trust me, I know, I mean, right? You go out on a date with me, the thing to do is let me pick the restaurant and this place is nice, a high-end bistro so it's not outrageous, but the food is delicious — there's only two things on the menu that are not worth trying, the calf's liver, and OK, they actually do a cow's head, which, I'm sorry, but this is America, nobody is going to order that. Anyway, so there we are, bad start but the restaurant could not be lovelier, candlelight, flowers — Beautiful. The service is excellent, the wine, a ninety-five bordeaux, I pick it because I know this stuff and it's just a lovely bottle with so many colors, berries and chocolate and just the right hint of smokiness around the edges, you know, it's almost an Amarone but it's French, it's one of those bottles that have no right to exist and yet there they are. So everything that I have contributed to this evening, I think, is rather good. This is a date I think many people would like to go on. And this guy is sitting there, looking at the menu and says, there's probably butter in all this stuff, isn't there?

(Beat. She looks at the audience, pissed.)

It's a Goddamn French restaurant! Of course there's butter! And then we go down the list, item by item we study the menu and and he talks about every single one of these positively brilliant offerings to the God of Food, and he wonders what might be in it, you know, "Do you think that has cream in it?" And he turns up his nose at it all and talks about how bad cream and butter are, and then I hear about his cholesterol.

(Beat.)

Let me tell you something. The first topic on a first date should not be cholesterol. Besides which I'm sitting there thinking, then order the salmon! How is this a real subject? If you're worried about your cholesterol, then order the fish! It's grilled! It says right on the menu, all our fish are grilled! BUT NO. We have to have an endless — and all of it, you know, is complicated by some sort of neurosis he has about numbers. Like, the normal number for a man his age would be this, but his doctor feels that his muscle mass is more appropriate to a younger man — of course he found a doctor out there who told him he wasn't as old as he actually is — so they calculated the cholesterol according to some other schedule and then sub-selected half of the difference, blah blah blah, so that means he has to watch his cholesterol but not really.

So then, I kid you not, he orders the Coquille Saint Jacques — Scallops, wrapped in bacon, swimming in cream sauce, topped with toasted cheese.

And then through the entire first course, we continue to talk about cholesterol, only then we move on to his colon, apparently his battle with cholesterol has had an extremely negative impact on his COLON. So I got to hear about that, and I will spare you the details, although he did not.

(Beat.)

So I'm like, OK, this is just a date that's not going to work out. That's obvious and it's not the end of the world, frankly, I didn't actually think the first guy I went out with would be "the one for me" or anything like that, I was just trying to go on a date. So I'm OK with the fact that this is largely pretty damn stupid. And then, there's actually a point in the evening where having given up on this guy I sort of perversely got interested in his story, in a very remote way — he starts talking about his ex-girlfriend. And the more he talks about her, the clearer it becomes that he's still, really, kind of in love with her. And the more I listen to him, the more I realize that this is more or less a first date for him, too, he's recently broken up with this woman he really loved, and now he's trying to get back on the horse. And this thought honestly makes me feel a little warmly toward him, I sense that we are fellow travelers. And so I say to him, as a fellow traveler, well, why did you break up? And he tells me this story about how — that your relationship with a person is like a movie. That when you're in a relationship, you see the movie, in your head, and that you need to see how the rest of the movie is going to go. And he realized that he couldn't see where the movie was going. He didn't know the end of the movie, with this woman. So that's why he broke up. And he looked so sad. Meanwhile, I'm listening to this, and trying to understand, so I say, What do you mean, a movie? And he goes through the whole thing again, about looking for the end of the movie, and your life with someone, and the relationship, and the end of the movie, so I say, you mean like death? Looking for the end of the movie, you're thinking about dying? And he says, No no no, it's not about death. It's about the End of the Movie. And we go around in circles like that for a while, and finally I say to him, I don't know, is it possible that you broke up with the woman you loved because of some insane metaphor? And then he got mad at me. I don't blame him. I definitely was getting too personal. And I honestly had a moment when I thought, if you're siding with the guy's ex-girlfriend? It's not a good date. So then things were uncomfortable, and they kind of went from bad to worse, and by the end of the evening we were really annoyed with each other, and I let him stick his tongue in my mouth, anyway.

(She shakes her head, and goes looking for shoes again, piling a whole lot of them on the bed. She picks out two pair and steps into the hall, knocks on Vera's door. Vera's music comes up.)

Vera! I need you to tell me what shoes to wear. These are the only choices. Good. Thanks. What? Well, can't you wear the blue skirt with, that top you have on right now is so cute, I think — you know, people don't really care about your clothes, Vera. Who you are on the inside is much more important than what . . . oh, never mind.

(She goes back into the room for a moment, and looks under her bed. She takes out a large shoe box, opens it, takes out a huge wad of cash, peels off several bills, then closes the box and pushes it back under the bed. She tucks several bills into her own purse, then goes to Vera's room.)

(Offstage.) This is all I can spare this week, so you're going to have to shop at Contrampo for once, or T. J. Maxx, it was good enough for me so — .

(She closes the door to Vera's room and comes back into her bedroom.)

Where was I? Oh. Right. Out in front of my building with Mr. Wonderful. There we are. Horrible, horrible evening, from start to finish, and yet he clearly expects to come up. I should have paid for myself, I offered, but I should have insisted because then you have a little more latitude to evade, you know, but I didn't, so I didn't have latitude, and there you have it. I am stuck with his tongue down my throat. It just, I have to say it shook me up, frankly, how quickly things progressed with this guy, on a date which was not by any means successful. I am not a prude, I think that's obvious but let's face it we clearly did not LIKE each other, but he was willing to sleep with me anyway! He was absolutely planning on it! What is that? Don't you think that's interesting, I think this is a true and extremely interesting point about the differences between the sexes: Men will happily have sex with someone they don't like. Women won't. Obviously that's not 100 percent true, but kind of it is, and why? Why are men sleeping with people they don't like? Is sex that much more fun for men than women, that they'd do it with just anyone? That would be one conclusion. The other would be that maybe men don't have enough to think about. Oh well, I'm not one to talk, I let someone I didn't like at all stick his tongue in my mouth.

(She sighs and looks at herself in the mirror. She is dressed in a very snakey little number, and looks really really hot.)

Now that's not bad for a woman who's as old as I am, I would say. If my mother saw me tonight, and said, "Are you going to wear that?" She would not mean you look old. She would mean go right back in there and take that off young lady. But I am not dressing to please my mother. I have another date.

(Blackout.)

SCENE THREE

Haley stands, in the same clothes, facing the audience. The room is as she left it — a mess.

HALEY: All right. I would just like to take this opportunity to admit that perhaps I have been, to some degree, indulging in male-bashing. And apologize to any men present, or even not present, for whatever amount of ill-humor, which may have offended you. Because tonight was an unmitigated disaster.

(She sits, as she tries to explain.)

This is what happened: I get to the restaurant. Now, the fact is, this time, it's a blind date. Which I don't generally, I am well aware that there is an entire subculture of people getting together with total strangers for fun and companionship, but that is not something I am as yet interested in. At the same time, after my last fiasco, I didn't actually think it was such a great idea to just go on a date with someone who asked me. I wanted some background, research, other people invested in the outcome. So, OK, I was talking to my mom on the phone, and I did in fact do a stupid thing and mentioned to her that I was starting to date, and kind of just, looking for guys, you know, to date. I actually said that to my mother. Who seemed sort of interested, in a casual, motherly way, and then called me back fourteen minutes after we hung up the phone, having already entirely arranged my next date. OK. Now, I did, for a moment, protest, because you know, who wants to go out on a date that their mother set up? But then I'm thinking, well, she made him sound kind of good, actually. He's from San Antonio, so he's Texan in a good way, you know, Texas but not too macho, and he's been living in New York four years. He's a professor. He teaches at Columbia. He's a professor at the law school. So I'm thinking — OK, I admit it: In spite of the fact that my mother set this date up, I am thinking George Stephanopolous with a cute southern accent. And I make no apologies for that. I have always believed that one should live with hope. So I call him up. And his accent is damn cute. He suggests that we go to my restaurant. I'm thinking well, that's like having dinner at home, far as I'm concerned, plus things are a little tense down there since I fired one of the busboys, Bibi, which was oh so necessary but always upset people, so I was looking forward to a night off. But then he goes on, how he's heard the place is so great and he's always wanted to go there and what a privilege it would be to dine with the artist who designed the entire experience.

(She takes a moment, pointing up the unmitigated pleasure of this.)
OK. He called me an artist. So I'm going, yes! We can have dinner at the restaurant. I certainly know the wine cellar there, and this is a man who will appreciate the bottle of wine I am going to pick out for him. This man teaches in the Law School at Columbia. He may or may not look like George Stephanopolous. And we're going to have a good conversation about I don't know, civil rights, the supreme court, I don't actually know what kind of law he teaches and I don't care 'cause the point is, I'm not going to be talking about colonoscopies all night. And I'm not going to make the mistake of looking ten years older than I actually am on this date. So I get myself dressed — I am dressed, am I not? And I go to the restaurant.

(She starts to act this out.)
And Eileen, she's as I said, the bartender but nights I'm not in, she does the front desk. So she says to me, your friend is waiting at the bar. And she has a kind of great look in her eye, Eileen is a connoisseur, so I go oh boy, this guy is way cute. So I'm feeling good now, and I go to the bar to meet my date, and . . . he's gay. He's cute, but he's also — gay. I mean, I am not — but he's gay! I am on a date with a gay man! And I mean, look, he's the kind of person, you can tell when you meet him. You shake his hand, he's gay. I'm thinking, why did my mother send me on a date with a gay man? Oh what a stupid question that is. And I am really mad at my mother for a moment, and then I'm thinking well why is he having his mother set him up on dates with straight women? Has he not told his mother yet? Does he possibly think she doesn't know? Maybe she doesn't know, which brings us back to why hasn't he told her? He's got tenure at Columbia and he can't tell his mom he dates boys?

And then I'm also thinking, even if you can't tell your mom because of whatever, that doesn't necessarily mean you let her set you up on dates with girls!

(She sits, fuming.)

And then I'm thinking —

(Gestures to her snakey outfit.)

Wasted. Snakiest outfit I've worn in eight years, wasted. And I looked good, man, I thought I really looked good.

(She sighs, stares at the ceiling for a moment, starts to undress.)

So, there was a bad moment, right at the beginning, that I don't think either one of us ever really recovered from. 'Cause I am sure that my disappointment was to some degree palpable. Well, I was on a date with a gay man! Of course I was disappointed! And then he clearly thought, oh look at this stupid pathetic straight woman, desperate to get laid by someone who could not be less interested, but how was I to know that? I don't know what he thought. Because we both got real polite real fast. I had Eileen show us to our table and I order a great merlot. I mean, I'm trying now, to be lovely, while I regroup, and he's attentive and appreciative, but a little tense, you know. So then I'm thinking for half a second, well, maybe he's disappointed because he saw that I was disappointed, so maybe he doesn't know he's gay. Or maybe he's not gay and I'm doing one of those horrible snap judgment things, people say you can always tell, but I don't think that's necessarily true. My brother B.J.'s gay, and nobody had a clue, when he told me I thought he was pulling my leg.

(She puts her hand over her face, remembering.)

Oh, it was horrible, he told me and I laughed, and he kept saying "no really" and I swear I just kept laughing 'cause that's kind of his sense of humor to do something like that, but this time he wasn't — anyway, it was just horrible, I had to apologize for days and then he got me back 'cause he was too big a chicken to tell Mom, so I had to tell her for him, which was — Anyway. So I'm thinking now, maybe you can't tell, maybe this guy just seems gay, but really he's just a nice sensitive person with excellent taste, who teaches at Columbia and is unmarried at forty-three, and says, "what a privilege it would be to dine with the artist who designed the entire experience."

(She rolls her eyes; she knows this sounds dumb. She picks up the phone and starts to dial.)

So me thinking maybe I've leapt to a wrong conclusion lasts for maybe twenty seconds, which is about when I notice that he's flirting with the waiter. And then I just have to give myself over to it, just say OK, tonight I am on a date with a gay man.

(Into phone.)

Hey B.J. it's me. Get this. You know that date Mom set me up on? He was a big old homo. I know!

(Starting to laugh along with him.)

No yes he was cute, he was just no fun. Of course as long as she was looking, Mom would find the least fun homosexual in the world. No I'm not giving you his number he was too mean. You have to ask Mom for it. Byyye.

(She hangs up, laughing.)

So anyway, the fact is Mr. Columbia Law Professor, whether or not he is gay, which he is, is finally less pertinent than the fact that he's snobby and kind of mean. He asks me how old I am, which I decline to answer, because I'm sorry, he's on a pretend date with a girl, and he still thinks he has the right to ask that? It's rude even on a real date! So I just come out and say I'm not telling you that and he says, why, is it a problem for you? Can you imagine? I ask him what he teaches, and he says "law." I'm not kidding. "Law." So I say, yeah, my mom told me that part, what kind of law? And he says, "It's pretty technical." And then he just keeps reading the menu. So then I just say, well, what, you think I'm too damn stupid to understand? And he gives me this look, offended, like I'm some sort of annoying bug, and instead of answering me, he says, "The menu here is really rather limited, isn't it?" And then before I can stab him through the heart with my fork, the waiter shows up with the mineral water and he gets all charming again!

(She sighs. Her cleaning has mostly amounted to shoving piles of things into closets, or under the bed. She now pulls out an oversized T-shirt and proceeds to get undressed, ready for bed.)

I mean it's not my fault he said he'd go on a date with a woman. Then I thought, well, maybe he's mad at me 'cause he's mad at his mom, who he can't tell the simple facts of his life to.

So anyway, me and this guy were getting pretty pissy with each other. I had no moments when I thought of him as a fellow traveler, that's for damn sure. At one point I finally decided that he mostly came on this bad date so that he could get a free meal at restaurant he'd heard of, and I decided that I was going to make him pay for the whole thing, full price, and then act surprised that he didn't know that was the deal ahead of time. So there we are on dessert — yes of course even as hideous as the whole date has turned out to be, he of course has to order dessert and keep it all going for an extra half hour — so he's digging into his crême brûlée. So I'm sitting there, thinking about how to signal Eileen, to get her to bring over a check. Now I know that Eileen assumes there is no check. Why would she make up a check for me? I would only rip it up. But I am really thinking by this point, this asshole is not going to be rude to me all night, and then get off with a free meal. No fucking way. But I also don't want it to be obvious that I am pulling a devious maneuver, I don't want to stand up, go to Eileen, whisper to her angrily, point at the jerk, and then send her over with a whopping bill for this terrible date. I want to be more subtle than that so that the burden of this delightful embarrassment falls completely, and unexpectedly, on my wretched companion. So I casually lean over, as if I'm just casually looking around the restaurant, and I casually try to spot Eileen to give her some sort of bizarre message with my eyebrows: This guy's an asshole, nothing is on the house, bring the check.

(She makes the bizarre face, to show.)

And Eileen looks at me and goes like this.

(She makes one of those what are you doing faces and gestures.)

And I'm like —

(She makes another ridiculous face, showing how she tried to communicate with Eileen, all the way across the room.)

She doesn't get it. In the heat of the moment, I cannot imagine what her problem is, so I make a bigger face.

(She does.)

So there I am, I've turned my head so that everybody in the room can see me, except for Mr. Columbia law professor, and I'm making this incredibly childish, hideous face that's meant to communicate all sorts of ridiculous nonsense, I mean, I'm virtually —

(She makes a huge face now, hideous, and points, as if to someone across the the table from her.)

And who walks in right in, right in the front door, while I'm performing, for everyone, who should walk in my restaurant at that very moment but — Mr. Let's-hope-all-sentient-beings-someday-come-to-enlightenment. The Bug Guy.

(Beat.)

I am not kidding. This is what I look like.

(She makes another face, looking quite like a bug.)

And there he is. The Bug Guy. He sees the whole thing. He waves. Stunned, I wave back. He takes this as an invitation, and comes over to our table.

(She puts her head down for a moment, moaning.)

"Hellooooo," says wretched companion, practically squealing, because, as I think I mentioned before, Bug Guy is very cute, when he's not talking about bugs. And Bug Guy is also not shy. He pulls up a chair. He's in the neighborhood, saw my restaurant, remembered my spectacularly soggy performance at the Buddhist book benefit, apparently, and decided to stop in and see how my spiritual evolution was coming along! Ugh. So, I introduce them, and Bug Guy gets all excited because he's actually heard of Mr. Columbia law professor, who is both mean and famous, apparently! So in no time at all, Bug Guy and Wretched Companion are talking about politics and music and literature and all the things I dreamed of talking about on my dream date with a man who turned out to be gay.

(The phone rings. She picks it up.)

BJ? Is that you? Who is this? Bibi? Bibi, cut it out!

(She hangs up quickly, takes a breath, and gets it together.)

Uh oh. I may have done something rather . . . stupid. Whatever. Anyway. That is why, frankly, I felt the need to apologize to the men tonight. Because he was one of those guys who act like all women are stupid or something, and it made me feel so bad, and I would hate it if I started to act like that. And — you know, I did, I stuck him with that check. I did. You know what? Excuse me.

(She goes to her desk, and opens a drawer.)

(After a moment of quickly looking through a pile of business cards, she selects one, consults it, and dials the phone again. She is clearly nervous.)

HALEY: *(Continuing; on phone.)* Hi. It's Haley. Haley Walker? Yes. Um . . . I would like to see you. Could I see you?

(Blackout.)

SCENE FOUR

Haley's bedroom is much cleaner. She is wearing a robe over devastating lingerie, and she is practically purring.

HALEY: I went on a good date. No. I didn't go on a good date. I went on several good dates. More than two. I know, I know you may think that's impossible, that I would ever find a man who I could deem worthy, but I have done it. I have found a good man.

(Beat.)

Monty.

(She laughs.)

Remember Monty? The bad guy from Mildred Pierce! His name's not Monty, his name is Lewis. I like that name, don't you? Lewis. Elegant but accessible at the same time, Lewis. Like an Armani suit, in which, I might add, he looks fantastic. Because this is what happened: After my hideous date with the nasty gay law professor deteriorated into well, abysmal behavior, on my part, I felt that it was time to take drastic action. I thought, enough already with the passive girl act, going out with some total stranger just because he asked you, or even better, letting your mom set you up on a date with a gay guy! I'm not a kid! I'm an adult! I am in charge of my life! And so I thought I am going to call somebody who I am interested in having a date with, and I am going to ask him out. I am going to call Monty. I haven't seen him in five years, and I presume he's married by now, or at least moved on, but I am going to take a shot. Why not just take a shot? So I call him. And I invite him to stop by the restaurant for a drink. He agrees. So on the appointed day I'm in there, before the dinner rush, and I ask Eileen to make me a fresh lime vodka gimlet, which she does extremely well, I think she puts triple sec in it, I can't remember, but it's delicious. Anyway, I am relaxing in the bar with my very adult drink, when this incredible man walks in the door.

(She laughs, delighted.)

I didn't recognize him at first, I was just thinking who is this, and then he sees me and he smiles.

(She stands up and does a little dance.)

He smiles at me! He's thrilled to see me! He comes over and tells me how great I look, what have I been doing, I'm sitting there trying to think straight, wondering what the hell I was thinking when I walked away from this? I had some massively ill-conceived theory about Mildred Pierce running through my head, is all I can recall. Well I can't go into that, of course, so I just say, what have you been doing, and so he talks, for a little while, about his work, which has something to do with Wall Street and international real estate — I remember some of this from before — anyway then he says How's your daughter? So I tell him about Vera and how big she's getting and he says, She probably doesn't need quite as much of your attention, anymore, and then I think oh Lord, he understood what happened. And then he says Are you seeing anybody? And I say, no, how about you? And he says he was but it kind of went south, and I'm thinking, then she was a big fat moron, oh well so was I — and then he says well, I'm really glad you called. And then he goes.

(A beat.)

He just — leaves the bar. He just came in, talked to me for ten minutes and left. I mean, I knew I had just said a drink, but the drink was going well, I had done the adult thing and I was being rewarded, I had found, again, this wonderful man, who I once carelessly tossed aside with the same kind of stupid thinking I have relentlessly mocked in others. Remember, the guy who kept wanting to see the end of the movie and how dumb I thought he was? I was just as dumb, what was I thinking, Mildred Pierce? What does Mildred Pierce have to do with anything? Mildred Pierce is a movie! This person is a person! What was I thinking? But I'm not thinking that anymore! I'm an adult now! I'm thinking, Don't Go!

(She paces, restless.)

So my head is in a state. And then of course there's this other stuff that I can't go into, let me just say that work, as much fun as it is to run a restaurant, the restaurant world is not necessarily always the simplest snake pit to negotiate, and it has frankly occurred to me more than once that if a good man showed up to take me way from all this it wouldn't entirely — that's not to say that I'm secretly a fifties gal, just that some days — whatever.

(She shakes her head, paces.)

Then he called. He called! And he said, would you like to have dinner. And I said yes. He picked the restaurant, not mine, there was no discussion, he just picked a very good restaurant, Italian, in Brooklyn of all places but it was surprisingly — of course I've heard that about Brooklyn, it's nowhere near as bad as you think.

So he picks me up in his car. OK, who gets picked up for a date in New York in a car? No one. It was like being in high school again, and I was so nervous, to be in a car, with a man who I had such powerful feelings about, I mean, I am really attracted to this guy, and he is so in charge. I was positively silenced by all of it. I just felt, for fifteen minutes, I felt potentially safe, and I didn't want to say the wrong thing and ruin it.

(She thinks about this.)

So we get to the restaurant, which is perfect, small, maybe thirty setups, spectacular Venetian glass chandelier which you might have thought would be too big for such a small space, but just wasn't, pressed tin ceiling that's distressed, I usually don't like that kind of rustic ruin look, but the chandelier contradicted it beautifully. And the food was out of this world, in Brooklyn! So I asked, well of course I asked, the chef trained at Union Square and Lutece, then spent three years in Venice, where she met her husband, the Italian maitre'd with dimples and an accent. Anyway, the rabbit with olives and soft polenta is beyond brilliant; Lewis had the beef cheeks which were also very good. So the food is great, the room is charming, and Lewis is — it's not just him; it's both of us, together, it's magical, I know that sounds trite, but it wasn't trite. It was as if time just evaporated, and everything that had been there for us five years ago was there again, only it was even more wonderful because we had let it slip away, so it was like all those lost hours and days and months were just hovering somewhere in the background, like an echo, of of of loneliness, we were in the middle of something that was just the opposite of being lonely, and it was such a relief, that we both couldn't stop laughing. We talked until midnight, shut the place down. And then we left and drove all over the city and then we parked. We parked up by the George Washington Bridge and made out in the car for two hours, I kid you not. The next day Vera said to me what happened to your face? It was completely all chapped up, I would have been mortified but I was just too damn happy.

(She paces some more, restless and happy.)

So then I spent the whole morning thinking about having sex, and then I spent lunchtime thinking, Haley, you got to put the brakes on, then Lewis called, and the brakes went off, and then we hung up, and the brakes went back on, and then B. J. called and he thinks everybody should have sex constantly, so the brakes went back off in a big way, and then Lewis called again, and we talked for an hour and the brakes were way off and then I hung up and the brakes went back on. And I was definitely back in high school. You know, the good part of high school, just feeling on fire with things and hopeful and moody, and wanting to buy shoes all the time.

(She pulls a beautiful new pair of shoes out of a box, waves them around gleefully, then puts them on.)

Anyway, then we went out again, to this fantastic place — the most romantic little sushi joint you ever saw, and I am not someone who generally considers sushi romantic. And then we went out a third time. And we didn't go to a restaurant, we just met in the park in the middle of the day and had the most delicious hot dogs I have ever had in my life, and we talked some more and both of us admitted that it was frightening, a bit, how far things had gone, even though we hadn't even slept together yet. And I said, why don't you come over? Let's just stop thinking about it and get it over with! And he said he had appointments, he had to go back to work, but that we would tomorrow night. And now, tomorrow is here. It's here. Tomorrow is tonight.

(She looks at herself in the mirror for a long moment. Then, suddenly, she moves to the bed, reaches for the phone and dials.)

Hey, it's me. No, not yet, he's coming over tonight. B. J. — stop it, I'm too nervous, you can't make fun of me right now. Yes. Ha ha. Yes, of course I got rid of her, she's spending the night at Emily's. No, honey, he more than assumes, it's been stated specifically, the plan is that he comes over, we order Chinese take out and then actually do the deed on the living room floor before the food even gets here.

(She laughs.)

What? I guess.

(She checks her watch, moves, nervous.)

A little.

(Beat.)

A little, just a little, don't make a big thing, it's a little. OK, an hour, he's almost an hour late, but — oh don't do that silence thing. He's a busy guy, sometimes he's late. I'm not going to turn into one of those psycho girlfriends who thinks the worst when a guy's a little late.

(Beat.)

Shit.

(Beat.)

You think I should call him? It's just an hour. Of course I should call him. It's probably fine, right — yes I have his home number, I have his cell. I am not being stupid — B. J., stop it, would you — well, I will, I will call him. I will. Yes, I'll call you back of course I'll call you back.

(She hangs up the phone.)

(To herself.) Jerk.

(She paces now, nervous, picks up the phone, and starts to dial.)

(On phone.) Yeah, hi, Lewis? Uh, it's Haley, I was just wondering what happened to you. So, just give me a call when you get this, or you maybe I'll see you first. You're probably on your way. OK. Bye.

(She hangs up, embarrassed at herself, puts the phone down. After a moment,

she sits on the floor, putting her head between her legs, hyperventilating a little.)

Shit. Shit.

(She stands and moves around the room, nervous.)

He's just late. People are late all the time. I am late all the time, all the time, that's so not true, I am never late, I'm too paranoid to be late.

(She goes out into the hallway. After a moment, she returns with a phone book, sets it on the bed and opens it.)

Be here be here be here — yes.

(She finds the number, shuts the book, and dials. Pause.)

Oh. Hello! Ah, hello, I was wondering, is, um, Lewis there?

(Beat.)

Uh, Haley.

(There is a long beat. She looks up at the ceiling, trying to hold back tears, suddenly.)

Yes, hello, Lewis. I uh, was wondering what happened to you, I think we said eight o'clock, and — Uh huh. Oh. Uh huh.

(Beat.)

Yeah, no of course, I'm not — angry, I'm disappointed, that's all. But not, I just, uh . . . Listen, can I just ask, does that have anything to do with the woman who answered the phone?

(Beat.)

You did, yes, you told me about her but you said that you had, that that had "gone south", and —

(There is a pause. Haley listens and nods her head.)

Oh. Oh! You're living together. No, I, I'm sorry, I didn't understand that. I thought, "Went South" meant, "Went South."

(Quick beat.)

I'm not — accusing, oh Jesus, that's so — Listen, it's fine, I don't, I just thought something else was going on which obviously was my mistake. But I do, you know, I don't quite understand, why you didn't call. I mean, it sounds like you came to this decision sometime before this very instant. So my point being, were you even going to call and tell me about it? I mean, I've been waiting here for an hour and a half, expecting you to come over for some big romantic — and you clearly had no plans to come and were you just going to let me figure that out on my own in the most humiliating way possible? OK, yeah, I guess I am angry, I —

(She stops herself, trying not to lose it. After a moment, she takes a breath.)

You know what? I don't want to talk about this anymore. I have to go. And don't come into my restaurant, even if someone as stupid as me calls you and invites you, don't even think about it, because you know what? We don't serve lying deceitful cheating fucking cowards.

(She hangs up the phone. She goes into the bathroom, where she sobs good and hard, then comes back out, with a Kleenex.)

Well. That makes me the biggest idiot on the planet. I'm not an idiot. He lied, he was just a fucking liar, and I'm a fucking idiot because I didn't see it. Well, people lie to you in new and exciting ways all the time, I guess.

(She sees her shoes then takes them off, puts them back in their box.)

Oh, God. Now I'm never going to be able to wear these shoes without feeling like shit and they cost me four hundred dollars. Well, that's too bad. They're pretty, too.

(Beat.)

How the hell did I not see that? Guy takes me all the way to Brooklyn for dinner because he's a big old romantic? Like, it didn't even occur to me that maybe he didn't want to be caught? My powers of delusion are really noteworthy. Brooklyn.

(The phone rings. She turns to look at it, exhausted, and then goes to pick it up.)

Listen B. J., I can't talk right now.

(Beat.)

Who is this? Eileen? Eileen, it's not a good time, Eileen, I just feel like shit, so — what? I can't hear you, what —

(Beat.)

Shit.

(She sits down.)

What did he say?

(Beat.)

No no don't give him the phone, don't —

(Sudden shift in voice.)

Hi, hi Veljko, how you doing? Wow, it's amazing to hear from you. Yeah, yes, we've been working hard, it's, the place is really humming and — so when'd you get out?

(She listens, nodding.)

Mmmm hmmm. Mmmmmm. Yes well listen, I fired Bibi because he was stealing, Veljko, it had gotten real — no, no — did he tell you that? Because that is completely, uh — Veljko, Veljko, look, there's no point

in getting worked up over what some third party has told you, I'd be happy to walk you through the books, that's not a problem. Why don't you come by tomorrow afternoon, I was gonna be in about —
(Beat.)
No, actually I'm not doing anything right now. You want me to come in right now, sure I can do that.
(Beat.)
No, you don't need to send anybody. I'll be there in half an hour. Yeah, I understand that, Veljko. I'll be there.
(She hangs up the phone and sits, silent.)
Well, this is turning out to be quite a night.
(She starts to move, fast now.)
As I said before, I have in fact done some rather stupid things in the name of survival which may in fact have been even more unwise than I first suspected.
(She changes clothes, quickly, into jeans and a sweatshirt.)
The fact is, and this is a fact worth knowing, the only reason for a restaurant to have a cash-only policy is for purposes of tax evasion and, um, in addition, possibly, money laundering, as I reported earlier. Not that I have been, on the contrary, but in addition to the aforementioned activities, it is possible to, how shall I put this. Cash only business, it's pretty easy to start dipping into the till.
(She goes to the bed, takes out the shoebox full of money, sets it on the bed, opens it, dumps it into a bag.)
It's just, a temptation for someone who's on her own and trying to be capable, it's not always easy for a single woman to be just capable without resorting to criminal behavior. I mean, I am not the first woman who stretched the legality of any given situation. Mildred Pierce, right?
(She takes two big books out from under the bed, goes to the closet, pulls out some really practical shoes and puts them on quickly. She picks up the phone and dials.)
HALEY: *(Continuing; bright.)* Emily? Hi, it's Vera's mom, can I talk to her? Thanks.
(Beat.)
Hi, honey. No, everything's great. Oh. Yeah, he's here, we're having Chinese food, everything's great. But now listen, sweetie, I have to come pick you up, OK? No, nothing serious, it's just some things have come up so I have to come get you and you should be dressed, all right. Vera,

really, I can't — I CANNOT ARGUE ABOUT THIS, VERA. I'M
COMING TO GET YOU NOW.
(She stops herself, sudden. Bites her lip.)
I'm sorry. I'm sorry, sweetie. I'll tell you about it when I get there.
Everything's fine, but I have to come get you, and um, wait inside, OK?
Don't, just tell Emily's mom I'll come up. Don't wait downstairs. I'll
come up.
(Beat.)
I love you, too.
(She hangs up the phone.)
It's fine. I'm not afraid. Everything's fine.
(She picks up the wads of cash from the bed, shoves them into her purse, grabs
her coat, and goes. Blackout.)

SCENE FIVE

*The following morning. Haley stands at the window, letting the light stream
over her. She wears the same clothing from the night before, and looks
exhausted.*

HALEY: I was used to doing things by myself. What is that thing they always
talk about, one of the things people sometimes like about Americans, is
their rugged independence. Pull yourself up by your bootstraps. Don't
be a big baby, ever. There's nothing wrong with that except that when
you make a mistake you're on your own. Because that's the way you
made your life.
(She sits, starts to take off her shoes, exhausted.)
The thing is, they eventually went back to it. The money laundering?
Those Romanians? Not that they involved me. I ran the restaurant, they
let me do what I needed to do to make that place hum, that was just a
front to them, they didn't care. But I did. And they weren't paying their
taxes. They weren't protecting the restaurant. So if the Feds ever came
back, they could shut the whole place down. Seventeen people work in
that place. That's not counting me. We all built it together. So — I kept
another set of books, myself. And I paid the taxes behind their backs. So
that if the law ever did show up again, and those nice criminals, who let
me run my own restaurant, if they ever got in trouble again, the restaurant would be safe. That's how it started. I was paying the taxes. And

then — OK. It went a little further than that. I have a kid. I wanted her in a good school, and you know, you have this kid, you want to give her things. A nice coat, once in a while. A drum set at Christmas. Although, the drum set was a mistake.

(She starts to take her clothes off.)

But it was mostly for the taxes. Some of the waiters knew. Eileen always knew. One of the cooks. I don't think anyone deliberately ratted me out to that little piece of shit Bibi, nobody liked him. But somehow, unbeknownst to me, he put two and two together. Believe me, if I knew he knew, I would not have fired his sorry ass. It was risky anyway, because he's related to all those Romanians, but I was pretty sick of him, it was a risk I was willing to take. I just didn't count on Veljko getting out of prison at this opportune moment. I knew he was getting out soon, I was nervous about that, but I didn't know when. And then — it had gone so far for so many years, there was no way you could explain. "I've been stealing from the business to pay the taxes." Try saying that to a criminal. So last night when he called . . .

(She thinks about this.)

I didn't have a lot of choices. I didn't have anybody to go to. So, I was gonna run. I was gonna grab my kid and catch a train and go. That's what I did before. When Roger turned into such a psychopath. Just get out of town. Go start someplace new. No one's gonna help you. You don't have anyone to help you.

(She stands, tries to shake this off.)

So I don't know why I went to the cops instead. I truly do not know, and I also do not know, and did not know at the time, if what I had done would get me in trouble with them as well as with the Romanian mafia. What a lovely position to be in. Maybe the cops will try to arrest me, I have after all been stealing. Maybe the Feds will arrest me. Or maybe they'll just take all the information I have on criminal activity down at Romanian mob central, and then send me and my child back to my apartment, where the minions of the Romanian mafia would be waiting for us. I didn't know. So I don't know why I went there. Maybe I just needed to believe, finally, that there was help, you don't have to be alone, we live together in this huge city, so many of us, there has to be help out there. And why shouldn't it be the police? That's their job! So I show up, hysterical, looking like a sexually frustrated wreck, dragging an angry and frightened twelve-year-old girl, and babbling on about the Romanian mafia — it wasn't my most impressive moment. I think they would have most definitely tossed me back onto the street, had I not dumped fifteen thousand dollars in small bills all over somebody's dirty desk. Really, those police precincts are filthy, that's not something they just make up on television.

(She goes to the door.)

Vera, did you offer him coffee? Offer him coffee, and don't put those extra scoops in, that's just for me. Other people don't drink it like that.

(She goes to the bathroom, comes out with a toothbrush and toothpaste.)

So once I had their attention, things really started to rock. They take Vera somewhere, sit her in a corner and feed her ice cream and coke all night, that's what she told me later, you got to wonder about the common sense of something like that, but I didn't know anything about it at the time. 'Cause I'm off in one of those interrogation rooms and people are asking me this and that, names of people, how much money over the years, how much I knew, somebody brings in one of those mug books — those also look exactly like they do on television. I have to say, my whole experience sort of reassured me about what we're seeing on television, those cop shows are actually pretty accurate. Anyway, at some point one of them, this kind of round cop, says, you know, you maybe want to think about getting yourself a lawyer. And he says it kind of casual, and I was suddenly so afraid. 'Cause I remembered something else I learned from all those cop shows: Get the lawyer. I just remembered everybody always wanting the perps or the witnesses or whoever to never get a lawyer and the one stupid thing was not getting a lawyer. So I said, yes, I want that. Then there was more whispering and talking and then the round one says, due respect? You don't want a public defender. You're gonna need somebody good. And I just felt sick. I don't know any lawyers. It must have been three in the morning by then. I was so tired. They let me see Vera, at which point I became aware that they had been pumping her full of sugar for hours, so I told them to cut that out. And she said to me, what's going on, Mom, and I just held her hand and said, everything's fine. The biggest problem we got right now is you explaining to me how you can eat like that and not vomit on your shoes! And so she's kind of laughing with me about that, and holding onto me at the same time, and I'm just sitting there, resting, trying hard not to lose it, when who should walk in the front door of that dirty police station, but — the Bug Guy.

(Beat. She wipes her eyes.)

I kid you not. They decided I needed somebody good, that's the kind of mess I was in, and so that nice cop called one of his friends, who happened to be — the Bug Guy. Who's a lawyer. Which is how come he knew Mr. Columbia Law Professor, remember that? So there he is, in my hour of need. The Bug Guy. And I sat there, and I thought — there's something bigger going on here. I'm sorry. Please don't think I've lost my mind. It's been a long night. The Bug Guy — his name is — aw, I'm not going to tell you what his name is — he sits down next to me and says, Hi, how you doing? Like it's the most normal thing in the world to see someone you met in a Buddhist thunderstorm, at three in the morning in a police station. And I say, I'm fine, how are you? And he says, is this Vera? And I say, it is. And he introduces himself as a friend of mine, just came down when he heard I might need someone to talk to and that he was going to take us home. Like it was so clear and simple and not a problem, none of this, whatever mess I was in was just not a problem. He was so peaceful — well, he's kind of a peaceful guy, did I mention that? Maybe you assumed that, because of the Buddhist thing, or maybe you just thought he was a nut, that's what I thought — anyway, he just cuts through there and takes me right into the office of the chief, and he says, she's cooperating but she needs protection. Veljko gets picked up right now on the evidence she's already given, she doesn't take the stand, and however you work this, nothing comes back to her. Then the chief starts to argue, but the Bug Guy, he's so calm, he just explains it all and it makes so much sense, we're all just sitting there, calm, and more and more it seems like everybody's going to get what they want, just by being calm. Have you ever heard of a Zen lawyer? It's sort of like Phil Jackson without the sweat. Nobody's sweating. We're all calm. And then even a little cheerful. That's the thing, I always used to think that about those Buddhists whenever I'd see them on the cover of a book or something: They always seem so cheerful. We sure felt cheerful. And they just let me go home.

(Sitting, exhausted.)

I need to go talk to the Bug Guy. My own private Buddhist lawyer. I'm just a ding-a-ling. Remember that first time I met him? When I thought, you know, if you think the Bug Guy is cute, maybe it means it's been too long since you've been on a date? Well maybe that's not what it means. We don't always know what things mean. Your life unfolds. You think you're in the middle of the worst catastrophe imaginable, and then the Bug Guy shows up. It's mysterious. So maybe if you think the Bug Guy is cute, maybe it's because he is cute. Maybe thunderstorms are a gift of the Buddha. Maybe men and women weren't put on Earth to torture each other. Maybe we're here because we need each other.

(She thinks about this, yawns.)

I'm going to go have coffee with the Bug Guy.

(She goes. Blackout.)

END OF PLAY

THE BELLS

ORIGINAL PRODUCTION

The Bells was originally produced at The McCarter Theatre Center March 22, 2005. It was directed by Emily Mann and had the following cast:

XUIFEI . . . . Pun Bandhu
CHARLIE. . . . . Michael McCarty
JIM. . . . . Paul Butler
SALLY . . . . Fiona Gallagher
MATHIAS. . . . . Ted Marcoux
ANNETTE. . . . . Marin Ireland
BAPTISTE . . . . Christopher Innvar

Scenic Design . . . . Eugene Lee
Costume Design. . . . . Jennifer von Mayrhauser
Lighting Design . . . . Frances Aronson
Sound Design. . . . . Darron L. West
Fight Director . . . . J. Steven White
Dramaturg . . . . Liz Engelman
Producing Director. . . . . Mara Isaacs
Line Producer . . . . Scott French
Director of Production . . . . David York
Production Stage Manager. . . . . Mindy Richardson
Stage Manager . . . . Alison Cote
Artistic Director . . . . Emily Mann

CHARACTERS

XUIFEI: Chinese, late 20s, a ghost
CHARLIE: early 60s, an aging prospector
JIM: 50-60, African-American, a prospector, a drunk
SALLY: 40-50, a prostitute
MATHIAS: 50s, an innkeeper
ANNETTE: early 20s, his daughter
BAPTISTE: 30-40, French Canadian

SET

1915 and 1899. The Alaskan wilderness. Tavern.

ACT I
SCENE ONE

Xuifei stands alone.

XUIFEI: I never knew the world could be so cold. In my village, when the rains came, the cold would crawl into the bamboo and sleep in the pitch of our ceiling. The rain came in and sat with us at our meals, like a sorrowful friend, and the cold spoke softly to our bones. But this is a cold so deep and wild there is no word that names it. They told me not to come here, but there was a hole in my heart and I did not know how to stay in one place. I don't want to die here. I want to die in my home, where the cold is warm.

SCENE TWO

The street. Jim and Sally throw themselves on Charlie, struggling to get a bottle from him.

JIM: Give to me! Come on! Charlie, you've had enough now —

CHARLIE: Get off, you stinking drunk —

SALLY: You bastard! Give me the damn — owwww —

CHARLIE: No! No!

JIM: Give it to me!! Give it to me!

CHARLIE: *(Drinking.)* Go to hell, you stinking Goddamn stinking — it's my turn, I'm gonna take my damn turn, the both of you had your damn turns now it's my damn turn!

SALLY: *(Overlap.)* Owww — dammit, Charlie, now you — oooowwww — *(They roll and fight for a long moment until Sally grabs the bottle and threatens to smash Charlie in the head with it.)*

CHARLIE: Don't don't don't — Sally, come on, darlin' — don't — Sally! It's almost Christmas now, and Christmas is a time of year when people are kind and good to each other —

JIM: Have a little Christmas spirit, Sally — now now now, you're spilling the hootch now, Sally, honey. Now what's the point of that, darlin'. *(Sally looks at the bottle, rights it, takes a rather long drink. The two men are ready to leap on her. She takes a step back and takes another drink. Both of them howl.)*

JIM: *(Continuing.)* Oh, my God — that is — now, Sally — you had your turn now!

CHARLIE: *(Overlap.)* Jesus God above, you stinking greedy whore —

SALLY: I'm not a whore!

CHARLIE: Say that again, and you're a liar and a whore and a thief for that matter, stealing liquor from Mathias —

SALLY: I'm not a thief! Mathias give me this, for a Christmas present!

CHARLIE: You're lying, you're a liar and a whore and a thief —

JIM: A liar and a whore and a drunk and a thief. That's like a song, isn't it? *(Singing.)*
Sweet Sally Maguire, a whore and a liar —

CHARLIE: A thief, when it suited her needs. Went down to the river, 'cause a man wouldn't give her —

JIM: A drink — 'cause she's a drunk —

SALLY: You're a drunk you stinking drunk —

JIM: You're a drunk —

SALLY: No, you're a drunk —
(They fight over the bottle again. Sally makes off with the bottle. Jim grabs her by the ankle, yanks her back, and gets the bottle himself. It is empty.)

JIM: Goddamnit! You drunken thievin' whore!

SALLY: Least I never . . .
(This stops Jim in his tracks.)

JIM: What'd you say?

CHARLIE: She didn't say nothing.

SALLY: The hell I didn't.

JIM: The hell she didn't —

CHARLIE: Come on now, it's Christmas, what you want to be dragging that up for?

SALLY: *(Insistent.)* Show me your palm! Show it to me!

JIM: I don't have to show you nothin' you crazy drunken whore!

CHARLIE: Come on, now! It's Christmas! Christmas is a holiday of good will and brotherhood, we're all, Christ's birth and have a drink and all.
(He pulls a couple of more bottles out of his pockets and holds them out.)

SALLY: I know what I know, Charlie —

CHARLIE: Sally. Leave it be and have a drink. We're all friends, now. This is a friendly town, not like Skagway or nothing. You remember that guy? That guy in Skagway? Jim, you remember that guy?

JIM: What guy.

CHARLIE: You know, that guy. Back in, I can't remember the year, I went there. He was running that town ragged, evil as a snake, you went in for a couple of drinks, next thing you know he was threatening to kill you over fifty cents, an old pair of boots, just a foul mood was enough to set that guy off and he had the gang to do it for him, too. Everybody smiling, talking like friends, like old friends explaining we're gonna kill you like they're asking you over for dinner or something. That's the way things were that year. So much gold in the air it made the brain go hot with fever, even in sixty below, didn't even matter there was nothing to spend it on but cheap booze and women you couldn't hardly look at, everyone running up from wherever the world spit them out to come stand in the freezing cold, the heat in their blood driving them through the Chilkoot Pass like dead men on their way to hell. Pack horses driven so hard they was jumping off the trail into the abyss, first time in my life I ever saw a horse commit suicide but that's where it took us, all of us screaming for gold like it was gonna save you from what it meant to be human. No Goddamn wonder that guy could turn a town like Skagway into our own local version of Hades.

JIM: What year was this?

CHARLIE: Don't matter. My point is, this is a friendly town! Nothing like Skagway.

(They sit for a moment.)

JIM: You hungry?

SALLY: Yeah, I'm hungry.

JIM: Maybe Mathias give us something to eat.

CHARLIE: Better hope Annie's not looking. She is, we gonna have to get Sally, with her sticky fingers, do her magic.

SALLY: She gives me a pain.

JIM: Don't talk to her. Talk to Mathias.

CHARLIE: It's Christmas, he'll give us some eggs or something.

SALLY: 'Cause I offered to work it off with him. It's not natural, livin' like a priest when there's whores in the world.

JIM: *(Singing.)* Sweet Sally Maguire, she sings in the choir, and oh how the priests gather round.

CHARLIE: There's nothing quite finer than her sweet vaginer, for making that good Godly sound . . .

(They are off.)

SCENE THREE

ANNETTE: Pa! Where are you, Pa! Six, seven eight — Goddamn it, PA! PAAAAA — they been stealing from us again, PA!!!

(Annette at the inn. Annette is counting bottles at the bar.)

MATHIAS: Here I am, here I am! Just went out to see the Sun rise, soon as it showed over the horizon, there it goes again, back into the Earth. Wind's kicking up too, snow ghosts rising out of the mountains, fading as soon as they take shape. To hell with them, I say. Go on, get out of here! Six weeks of black don't scare us! We're going to light this town! I'm telling you, it's gonna work, this place is going to burn bright as the stars themselves! So that when the heavens look out, we are what they're gonna see, this place, shining like a star, past reason and hope, brighter than all of it, shining into the night.

ANNETTE: Wait a minute. That's why you bought all those lanterns in Dawson City? To light the whole town? Oh my God, you're just going to give them all away, aren't you?

MATHIAS: I bought so many because you got to believe in the light of us, Annie, you know what it is when the darkness is all we have, we're not meant to live like that. Good Lord tells us to light a candle, rather than curse the dark, that's what I'm doing.

(He lights the lamp.)

There you go. A single lamp, burning through the endless night.

ANNETTE: Not a single lamp, a whole mess of them, that you're just giving away to anybody who happens to need one —

MATHIAS: We'll put them in with the Christmas baskets.

ANNETTE: The Christmas baskets? How much is that going to run us this year? Don't tell me, I don't want to know. I want to talk to you about Sally and Charlie.

MATHIAS: Look how pretty you look. You do something different to your hair?

ANNETTE: I combed it.

MATHIAS: You should do that, more often.

ANNETTE: I counted before and now I'm counting again, and Sally and Charlie both been stealing liquor. They come in here, you make me wait on 'em, treat 'em like decent people —

MATHIAS: Their hearts are in the right place.

ANNETTE: They got no hearts! That Jim Lynch is just as bad, they're barely, there's dogs on the street more human than those three!

(He looks at her. She looks away.)

MATHIAS: Just because this place is wild doesn't mean you have to be.

ANNETTE: You tell me how to be any other way.

(There is a sad beat, then.)

MATHIAS: You're lonely, I know that.

ANNETTE: Pa, that's not — I don't want to talk about this.

MATHIAS: Annie.

ANNETTE: No, no, I'm fine. You're right, I'm just in a bad mood over nothing, I'm ashamed of myself. I'll finish cleaning this up and . . . come help you with those baskets.

MATHIAS: It's all right. I can —

ANNETTE: *(Snapping.)* Pa! I said I would help, would you just stop trying to take care of me all the time I'm fine I told you!

BAPTISTE: *(In doorway.)* Hello?

(Annette turns, furious again.)

ANNETTE: Jesus God above, what the hell are you doing? We're not open, all right?

BAPTISTE: I'm sorry.

(Annette stops. He is quite handsome.)

ANNETTE: Oh. I'm sorry. I thought you were someone else.

BAPTISTE: You are not open?

(And he's French. She's speechless.)

MATHIAS: Of course we're open! Come on in, have a seat. Annie. We have a customer.

(Mathias gestures to her to wait on him. Nervous, suddenly, she does.)

ANNETTE: Yes, of course. Excuse me. What can I get you? I mean, can I get you anything?

BAPTISTE: Food, you have food?

ANNETTE: Any particular kind of food?

BAPTISTE: No.

ANNETTE: OK, we have that. Anything to drink?

BAPTISTE: Wine? Do you have wine?

ANNETTE: Yes, we have that.

BAPTISTE: I would like some wine.

ANNETTE: I'll go get that then.

(Annette nods, goes to the bar. Mathias steps forward, friendly.)

MATHIAS: You're French.

BAPTISTE: Canadian.

MATHIAS: French Canadian. Annie speaks French.

BAPTISTE: *(Interested.)* Yes?

ANNETTE: *(Embarrassed.)* I don't . . .

MATHIAS: Yes, yes. Her French is beautiful. Go ahead.

ANNETTE: *(A beat, then.)* Bonjour. Como tallez vous?

BAPTISTE: Ah. Well. May I have my food now?

ANNETTE: Sure.

> *(Embarrassed now, she slams his drink on the table, and goes. After a moment, Mathias approaches.)*

MATHIAS: I haven't seen you around these parts. What's your name?

BAPTISTE: My name is Baptiste Carbonneau.

MATHIAS: Pleased to meet you, Mr. Carbonneau. I don't know what Annie's so touchy about.

BAPTISTE: She is a woman.

MATHIAS: Oh, no no — she's well of course yes, she's a woman. She just a little rough around the edges sometimes, and you can't blame her. There's not a lot of people come through here. So her manners can get a little raw, but she's a pure soul. I'm her father, you'll forgive me bragging a bit. So how is that stuff?

BAPTISTE: Fine, will you join me?

MATHIAS: Thanks, I think I will.

> *(Mathias pours himself a glass, refreshes Baptiste's, then sets the bottle on the counter.)*

MATHIAS: *(Continuing.)* So, you're from Canada. What are you looking for in these parts?

BAPTISTE: What is any man looking for?

MATHIAS: Only one answer to that in the Yukon.

BAPTISTE: Yes, well.

MATHIAS: You don't look like a prospector, though.

BAPTISTE: All the gold is gone, that is what I have been told.

MATHIAS: People look for it all the same. But you're right, you missed the action by nigh on twenty years.

BAPTISTE: You were here for the fever, then?

MATHIAS: We were here. And between you and me, I'm not sorry those days are behind us. Where are you from, Carbonneau?

BAPTISTE: I was raised in Montreal.

MATHIAS: Nice city?

BAPTISTE: Quite beautiful. Elegant, even.

MATHIAS: Educated?

BAPTISTE: The city is quite educated, yes.

MATHIAS: You, I meant.

BAPTISTE: Both the city of Montreal and myself have been educated.

MATHIAS: Well, you've come a long way. What brings you out here again? I didn't catch that.

BAPTISTE: I did not say.

MATHIAS: I know you didn't, that's why I'm trying to pry it out of you. No no. You don't want to say, I'm not going to push you.

BAPTISTE: And yet you ask me twice.

MATHIAS: *(Laughing.)* Curiosity is a virtue! Didn't you ever hear that?

BAPTISTE: I have heard many things. Some of them are true. But not all.

MATHIAS: You're a philosopher.

BAPTISTE: Was that philosophical? I suppose it passes as such in Yukon.

MATHIAS: No no. You can't be cynical here. The weather won't stand for it. Fifty degrees below and the wind blowing at you straight out of the netherworld, you learn pretty damn fast that cynicism is one of the luxuries of civilization.

BAPTISTE: Then you are a philosopher yourself.

MATHIAS: I am! Come a long winter's night, and out here the nights are long, you have time to ask yourself, what does it mean to be human, in the wilderness?

BAPTISTE: Some would say, to be human is to follow the laws of God. Just as the cosmos follows natural law, physical law, so must we follow the laws of the God in whose image we are made.

MATHIAS: Who would say that?

BAPTISTE: Some would say, it is known. Our reality is from God's decree, ordered, and this order represents the perfected nature of that God who has brought everything about, including the law itself.
(He laughs.)

MATHIAS: That's funny?

BAPTISTE: It is, a bit. The things we are taught, in our youth. And the things we learn elsewhere. Humanity is holy. Humanity is shit. So yes, I am educated, for all it is worth. You tell me yourself, in the Yukon, it is worth nothing at all.

MATHIAS: I didn't say that.

BAPTISTE: No? I thought you did.
(A beat.)

MATHIAS: So what are you doing here, Carbonneau?

BAPTISTE: I am having a glass of wine. Perhaps some food, if your pretty daughter deigns to feed me, and then I go to Minto Landing.

MATHIAS: That trail's under six feet of snow this time of year. What fool sent you there?

BAPTISTE: I am my own fool.

(Annette enters, carrying two plates of food. She takes them to the table, sets them down, shy.)

ANNETTE: Here's your food. We had some chicken and carrots . . .

(Then, simple and sweet, schoolgirl french.)

C'est un peu simple, mais j'espere que vous l'aimez.

BAPTISTE: (Surprised.) Merci bien, mademoiselle.

ANNETTE: De rien.

(She goes back to the bar, pleased with herself.)

BAPTISTE: (To Annette.) It is very good.

ANNETTE: Thank you.

(She starts to shove things back into the cabinets.)

MATHIAS: Annie, go on and make up a room for Mr. Carbonneau.

BAPTISTE: No, excuse me, I cannot stay.

MATHIAS: As my guest. We let you walk out that door tonight, it'd be just this side of murder. Amount to the same thing. Annie.

ANNETTE: (Embarrassed.) If he doesn't want to stay, Pa —

MATHIAS: Annie. Make up a room.

ANNETTE: He is right, Mr. Carbonneau, you won't see sun now till almost midday tomorrow. You'd need a strong reason to go out there and face all that dark.

BAPTISTE: Perhaps not, then. My reasons for staying seem strong as well.

(Baptiste brings his empty wine glass to the bar, reaches for the bottle. Abashed, Annette takes the glass from him.)

ANNETTE: Here, let me get that for you.

BAPTISTE: What is this?

(He looks at the counter, picks up a small open box that rests there, as she pours the wine.)

ANNETTE: Oh, that's nothing. Someone gave that to me a long time ago. I forgot it was back there.

BAPTISTE: What is it?

ANNETTE: It's bells. A Chinaman gave them to me, when I was just a little girl.

BAPTISTE: A Chinaman? What happened to him?

MATHIAS: He went back to China.

(Lights shift.)

SCENE FOUR

Xuifei.

XUIFEI: There was a girl in my village. When you looked at her, she would return your gaze like a young animal. Her hair fell to her shoulders like water, and although she rarely laughed, her smile was quick. I loved this girl. I wished to marry her. But her family was poor. My love had gone to someone so poor she could never marry and eventually she was sold, by her parents, to a house of prostitution. My brother, knowing my pain, came to me with this news as a gift. See, he said, I will give you money and now you can have her whenever you please. And that is what I did. Night after night I went into the village, and paid for the right to have her. But even that brought me no rest, and I could no longer bear the sight of her face. And so I left my home. I left my home.
(It is night. Mathias is alone in the inn. He has clearly been drinking. Annette enters the scene behind him, as does Xuifei.)

ANNETTE: I can't do it!

XUIFEI: Kuh-yi, kuh-yi.
(Xuifei rubs the balls expertly. She goes to watch him.)

ANNETTE: Show me!
(He does. She laughs, delighted, as he holds her hands and shows her how to rub the balls together.)

XUIFEI: Hao, hun hao!

ANNETTE: Pa, look! I can do it, too!

MATHIAS: Get out of here!
(Xuifei disappears. Annette turns, looks at Mathias, surprised.)

ANNETTE: You all right?

MATHIAS: *(Beat.)* I'm fine, I'm fine. I'm just doing some bills, you got me so worked up about the money this afternoon, thought I'd see what we had in the till.

ANNETTE: You want me to stay with you?

MATHIAS: No, no. You go to sleep.
(She starts to go. He calls to her.)

MATHIAS: *(Continuing.)* Annie?

ANNETTE: Yeah, Pa.

MATHIAS: This Canadian. You like him?

ANNETTE: Oh my God.

MATHIAS: He's educated. Good-looking. French.

ANNETTE: Go to bed, Pa.

MATHIAS: Best-looking guy I've seen around here in years —

ANNETTE: GO TO BED.

MATHIAS: In a minute.

(She goes. Mathias looks at bills that have been left by the cash register, or on the counter.)

MATHIAS: *(Continuing.)* Two, two fifty, four, six — six hundred, just last month — that's down a bit from October, but still enough to put two hundred in the bank, which brings the savings up to over thirty thousand . . .

(After a moment, the sound of the bells, far off, can be heard. He turns, then turns back to his counting. The sound continues to rise as he counts.)

MATHIAS: *(Continuing.)* Thirty thousand dollars, that's nothing to sneeze at, coming from nothing, most everybody else run through it all overnight, but Annette is going to have — her children are going to have more than I ever did. That's what matters. That's what matters!

(He stands, abrupt, listening. The sound fades. He takes another long drink.)

MATHIAS: *(Continuing.)* People showing up out of nowhere, talk about nonsense, it's just the night. Night's so long now. So damn long . . .

(He goes to the counter, turns up the light, which gets brighter and brighter until it suddenly goes out. Blackout.)

SCENE FIVE

Charlie wandering in the windy night, with Sally and Jim behind him. He is going on. They are drinking and shoving each other, behind him. At some point they simply collapse in a drunken stupor.

CHARLIE: I saw a bird. Last night of my life I slept in a real hotel, this place was swank, people wearing silk clothes, chairs with cushions on 'em. That bird was smart, it could talk in six different languages, some seaman taught him all this shit, then died on him, bird got dumped in this hotel in the wilderness, no one knew much more than that. So I go up to it — and I say, Hey bird! I hear you can talk! What do you have to say for yourself? And the bird just stares at me. So finally I think what the hell, and I turn around, and the bird says, "Thank God he's leaving. Boring old shit head." Turns out he won't talk to nobody unless you're walking away from him. I finally got sick of it, went off and got drunk.

Come back, it's three in the morning maybe, I'm climbing the steps to the porch of this place and I hear a woman singing, this song of such purity, it's like a breeze from a far country, moving through the night, a dream of a better time. I never heard anything like it, before or since. And I look through the window, and it's that damn bird. All alone. Singing — well later they told me it was from some opera, that damn bird could sing opera on top of everything else. So the bird finally finishes this — song — and I say to it through the window — Bird, if you can do that — you can sing like that — how come you're so perverse? And that bird looks me in the eye and says, "'Cause you're all sons of bitches."

(He stops, takes a drink. After a moment, Sally laughs, long and hard.)

SALLY: That bird said that?

CHARLIE: *(Laughing.)* It did. "Sons of bitches."

SALLY: That is a smart bird.

(She collapses again. Jim sits up.)

JIM: Where are we?

CHARLIE: We're right about here, you know. There's a windbreak up another half mile, we'll camp there.

JIM: We're sleeping out here? It's cold.

CHARLIE: Dammit Jim, I told you, we're going out to work that old stake Stu Campbell told us on!

JIM: No, come on.

CHARLIE: What'd you think we were doing, you damn drunk?

JIM: You just said . . . I need a drink.

(He staggers over to Charlie, looks for a bottle. Charlie tosses the bottle.)

CHARLIE: We're working now. That stake is still going strong. Stu used to swear on it.

JIM: It's going so good, how come he ain't out there working it?

CHARLIE: What do you care why? Nothing left for any of us in the town.

JIM: Mathias takes care of us.

CHARLIE: I don't want to be taken care of! Goddamn it, I'm not ready to just drink away my last years. I want to do something. I want to feel yearning in my heart. I want to climb into some freezing hellhole and look for gold. Remember that feeling?

JIM: Yeah, I remember it. That's why I drink, to forget it.

SALLY: *(Sitting up.)* I'm not working any fool ass claim. There's no more gold out there, you fool.

CHARLIE: 'Cording to Stu Campbell there is. He said he and that Chinaman took near six thousand dollars out of the ground up there.

SALLY: That was a long time ago!

JIM: That where we're going?

CHARLIE: I told you this, Jim!

JIM: 'Cause I'm not going there.

SALLY: Jesus God above.

(She looks beyond them. Mathias stands in the snow, covered in blood. They turn and see what she sees. Mathias takes a step forward and tries to speak to them. After a moment, he collapses. They go to him, pick him up and help him stagger off.)

CHARLIE: Mathias!

SALLY: Oh my God, Mathias! What happened to him?

JIM: Mathias!

CHARLIE: Mathias!

SALLY: Look at all the blood, what happened?

JIM: Can he walk?

CHARLIE: Mathias, can you walk?

SALLY: What's he doing all the way out here? Mathias, what are you doing out here?

CHARLIE: You got him? You got him?

(In dark, Annette rushes through the night.)

ANNETTE: Bring him upstairs, upstairs Mr. Carbonneau! Where did you find him? Oh my God, there's so much blood — somebody make coffee — blankets, I need blankets!

SCENE SIX

Baptiste alone in the bar. He peers through the curtain into the back of the house, sees there is no one about, and starts to search the bar area. He pours himself a drink as he searches, then ducks back behind the bar itself, looking. Annette comes out of the house, sees him behind the bar. He does not see her. After a moment, she speaks.

ANNETTE: Can I help you?

(Baptiste stands, startled.)

BAPTISTE: No, no, I . . . ah, no.

(He goes to the other side of the bar. Annette looks back at where he was looking, then looks up at him.)

ANNETTE: Looks like supplies are getting a bit thin back here.

(She pours him a drink.)

BAPTISTE: The prospectors who found your father on the trail, they came here once or twice, you were occupied, caring for him —

ANNETTE: So basically you just let them raid the place for a day and a half.

BAPTISTE: *(A shrug.)* How is he?

ANNETTE: He'll be all right. I guess. I don't know. I haven't thanked you for what you did, Mr. Carbonneau.

(She brings him the drink she poured. He looks at her.)

BAPTISTE: I expected no thanks.

ANNETTE: You carry a man half a mile in the snow, and you don't expect thanks?

BAPTISTE: Expectations are wearisome.

ANNETTE: So are you.

(She turns, upset.)

BAPTISTE: Why are you so angry?

ANNETTE: I'm not angry. I'm grateful. I'm grateful! And I just thought I'd mention that, that I'm grateful that you saved my father's life, 'cause I thought it might be something that was worth saying, thank you, thank you for saving my father's life.

(She pours herself a stiff drink, lifts the glass to toast him.)

ANNETTE: *(Continuing.)* So, thank you!

(He stops her hand. She looks at him.)

BAPTISTE: You're welcome.

(He takes the drink from her and drinks it himself.)

BAPTISTE: *(Continuing.)* You must not drink. It will not help you.

(Beat.)

You are worried for him. Yes? You are worried. For your father.

ANNETTE: I just don't understand what happened. He's been running on about the axe, and it's gone from the woodpile, but I can't make sense of any of it.

BAPTISTE: That is what he used to cut himself?

ANNETTE: It must be, but he says he doesn't remember. I don't know.

BAPTISTE: What was he doing so far out?

ANNETTE: He says he doesn't remember.

(Beat, tearing up.)

I don't know what would happen to me, if anything happened to him. Sorry. I'm just scared.

(Wiping her eyes.)

Do you have family, Mr. Carbonneau?

BAPTISTE: (Surprised.) I? What makes you ask?

ANNETTE: I just can't make out why you'd be here. If you did. Why you'd leave them. The world is so lonely, even with there being just one person, that you love. At least my pa and I . . . we have each other.

BAPTISTE: You have your father? And that makes it not lonely?

(She shrugs.)

ANNETTE: No, it's still lonely. I don't know what I mean. It's this place, maybe. I don't know.

BAPTISTE: You think it is not so lonely elsewhere?

ANNETTE: I don't know what it's like, anywhere else, I only ever been here. And everything is so big and . . . distant, here. The mountains and the snow and the black nights can be so black.

BAPTISTE: And you feel alone.

ANNETTE: It is that, but not only that. There's the cold, too, sometimes it's so bitter it reaches right down to the heart of you, and you're thinking you must be a strong person, to bear something so otherworldly, and then the wind comes and you know you can't bear it, you're not strong, you're just like a ghost already, it takes the breath right out of you, just like that. Like death, that's how it feels. So you're going along and feeling that, and wondering how God could make a place so horrible, and you don't know if there is a God, you don't know if there's anything except the cold and the black and the wind, and then the lights come, blue and green and shimmering, all over the night sky. They just come, all at once. You see the stars again. And the mountains are so beautiful, the air is so strong, and you realize this terrible place is where God put his hand, back at the dawn of time. He just reached down and touched the Earth, right here, that's why it's so strong. And then you're not lonely at all.

(Beat.)

But you don't have anyone to tell that to. Which makes it a little lonely, I guess.

(A short beat, then — .)

BAPTISTE: My father was a schoolteacher. He was well taught, by the Jesuits; at night he would play badly on the violin, he would quote endlessly from poets whose names are now lost. He was a good man who died needlessly when I was fourteen. My mother married again, a man who drank and beat her children. My sister, one night, he struck her so cruelly. Her face, her body. She was very young. He was a large man, I could not stop him. After her death, I would not stay.

(He pours himself another drink.)

ANNETTE: *(Quiet.)* I'm so sorry.

BAPTISTE: I have seen worse since.

(As he is about to down another drink, she reaches out and places her hand on his, in a small gesture of comfort. He looks up at her, startled. They consider each other. After a moment, Sally and Jim and Charlie enter.)

CHARLIE: How is he?

ANNETTE: He's fine. Just took a couple of nasty cuts, on his arm. That's how come all the blood. He's been unconscious, mostly. I won't say I wasn't real worried there for a minute, but he's come out of it now.

(Then.)

I know you all been helping yourself around here.

SALLY/CHARLIE/JIM: No, no, no —

ANNETTE: No, I was going to say, it's fine. I'm real thankful for your help. Jim Lynch, you take a seat. Sally, let me get you something. What can I get you?

MATHIAS: *(Offstage.)* Annie?

(Annette turns, startled, as Mathias appears in the interior doorway.)

ANNETTE: Pa, what are you doing up? You have to stay in bed.

MATHIAS: I'm all right.

ANNETTE: You're not all right.

MATHIAS: *(Sees Baptiste, bewildered.)* What's he doing here?

ANNETTE: You asked him to stay. He was here, sleeping here, when Sally came and said they found you. On the trail.

SALLY: We found you out on the trail, Mathias, don't you remember? Couldn't carry you back the whole way. So Mr. Carbonneau, he come out and brought you in.

ANNETTE: He saved your life, Pa. Don't you remember any of this?

MATHIAS: Course I do. I'm just tired, is all. Little out of my head, I guess. Sorry.

BAPTISTE: How is your arm?

MATHIAS: Fine. Thanks for your help. Like a drink? Let me get you a drink. Jim, Charlie. She taking care of you? Let me take care of you.

(He goes to the bar, pours drinks.)

ANNETTE: Pa —

MATHIAS: How long I been sleeping?

ANNETTE: A day and a half.

MATHIAS: Guess I was tired. Charlie, Sally — how you holding up for food? You want some eggs, or something?

CHARLIE: I won't say no to a plate of eggs.

MATHIAS: She hasn't fed you yet? Annie, where are your manners?

ANNETTE: I've had a few things on my mind, Pa. And I don't think —

MATHIAS: What?

ANNETTE: I just don't want you to, to, to — Pa, really, you have to —

MATHIAS: I'm all right!

(He hands a glass of wine to Baptiste, pours himself a glass.)

MATHIAS: *(Continuing.)* I'm embarrassed, mostly. Go out to chop some wood for the stove and end up slicing up my own arm, the drunks from the town finding me wandering around the snow like some crazy prospector been lost in the hills since the fever hit.

BAPTISTE: You were a long way out.

MATHIAS: All that white, it's near impossible to find yourself once you're off the landmarks. Wind kicks up, there's no real way of knowing where you are. Isn't that right, Jim?

JIM: That's what I been saying, to Charlie, there ain't none of us in any shape to go out there no more. He's got some crazy idea.

CHARLIE: There's gold out there. Stu Campbell —

MATHIAS: Not tonight, Charlie. Let's just be grateful we're all safe and warm tonight. Annie, what about those eggs?

ANNETTE: *(To Baptiste.)* Don't let him drink too much.

(She takes a moment, then goes. Baptiste watches. Mathias watches him.)

BAPTISTE: *(Off the others.)* She did care for them. While you were sleeping. You've taught her well; she has a generous heart.

MATHIAS: Thank you.

BAPTISTE: Can I ask you about these?

(He holds out the bells. Mathias stares at them for a moment, reaches for them, and takes them from Baptiste, firm.)

MATHIAS: Those things are still lying around, huh? Annie's gonna end up losing them, she's not careful.

(He takes the bells, starts to put them back in their box.)

BAPTISTE: She says it was a Chinaman who gave them to her. A prospector, Stu Campbell, he told me about this Chinaman as well. They worked a stake together, not far from here.

MATHIAS: *(Slight pause.)* You've met Stu Campbell.

BAPTISTE: He said he was a good man. His name was Lin Xuifei. They were friends, it seems, and Campbell thinks something terrible must have happened to him; they had agreed to meet at Minto Landing, and the Chinaman never came.

MATHIAS: And why do you care about that?

BAPTISTE: I was paid to find him.

(A beat.)

MATHIAS: You're a bounty hunter, then.

BAPTISTE: Yes. I am a bounty hunter.

JIM: *(Perplexed.)* Someone put a bounty on the Chinaman? What for? He's been dead —

(Baptiste turns and looks at him. Jim looks at him.)

BAPTISTE: Why do you say that?

JIM: You're the one who said it. You said, Stu thinks something terrible happened to him. I don't know what happened to him.

MATHIAS: I don't know what any of us can tell you. It was a long time ago. None of us knew the man.

BAPTISTE: But he gave your daughter these bells.

(Xuifei appears, holding bells out.)

XUIFEI: Shr-ni-da. Na ba. Na ba.

(Annette enters, takes a step toward him, tentative.)

ANNETTE: What's he saying, Pa?

XUIFEI: Na ba! Na ba!

(Mathias casually takes up the other set of bells.)

MATHIAS: That's right, he came through, he gave those things to Annie, and then he left. Never got them to make that sound again and Lord knows we tried. Charlie, you remember, how long were we trying to get these things to make that sound for her?

CHARLIE: Oh Lord, it was months.

ANNETTE: Show me!

XUIFEI: Hao —

(Xuifei holds her hands and shows her how to make the bells ring.)

MATHIAS: Annie was heartbroken, everybody in town trying to get these damn bells to sing, nobody can do it. Sally —

SALLY: *(Cool.)* I couldn't do it.

JIM: Just didn't have the touch, not a one of us. She was such a sweet little thing, you hated to disappoint her.

ANNETTE: You try it, Pa!

(She holds her set of bells out to him. He does not turn.)

MATHIAS: I still can't do it. Here, you give it a try.

(He hands his set of bells to Baptiste, who looks at them, considers them, then sets them down.)

(Annette turns back to Xuifei, hands him the bells. He shakes his head, and gives them back to her.)

XUIFEI: Jeige. Wo geh ni. Wo geh ni.

BAPTISTE: Stu Campbell, this prospector —

MATHIAS: A prospector! You're taking the word of a prospector, each and every one of them bone mad with gold fever to begin with — no offense, Charlie —

CHARLIE: None taken —

MATHIAS: By the time they make it through the Chilkoot Pass or whatnot, their brains and their hearts and their souls are frozen solid and blasted through, not a one of them even resembles a human being by the time they make it up here, that's who's telling you, what'd he say?

BAPTISTE: He said the Chinaman was carrying three thousand dollars in gold. Do you remember that?

(Xuifei empties a bag of gold onto his table.)

ANNETTE: Pa, look!

(Xuifei laughs, and gestures her to see it.)

XUIFEI: Ni kan ba. Pyaon lian, shr bu shr?

JIM: That what you're looking for? You talked to Stu, you're thinking that Chinaman froze out there, the gold's still out there?

(Xuifei holds a piece up, shows Annette.)

XUIFEI: Wo gei ni.

JIM: That gold is gone!

BAPTISTE: You know that for a fact?

JIM: Everybody knows it! How long ago was that, Sally?

SALLY: Eighteen years.

JIM: That's what I mean!

CHARLIE: There's gold out there still! Stu told me, they never came to the bottom of that claim. We're gonna work it, me Sally and Jim.

SALLY: Have a drink, Charlie.

MATHIAS: Gold everywhere. Where is your God in so much gold, Carbonneau?

BAPTISTE: My God? I have no relations with God. Do you?

MATHIAS: I fear the Lord. But I question him, too. What I saw those years. Men driven mad with the wanting and the having and the losing of it. Standing in the icy waters day in day out, the one becomes rich, the next dies of grief and loss, starvation, how many of us, dying of cold and starvation, scurvy. You ever see anyone die of scurvy? The blood turns thin. Legs go lame. Your gums swell and bleed until your teeth drop out, your skin mottles and putrefies — worthy men and women turning into lepers around us, my wife, my wife dying an unimaginable death, meanwhile God is showering gold without end on men living like animals. What kind of God is that?

(Baptiste does not answer. The two men look at each other, consider each other. Xuifei stands and slowly leaves the room. Annette takes her bells and leaves as well.)

MATHIAS: *(Continuing.)* As to this Chinaman and his gold — I couldn't likely say one way or the other, what happened.

BAPTISTE: What year was this? Ninety-nine, ninety-eight?

MATHIAS: Ninety-nine.

BAPTISTE: Was that the year your wife died?

(Mathias looks at him, pours another drink.)

MATHIAS: Yeah, so I had other things to think about.

BAPTISTE: How big was the town at that time, do you remember?

MATHIAS: Lot of people coming through, those years.

BAPTISTE: But those who stayed, those who lived here. How many, thirty, forty?

MATHIAS: That sounds about right.

BAPTISTE: It was a hard winter.

MATHIAS: Yeah, it was.

BAPTISTE: People were starving, you said.

MATHIAS: Yes.

BAPTISTE: How did you make it through?

MATHIAS: You just do! I'm sorry. I don't mean to be so abrupt. It was a hard time. Hard to look back at it. We weren't here long ourselves, just arrived the year before, none of it looking like anything you thought. How could it? People tell you stories of gold without end, they don't tell you the rest, somehow. Met one guy, talked about the Yukon, he called it Eldorado. You hear that, you don't think about ragged men, living in shacks, held against the Northern wind with newspaper and glue. You don't think about the cold, going so deep for so long the memory of warmth moves to a distant place, it becomes the fantasy, a little girl's bedtime story, There once was a place where the sun shone, and things grew. You don't think, how can a woman and a child live in a place like that?

BAPTISTE: Your conscience bothers you, with regard to what you did?

MATHIAS: My conscience?

(A beat.)

BAPTISTE: Bringing them, your wife and child, to this dreadful place.

(A beat.)

MATHIAS: We were poor enough before we came here. I got no way of knowing what my life would've been if we never came. Just as you won't ever know what your life may've been, if you'd lingered on in the elegant city of Montreal, pondering the history of civilization.

(Annette enters, carrying a bowl of eggs and sausages, for Jim and Sally and Charlie.)

ANNETTE: Here you go! It's not much, I did what I could with what was in the kitchen — Pa. What's the matter?

MATHIAS: What?

(Annette sets the food down, worried.)

ANNETTE: Look at you, you're all flushed, you look about to faint —

MATHIAS: I'm fine —

ANNETTE: You're not fine!

(Sharp to Baptiste.)

I told you not to let him drink, it's making him sick. You shouldn't be drinking that stuff, it's been around I don't know how long, it's making you crazy, Pa.

MATHIAS: Guess I'm not used to it.

ANNETTE: Guess not. You're going back to bed right now.

(Annette takes Mathias out. Baptiste turns to the others.)

CHARLIE: I'm sorry we can't help you, son. But no one here really knew that Chinaman. What'd you say his name was?

BAPTISTE: Xuifei. It means "snow."

CHARLIE: Well, that's an interesting fact, but you're missing my point here. We didn't even know his name. We all heard him and Stu were having some good fortune up there on that claim they struck, but he didn't come down here into town but a few times. Kept to himself, mostly. Didn't even speak English. There's not much more to say.

BAPTISTE: There is a good deal more to say, I think. Thank you for your help.

(Baptiste puts his rucksack on his shoulder and goes. There is silence for a moment. Charlie eats.)

SALLY: We got to get out of here.

JIM: That guy's an idiot. He's not gonna find him.

SALLY: He's no idiot.

JIM: You just like him, 'cause he's French.

CHARLIE: What do you want to stick around here for, Jim? I'm telling you, that claim is still out there and that cabin is snug. On top of, Stu left his traps! Catch us a few jackrabbits, steal a couple bottles of hootch from Mathias, we got everything we need.

JIM: *(Abrupt.)* 'Member that Chinaman, how much gold he had? You and me working day and night, we didn't come up with four dollars between us. And he comes in here, a Chinaman, he don't even speak English, and the gold just come out of the earth for him. Rising up, out of the earth, like a bad dream.

(The lights shift.)

SCENE SEVEN

Xuifei.

XUIFEI: My grief made me alone in the world. The desolation of the sea, the exhaustion which came with the loading and unloading of the vessels, the ebb and flow of tide, men, seasons, such days suited my bewildered spirit. But the nights of drinking and laughter were a torment to me. The women came at night and my heart filled with rage at the careless-ness of empty pleasure. Even here, among a breed of men who were homeless in all the world, even here I could not stay. A ship came, sail-ing as far as anyone had heard. To a land of monumental mountains. Endless darkness. Cold beyond dreaming. Why would anyone go to such a place?

SCENE EIGHT

Jim starts to sing. As the song progresses, the others join in.

JIM: Hark the herald angels sinngg. Glory to, the newborn king. Peace on Earth, and mercy mild. God and sinnnners reconciled. Joyful all ye nations rise, join the triumph of the skiiiies, with angelic host proclaim, Christ is born in Bethlehem! Hark the Herald Angels sing, Glory to the newborn king.

(It is Christmas day. At the end of the song, there is a burst of applause from Charlie, Sally, Annette, and Mathias.)

ANNETTE: That was beautiful, Jim.

JIM: Thank you.

MATHIAS: And it calls for another round. Annie!

ANNETTE: Pa —

MATHIAS: It's Christmas day, Annie. On Christmas day, one may be forgiven some small indulgence. The winter goes on a long time 'round here.

CHARLIE: That's the truth.

MATHIAS: Come on now, make everyone feel welcome, and I'll give you your present.

ANNETTE: A present!

MATHIAS: And what else, on Christmas?

(He reaches under the tree and picks up a box. He turns and hands it to her.)

ANNETTE: What is it?

MATHIAS: Open the box.

(She opens the box and takes out a beautiful hat, with gold and stars on it.)

ANNETTE: Oh, how pretty! And it's for me?

MATHIAS: For whom else could it be? Not for Charlie!

(The others laugh as she puts the hat on, looking at herself in the mirror.)

ANNETTE: Oh, it's . . . I never saw anything so pretty . . .

SALLY: *(Dry.)* I wonder what that Canadian will say?

JIM: He'll say she's the prettiest girl in the territory.

ANNETTE: Stop it! You're nothing but a bunch of lying, drunken — fools.

MATHIAS: No, they're not. They're telling you the truth. And you're a young lady now, you can just learn to accept a compliment. I didn't think it was possible anything could grow in this wild place, but it's like the whole land, the mountains and the air, just move through you and suddenly there's a spirit, right before you, where a child was a moment ago.

(A beat.)

ANNETTE: Thank you, Pa.

(She hugs him.)

MATHIAS: It's my wedding present, Annie. The day of your marriage, I want you to wear it, and preserve it forever. You hear me? In twenty years, you promise me, you'll remember it was me who gave it to you?

ANNETTE: Now you're talking crazy.

MATHIAS: I don't think I am. Come on, everybody, drink, what the hell is the matter with you? Charlie, it's Christmas day and after I get you good and drunk you're going to tell us all that story about that dogsled race on Upper Bonanza.

(He pours more drinks.)

CHARLIE: That's a good story.

JIM: I heard that story so many times I think I'm gonna kill myself, I have to listen to it again.

MATHIAS: All right, not the dogsled story. What story we gonna get him to tell? Annie, what story you want to hear?

ANNETTE: Oh, I like all Charlie's stories.

MATHIAS: Well, pick one.

ANNETTE: I don't know.

(She goes to the tree, pulling out presents.)

SALLY: (Dry.) So where'd that Canadian go, anyway?

ANNETTE: He disappeared two days ago, no one's seen hide nor hair of him since. Good riddance, I say.

JIM: He's still off looking for that Chinaman?

(The sound of bells. Mathias turns, distracted, tries to focus. This is bad news.)

ANNETTE: He didn't say one way or the other, he just went. Coming here and stirring up a lot of trouble over nothing. Here, Pa, there's still presents. You open yours.

(She hands him a present.)

MATHIAS: It's not enough.

ANNETTE: What do you mean?

(Beat.)

Pa? Aren't you going to open it?

(The sound of the bells continues to grow.)

ANNETTE: (Continuing.) Pa?

MATHIAS: I don't need any gifts, I tell you. It's not enough.

ANNETTE: You give so much to everyone. It's just a little thing. Look, it's a scarf. I made it myself.

(She shows it to him. He looks at her, suddenly hugs her.)

MATHIAS: Annie.

JIM: Mathias, you all right?

ANNETTE: He's OK, of course he's OK. It's OK, Pa. You're just drinking too much these days.

(Mathias tears the scarf off his head.)

MATHIAS: I'm fine, I'm fine —

(He reaches for the bottle.)

ANNETTE: Oh, Pa —

MATHIAS: I'm fine, I said! It's Christmas, I can have a drink, can't I?

(He drinks from the bottle. Annette looks down.)

MATHIAS: *(Continuing.)* I'm sorry. I'm sorry, Annie, you're right, I guess I am a little — God, what the hell is —
(Frantic now.)
What the hell you all staring at? It's Christmas, the day of our Lord's birth, how come you're not — we should bow our heads to the Lord, in prayer. That's what we need to do, now. Everybody, now, join me —
(He kneels. The others do too. The sound of the bells continue throughout.)
MATHIAS: *(Continuing.)* Oh, Lord — Lord we thank you for our life's many blessings. You guide and protect us in the wilderness, and bring us out of our — out of our grief and despair, your strong right hand protects us oh God — God, don't you hear it? Doesn't anyone hear it?
(He stands, sudden. The bar fades in darkness. The walls fall apart, revealing two men, in the distance, in the snow. One sits next to a small campfire. The other takes a step forward, raises an axe.)

END OF ACT I

ACT II
SCENE NINE

There is a campfire. Directly alongside, Mathias sits alone at the bar. The walls are gone. Xuifei stands alone, speaks.

XUIFEI: The way is a limitless vessel. Used by the self, it is not filled by the world. Such is what I was taught. I could not be of the world. And yet the world overwhelmed me. Nature is not kind, it treats all things impartially. Neither is man kind. In the wilderness of nature, we learn who we are.

(He turns and goes to the campfire, sits next to it. Mathias looks over at him, then looks away.)

MATHIAS: You don't have to think about that.

(He goes to the bar, pours himself a glass of wine. As he speaks the walls close in over the image, restoring the bar.)

MATHIAS: *(Continuing.)* That was a long time ago. You carried it long enough, it don't have to mean everything. A life is more than one moment, one day, that's not a life. Every good you do isn't erased by one necessity, that's what it was, a single necessity, no one said they wanted it. I didn't want it. Last moment I ever felt truly alive, all the hammering, pushing it away, you think a man wants that to be what is? I didn't ask for this. It had to happen, someone had to do it, it fell to me. Last moment I ever felt alive. Who would choose that? But somebody had to. Both of us a sacrifice. For all the rest.

(In shadow, a figure stands at the open door.)

MATHIAS: *(Continuing.)* Not just Annette, but all of them, how many lives was that winter meant to take? She was starving, every last one of us looking death in the eye. Somebody had to do something.

JIM: Mathias?

(The figure steps into the light. It's Jim.)

MATHIAS: *(Turning, startled.)* Jim Lynch! Come on in, what are you doing out there on a night like this?

JIM: Who you talking to?

MATHIAS: Just myself. What can I get you, a cup of whiskey?

JIM: Well, I wouldn't say no to that. Never could, you know that.

(Mathias pours him a drink.)

JIM: *(Continuing.)* I heard you talking in here, thought maybe that Canadian came back, or something. Thought that maybe was who you were talking to.

MATHIAS: No, haven't seen him.

JIM: How long's it been now?

MATHIAS: Don't know, three days maybe.

JIM: Damn cold out there, too. Maybe he froze or something.

MATHIAS: Maybe.

JIM: Anyway, that's who I thought you was talking to. He's a talker, that one, isn't he?

MATHIAS: You been talking to him, Jim?

JIM: No, now you know I wouldn't do that. I was just thinking about the other night. Before he took off. You two were kind of going at it. He had a lot of questions. He's a persistent guy.

MATHIAS: *(Acknowledging the truth of this.)* He'd've been a prospector, I'd lay odds on his chances, hitting something eventually.

JIM: I was thinking that myself.

MATHIAS: You need another drink?

(He pours them both another round.)

JIM: Can't pay you for it. I'm plumb broke, Mathias, and that's a fact.

MATHIAS: Don't worry about it. Your money's no good here.

JIM: I don't have any money.

MATHIAS: That's fine, Jim.

(Jim downs the second drink.)

JIM: Of course, regarding this matter I don't think he's gonna be able to find nothin'. After all this time? You got to ask yourself, if there was anything out there anymore, somebody would've found it by now. Every inch of this land been racked and raped clean, Alaska ain't so big we couldn't suck dry every inch of it, all that gold in the ground. This place sure is cozy! You built it up nice, over the years. Got your own little kingdom up here. Be a shame if anything happened to take that away, considering what you had to do to get it.

(Beat.)

I'd like another drink, Mathias.

(Mathias considers this, now, then pours the drink.)

MATHIAS: You been mentioning these thoughts to anyone, Jim? Sally, or Charlie, maybe?

JIM: No, no.

MATHIAS: It's just I haven't seen much of them, since the Christmas party.

JIM: They're scared, Mathias.

MATHIAS: What are they scared of?

JIM: That's what I said! But Charlie, he's all, gonna go work that stake again, up by Fortymile. The one Stu Campbell, and that Chinaman worked. He wants gold. I understand that. I just don't want to go back out into the wilderness, to get it.

(A beat.)

MATHIAS: Don't I take care of you, Jim?

JIM: Maybe I don't want to be taken care of no more. You ever think about that? Feels good to be the king, don't it, always doling out favors. Never crosses your mind, maybe a man would want more than that.

MATHIAS: Don't do this, Jim. What happened was a necessity. Good for all of us then and now. A man can't be held responsible for something that had to happen anyway. Let it rest. I'm begging you. Let it rest.

(The two men consider each other.)

JIM: *(Not unkind.)* It's not in my interest, Mathias. You ever think about that? Course you didn't. You never had to, till now.

MATHIAS: You gonna make me go back there, Jim? I kept it at bay all this time and now you're going to make me go back?

JIM: Don't talk to me, talk to that Canadian. All these years, no one ever wanted to know. But he wants to know now. So whyn't you open the till there, see how much you got on hand. Then we'll talk about what's in the bank.

(Mathias nods, brief, backs away.)

MATHIAS: That's Annie's money. Money for her children. Yours I put elsewhere.

JIM: What do you mean?

MATHIAS: All of a sudden you're rich? Where'd you get the money from, so suddenly? That Canadian makes it back here, you're the one he's gonna be looking at. You and me both.

JIM: We'll tell him I hit a stake.

MATHIAS: That's exactly right. That's it, Jim. That's why I prepared for this. Knowing this day was coming. Your share is out there. We just got to go get it.

(The walls start to shift, as Jim considers the wilderness.)

JIM: What do you mean, we got to get it?

MATHIAS: Where does gold come from, Jim? Ask yourself. Where does it come from?

SCENE TEN

Lights shift. The wilderness. Xuifei, in the snow.

XUIFEI: The gold came out of the earth for me. I did not ask it to. I was so lost in my own mind, this wild place seemed to suit me, for a time, and I was uncomplaining. Silence was my way. Grief and private bitterness were my way, until the gold came. And then I saw envy in the faces of all who looked on me. The hunger of men half dead with exhaustion, hunger not for food or warmth or wisdom or peace, but hunger for these lumps of stone which I held so carelessly. These stones held meanings for them which I could not comprehend. This was not my heart's desire. The truth of this overwhelmed me, and I knew, I must go home. I must take this strange fortune, given to me by the earth itself, and buy the girl I loved and defiled, buy her and bring her to my home, and make my life with her. That was my intent.

(Behind him, a body stirs, moves.)

BAPTISTE: *(Hoarse.)* Is someone there? Who is there? Help me, please.

(Baptiste tries to sit up and look around, lost, blinded by the the snow and the dark. He babbles for a long moment in French, then, delirious, reaches into his pack and takes out a gun. He swings it around, points it at Xuifei. Xuifei looks at him. Baptiste stares.)

BAPTISTE: *(Continuing.)* It cannot be.

XUIFEI: A weapon will not help you here.

BAPTISTE: The Chinaman. You are the Chinaman.

XUIFEI: This place will take you. The darkness without end. The cold there is no name for. This is death, I tell you. I know it now as I know myself.

(He starts to go. Baptiste crawls after him.)

BAPTISTE: Help me. Help me, please. I am lost. Help me find my way. I will freeze, here, I will die, please —

(Xuifei turns on him, angry.)

XUIFEI: Pain and disappointment are meant to cleanse the heart. Yours have lead you astray! There is no place on Earth that offers rest for such as you. There is no place for any of us. I cannot help you now.

BAPTISTE: I am here for you. I came for you.

XUIFEI: You came for desolation! You came for the hope that your empty spirit might be filled by a place so wild and cold and evil that God himself cannot utter a curse to contain it. You came as I did, in love with your own self-pity. You are beyond help.

(But as he tries to turn again, Baptiste grabs him and wrestles him to the ground. The two men fight again, until Baptiste falls backward, into the snow. Xuifei stands.)

BAPTISTE: I would live. I would not die here. It is so cold. I would die, where the warmth of the sun might find me one last day. Where the heart might leap with joy at the sight of a woman's face. I would see a woman gaze upon me with kindness, one last time. Can you have no compassion?

(Xuifei looks at him, mournful. After a moment, he speaks.)

XUIFEI: It is a poor thing, from this side of the grave, but I would have justice.

BAPTISTE: I will bring you justice. Please. Let me live.

XUIFEI: He who regards himself as the world may accept the world. I would not have you die here. It is too lonely.

(Xuifei points in the opposite direction. Baptiste turns, sees light.)

BAPTISTE: *(Hoarse.)* C'est une lumière. Je le vois. La lumière.

(Xuifei goes in the direction of the light. Baptiste follows, first crawling, then standing and staggering off.)

SCENE ELEVEN

In the snow, Mathias appears, with Jim. Mathias carries an axe, and a pack. Jim carries a bottle.

JIM: It can't be this far. You didn't say it was this far.

MATHIAS: We're there now. We're here, it's right here.

(A flash. Xuifei is watching them.)

JIM: God, it's just like it was. You buried it? Goddamn it, Mathias, you buried it?

(Mathias reaches into his pack, hands Jim another bottle.)

MATHIAS: We'll take turns.

JIM: Digging in the ground for gold. I told Charlie I never would come back here.

(A flash, Charlie in the distance.)

CHARLIE: There's gold out there, Jim. Only thing that's gonna save any of us.

JIM: Where is he? You hear that? Charlie?

MATHIAS: No one there, Jim. Have another drink, it'll warm you up.

(Jim drinks.)

JIM: *(Desperate.)* Shouldn't be out here. You missed it, Mathias!

MATHIAS: I didn't, it's right here!

JIM: I don't see no markings! How can you tell anything, all this white. Nothing. It's just blank nothing.

(He drinks. A flash, Sally appears.)

SALLY: We got to get out of here, Jim! You more than anybody!

JIM: Sally? Sally! Charlie!

MATHIAS: They're not here. We're the only ones here, Jim.

SALLY: I don't know what happened, and I don't want to know! I don't want to look at your palm no more, you don't have to show me nothin'!

JIM: It wasn't me, Sally. I didn't do it!

MATHIAS: Jim, your brain's half mad with that stuff.

JIM: You remember the horses? On the dead horse trail? Just moving through the night, dumb beasts beat so hard they was half mad with it, almost human with all that suffering. So many dying those years. What would it matter, one more? What does one more matter?

MATHIAS: Have another drink, Jim! You don't have to think about that now!

JIM: Why'd we ever come here, Mathias? Do you remember?

(A flash, Xuifei appears, watching, and disappears again.)

MATHIAS: I remember the streets of Seattle. The word, that gold was here. The hope that come up in your chest, that there was a chance of life opening up in new ways, that somehow the size of this place would mean . . .

(A flash on Annette, wearing her hat, in the snow, looking at the sky.)

JIM: Mean what?

MATHIAS: Everything.

JIM: I didn't come for that. I came for gold.

(He grabs the pickaxe, drunk, tries to raise it to dig. Another flash on Xuifei. Jim backs away, startled.)

JIM: *(Continuing.)* Did you see him? He's out here! Mathias, the Chinaman is out here!

MATHIAS: Now you're talking crazy.

JIM: You take me back. How do I get back?

SALLY: Jim!

CHARLIE: Jim!

JIM: Charlie? Sally!

MATHIAS: It's the wind.

JIM: *(Starting to cry.)* Take me home, Mathias. I want to go home.

(A flash, Xuifei appears, watching.)

MATHIAS: Have another drink, my friend.

(He hands the bottle to Jim, who falls into the snow, sobbing.)

JIM: It's cold.

(Jim continues to sob. Mathias comforts him.)

MATHIAS: It's all right, Jim. It's time to just slow down, let everything slow down for you. Just go to sleep. Everything's fine. You've known a long time that this place would finally get you. Been here so long you're a part of it. I know I am.

(He stands, moves away, looks around him.)

MATHIAS: *(Continuing.)* Night, day. Wind. Stars. Seasons. It's a dance, isn't it, Jim? And our task, maybe — maybe our task is simply to find our place in it. Don't argue with it. Don't try to understand the whole of it. Just find your place, and move with it. What did the ancients say about movement? That Canadian would know. He's a smart one, he thinks he's going to trick me into admitting, what? What do you think he thinks I did? Why does he want to know? He made me angry, I admit it, and anger is the enemy. But I've had a lot of time to prepare for all of this. Obviously I couldn't just pretend it wasn't going to happen. I hoped, of course, one always hopes, but hope is the frailest of virtues. I don't know that it isn't a failing, finally. Hope. Ah, I'm wandering. I'm tired, Jim. I got to be honest, I was relieved when you came to me tonight. Not that I've been looking forward to this, far from it. But that I knew it would finally be over. Another necessity. A hard one, one I deeply regret, but I was worn down by the, what, the inevitability of it. Your coming, in the night. You were always going to come, alone, in the night. It was in your nature, my friend! Your part of the dance. And I was just the agent. I fought it, you can't deny that, I begged you not to bring us out here again, I've been fighting the whole of it all along, but some things will not be denied. I'm stating the obvious. This is boring, I'm boring you! But the fact is, if you hadn't come, it wouldn't have been fated, don't you see? It would have just been my imagination going haywire all these years, eating itself up with worry for no cause. That's all it would have been! Tracks in my mind, grooves where my thoughts wore down whatever it was used to be in there. Horror. Goodness. I'm still good. I did not, the proof being it meant something to me. It was a sacrifice. It's not the goodness that's gone, it's the horror, that's what I faced. Alone. All these years. You didn't have to face any of it. You just reaped the benefits.

You and Charlie and Sally and all the rest, who knew! We all knew together, and you didn't want the knowledge, you couldn't face it, that's why you didn't see this coming. But I did. I did. Because I understand treasure. The idea of treasure, I saw it work on too many minds. I saw reason itself bend under the weight of it. Bend so far that the universe itself ceases to exist! The mind. So many things flashing like lightning through the mind. This world isn't so big we can't erase it altogether! With hunger. Fear. Greed. Memory. Not memory, the past doesn't exist if you don't let it. There's no such thing as memory! Tracks. But it's a battle. Because that's what happens, isn't it? When you spin. You work it all out. Again, and again and again, you catch yourself, two people, all the time, the one watching and planning and holding the rest at bay, I'm not looking at that, the not looking itself is exhausting, and so lonely, in the middle of so much accomplishment, to be so alone, you can't deny all of it was an accomplishment. Annie. The lives of, all life, what I did, and to never rest, you don't even know how lucky you are, this is an easy destiny, quiet, falling silent, sleep-drenched, into the snow. It's a kindness. Becoming a part of the world you threw away, and for what? Gold? Liquor? A kindness. I mean to be kind. No. I am not apologizing to anyone! Goddamned Chinaman can go to hell. There is no Chinaman. He's a track, in my mind. Eighteen years. Every second, a lifetime. I'm not looking at that. The world is so pretty. The stars are so pretty. Beautiful. Even in the dead of night, the snow shines, the mountains, black against black, all of it a wonder and it's always here. Look at it, Jim! And we can't hardly ever even see it, because there's too much going on in the mind. Look, Jim! The lights! The world is so beautiful, and so alone. It's lonely. It's lonely for us. I see that now. I see that.

(He turns and sees Xuifei, watching.)

MATHIAS: *(Continuing.)* You're here. I knew you would be.

(Beat.) Look over him. Look over him.

(He heads off. Xuifei watches him go.)

SCENE TWELVE

Sally and Charlie make their way through the snow.

SALLY: We got to go in, Charlie. It's too cold.

CHARLIE: We got to find Jim!

SALLY: What did he come out here for anyway?

CHARLIE: I don't know, but we got to find him before we go back!

SALLY: I can't keep going! Charlie —

(She stops. Xuifei is there. Charlie comes up behind her.)

CHARLIE: Good God.

SALLY: It's the Chinaman.

CHARLIE: You see him too?

SALLY: Please don't hurt us. We didn't know what happened. We just didn't ever really know.

(She falls to her knees. Xuifei steps forward.)

CHARLIE: What do you want? What do you want, Ghost?

(Xuifei holds out his hand to her, palm upward.)

SALLY: You want me to read your palm? I can't read your palm, Ghost.

(Xuifei continues to hold out his palm.)

CHARLIE: Do it, Sally.

SALLY: That's just a trick, Charlie! I can't really do it under the best of circumstances!

CHARLIE: What is it you want us to know, Ghost?

(Xuifei looks at them, looks at his palm.)

SALLY: What's he saying, Charlie?

CHARLIE: I don't hear nothing but the wind.

(Xuifei looks at them, desolate. Sally takes a step forward.)

SALLY: Look at him, he's crying. Don't cry, Ghost.

CHARLIE: Ghost, let me tell you a story, Ghost. About an old prospector, one day he wakes up, starts to make himself some coffee, turns around and there's another prospector, heading down the road, moving away from him, and the first one says come on over here, let me make you some coffee and biscuit! So the stranger comes on over, sits by the fire and the prospector looks at him and says, you know what friend, I think I know you. All my life, he said, I been out here searching for treasure. I have sought it on mountaintops and in valleys of snow and ice. I have sought it in the wind and the cold, in the roiling waters falling to the sea, I have sought it deep in the earth itself — and yet have not found it. Instead, at the end of every trail, I have found you. Nothing else. No one else. And I cannot yet say who you are. Tell me, stranger. Who are you?

(A beat.)

SALLY: What did the stranger say?

CHARLIE: He knows what he said.

(Xuifei points to Jim's body.)

SALLY: Jim?

(Charlie and Sally hurry to the place where Jim's body has been revealed.)

SALLY: *(Continuing.)* Jim? Jim!

CHARLIE: Aw, Jim.

XUIFEI: You must bury him.

SALLY: How can we bury him? The ground is frozen solid.

XUIFEI: You must bury him, or he will never rest.

(As they kneel before Jim, the walls of the bar move forward. Annette stands at the doorway, facing the howling wind.)

SCENE THIRTEEN

ANNETTE: Is someone there? Who is there? Who is it? Who is it?

(A figure staggers forward and collapses on her.)

BAPTISTE: Je te supli — la lumière —

ANNETTE: Mr. Carbonneau —

BAPTISTE: Annette —

ANNETTE: Oh my God — you've been out there this whole time —

BAPTISTE: I did not understand. To love death, that is a sin. But perhaps, to find meaning at the edge of death —

ANNETTE: Mr. Carbonneau — you stop now, stop — we got to get you inside —

(Mathias appears at the edge of the clearing. He watches and listens as she takes Baptiste inside.)

BAPTISTE: *(Overlap.)* What I was told, as a child, the promise of meaning and justice, why is that taken from us, Annette?

ANNETTE: *(Overlap.)* Mr. Carbonneau, you're froze, please let me help you, please —

(He suddenly kisses her. She resists, then kisses him back. Mathias enters, sees this, unseen.)

ANNETTE: *(Continuing.)* It's all right now. You're gonna be all right.

(Sees Mathias, embarrassed.)

Pa, there you are, where'd you go? Mr. Carbonneau came back, he's near froze —

BAPTISTE: I saw him. I tell you. I saw him.

MATHIAS: Baptiste. Son. Just let Annette take care of you now.

ANNETTE: I'm gonna take your boots off now. There's coffee in the kitchen, Pa —

MATHIAS: I'll get it. I'll get some blankets, too.

(He turns and goes into the next room.)

ANNETTE: *(Pulling off Carbonneau's boots.)* You got to be still, let us help you now.

(Calling.)

Pa, you got to heat up some water —

MATHIAS: *(Offstage.)* I know, I know —

BAPTISTE: *(To Annette.)* I came here with a bitter heart, I came for money alone, but now I understand —

ANNETTE: Wandering in the wilderness for three days, it's crazy, everybody's gone crazy lately — I said be still, now —

(Just then, the sound of the wind. Xuifei opens the door, comes into the room. He closes the door. Baptiste stands at the sound of it.)

BAPTISTE: Who is it? Who is there? Who is there?

(Mathias, reentering, sees Xuifei. He looks at Baptiste, surprised, shrewd.)

MATHIAS: You see something? What do you see?

BAPTISTE: You see him too.

MATHIAS: Annette, go get that coffee. Go on.

(She goes.)

BAPTISTE: I found the signs of what has been. The blasted earth. Snow and ice, the signs of fire!

MATHIAS: *(Reasonable.)* Prospectors burn the ground, so they can bring out the gold. It's the only way, the ground's so frozen, the only way to get it out is to scorch the earth.

(Baptiste reaches into his knapsack and pulls something out. Still shivering, he puts it on the table. It is a blackened skull. Annette returns with the coffee and sees this.)

BAPTISTE: I found him.

ANNETTE: What is that? Why do you bring that here?

BAPTISTE: Annette —

MATHIAS: Annette, go into the kitchen.

ANNETTE: *(Near tears.)* Pa.

MATHIAS: *(With compassion.)* Go on now, honey. Go heat some water, make up a bath. It'll be all right. Go on.

(Annette goes. Mathias pours coffee.)

MATHIAS: *(Continuing.)* Drink this. You need it.

(Baptiste ignores this, he shrugs.)

You're not interested in this coffee, how about a glass of wine?

BAPTISTE: I will tell them what you did.

MATHIAS: What I did? And what do you think you know about that?

BAPTISTE: I know he was here. He came to this place, he had three thousand dollars. He disappeared in the night, and you became a wealthy man.

MATHIAS: I see. This is about greed. I can't say I'm surprised, I've seen my share of that over the years. How much are they paying you? I can match it. I can double it.

BAPTISTE: I will not take your blood money!

MATHIAS: You came here for blood money! You got a price, you already admitted that much. My guess is, right about now your price is going up. Maybe I'll pay it, and maybe I won't.

BAPTISTE: *(Insistent.)* I will take this to the authorities. I will tell what I have seen, what I know. I will tell them the truths that you have been hiding —

MATHIAS: *(Laughing.)* There are so many truths! I didn't think I'd have to remind you of that. One truth is, we were starving. We supposed to die that way, like animals? Go from one night into the next, you telling me that's what life is meant to be? Because I don't believe that. I believe in the power and the flexibility and the resourcefulness of the human spirit. You find yourself in a far country, you learn to adapt. You forget what you learned in a previous life. Because if you cling to what it is you thought you knew? You die. And that was not going to happen.

BAPTISTE: Then you admit it.

MATHIAS: I admit that we were living with death, among the dead. Dreams come to you in the cold. Odd moments, you waken from a stupor, see the one you're meant to care for, and you know, this can't go on, you have to do something to stop it or it will be too late. It's not merely your own survival. And in those few moments you know that, survival becomes a bigger thing. Becomes part of the place itself.

BAPTISTE: What did you do, Mathias? To survive.

(Mathias looks at him. After a beat, he answers.)

MATHIAS: I wrote. To my wife's folks, after she died. That's how it ended. They sent money, for the baby. Lot of money. Enough for everybody.

BAPTISTE: I can write too. I can find out. It is the easiest thing in the world, to find out.

MATHIAS: Drink your wine. Go take a bath.

(He picks up the skull by the sockets of the eyes, and carries it casually to the bar, pours them both drinks.)

BAPTISTE: This is not a matter of a casual argument to be won or lost. The act of taking a man's life is not something to be toyed with, it is not a game —

MATHIAS: You're the one who keeps changing the rules.

BAPTISTE: *(Incensed now.)* I met the parents. They are good people. They have searched for their son for fifteen years. They carry their grief across oceans, through the insurmountable barriers of time and language and place so that they may find their son and bring him home, if, as they fear, he is dead, to bring him home so that he may be buried with his ancestors, in his home. With his people. His spirit cannot rest until he is brought home.

MATHIAS: Who told you that? God? Oh that's right, you and God don't get along. Reason then. "His spirit cannot rest" — maybe not reason. Superstition, then? Is that what we're arguing about now? Superstition?

BAPTISTE: It is an ancient belief. The Greeks themselves. The Egyptians. The necessity of a proper burial — It is a necessity —

MATHIAS: Life is full of necessities.

BAPTISTE: And death as well.

MATHIAS: *(Laughing.)* Meaning what?

BAPTISTE: *(Defiant.)* You ask me if it is my God or my reason that tells me the truth, and I tell you it is my heart. My heart tells me you killed him. You killed him, and I will see you brought to justice.

(A beat, and then, Annette calls from the other room.)

ANNETTE: Pa?

(Baptiste turns, at the sound of her voice.)

MATHIAS: *(Lighting on this.)* Is that all your heart tells you?

(Calling.)

It's OK, honey, I'll be right there.

(Turning back.)

What would you do for her? She was in danger, say, mortal danger, what would you do?

BAPTISTE: *(Deflecting.)* No, no —

MATHIAS: Would you kill for her? Think now, before you answer. Think about the way she's entered your heart. It's just starting, but it would take a blind man not to see it. Both of you are running through each other's spirits, like a river finding new ways. I don't begrudge you, you want to take her from me, I see that, and I don't begrudge you. I'm not a monster. I recognize what that is. So tell me. Would you kill for her?

BAPTISTE: No I would not. I would not.

MATHIAS: Course not.

BAPTISTE: You do not know me.

MATHIAS: I know when you're lying.

BAPTISTE: And I know your lies as well.

MATHIAS: I know you do. I just don't think you're really finally going to be able to do anything about it. For all your hunting and truth seeking out there on the blasted earth — I'm her father. You'd lose her forever, I'd see to that. And for what? Money? Oh that's right, this isn't about money anymore. This is about justice. Meaning. A dead man. None of it real. All of it tracks in the mind.

BAPTISTE: No. I know this now. Conscience. We cannot live without conscience. Perhaps it is not only justice we must seek. Perhaps it is redemption. If you only spoke the words. To no longer carry the burden alone. What about your soul, Mathias?

MATHIAS: My soul is steady. Yours, I think, is not. You went out there, to the edge of reason, and what did you see?

BAPTISTE: I saw Xuifei.

(There is another silence as the two men consider what this means.)

MATHIAS: You saw him. Alone, in the wilderness, you saw his spirit rising frozen from the grave. And you see him now, is that right? You're seeing ghosts, son. You keep pursuing this, that's what your life is going to be. Ghosts. Night. Desolation. Madness.

BAPTISTE: There's madness here.

MATHIAS: No. This is sanity I'm offering you now. Think about her. Tell me what you would do for her, if you loved her, if you came back to life just that far, what you know in your heart you'd be capable of doing, to protect her, and then think what if she were your child? You just take a minute and think about that. What having a child, protecting a child, what that might drive you to.

BAPTISTE: *(Quiet.)* Even so. If it drove me to kill. Unjustly. I would expect to hang for it. We cannot survive as a people if we look the other way when a man's life has been taken so cruelly.

MATHIAS: Just because your heart's made room for a little light, doesn't mean the darkness fades.

BAPTISTE: You cannot excuse what you did! I cannot excuse it —

MATHIAS: Nothing happened! Look around! What you got here is a town with a nameless crime without a victim. This is your evidence that something happened?

(Off the skull.)

The land is littered with them. It doesn't prove a thing. Men came here and died here and no one knows who they were, why they were, how they died, why they died. Why they lived. No one cares. Go ahead, take it up to the law at Fortymile, see for yourself. They'll laugh at you. They'll shrug. It doesn't mean anything.

BAPTISTE: I will tell her, then. If that is the only justice he can have, he will have it. I will tell her.

(Mathias freezes.)

MATHIAS: She won't believe you.

BAPTISTE: She knows it already. If the words were spoken, there would be no question inside of her. It would be known. Forever. By her. She would know you. As you are.

MATHIAS: I'll kill you. I'll — kill you.

(He takes him by the neck, and starts to strangle him. Baptiste puts up a fight, but Mathias has him.)

MATHIAS: *(Continuing.)* You'll die alone, and she'll die alone. Do you doubt it? Listen. Listen to what's out there. Silence. Doom. Madness. So, tell me. Do you want to live? Do you?

(He tosses him, sudden, to the floor. Baptiste chokes, gasping for breath. Mathias moves away.)

MATHIAS: *(Continuing.)* This land's not going to claim either one of you. Even if survival means the betrayal of everything you believe in, you'll survive. I'm telling the truth, now. You're a man who recognizes truth. It's going to happen. It's happened already.

(Annette reenters.)

ANNETTE: Pa — Baptiste — is he all right?

MATHIAS: He's just tired.

(She helps him up.)

MATHIAS: *(Continuing.)* You got something you want to say to Annie, Mr. Carbonneau?

BAPTISTE: *(Beat.)* No.

MATHIAS: Then I think she's made up a bath for you.

(Baptiste lets Annette take him off. Mathias turns to Xuifei.)

MATHIAS: *(Continuing.)* You need to go now. There's nothing for you here. He's staying here.

(Xuifei leaves. Lights fade.)

SCENE FOURTEEN

Mathias, in the bar, drinking alone, in the night. The skull is on the bar. Annette enters.

ANNETTE: I put him in your bed. He didn't want to go.

MATHIAS: He's half out of his head. I hope you insisted.

ANNETTE: I did, of course I did.

MATHIAS: Is he sleeping?

ANNETTE: Yes. Saying such God-awful crazy things, Pa. I'm glad you weren't up there, to hear him.

MATHIAS: A week in the cold, digging for bones in the scorched earth. That must have been some ordeal. He'll get through it. You go up there. You spend the night at his side. Don't listen to any of his crazy ramblings, he's out of his head, right now. When he wakes up, you just tell him you care for him. Hold onto his hands. Remind him who he is. He'll make it through.

ANNETTE: *(Quiet.)* What did you do, Pa?

MATHIAS: I didn't do anything.

(Beat.)

I didn't do anything.

(Beat.)

I love you.

(Annette backs away from him.)

ANNETTE: Please don't. I can't. I'm sorry. I can't.

(Unable to look at him, she goes. After a moment he goes to the bar, pours himself more wine.)

MATHIAS: What does it mean to be human in the wilderness? Might as soon ask what it means to be human anywhere, but that's not the question, is it. The question is here. What does it mean, in this crushing place. God knows it's not that I don't believe in the light of us, I know what it is when the darkness is all we have, we're not meant to live like that. If we were, death would mean nothing. Instead it looms. Like this place. And so we cling to the days, even as they disappear around us. Gather around the light of a fire. A Christmas tree, a young girl. A woman. We don't just give in to the night. We turn our faces to the sun. That's what it means. To be human. To live. Simply, to live.

(He picks up the skull, considers it.)

MATHIAS: *(Continuing.)* Not this. This doesn't look like anything at all.

(The sound of bells. Mathias freezes, shakes his head.)

MATHIAS: *(Continuing.)* I won't look any more. It's over.

JIM: How 'bout a drink, Mathias.

(Mathias turns. Jim is there. He holds the bells.)

MATHIAS: You get out of here, Jim. I did what I could for you. Just got rid of one ghost, I'm not taking up with another.

JIM: Then maybe you better stop killing people.

MATHIAS: Prove it. Nobody can prove it on either you nor the Chinaman. I didn't do anything.

JIM: You killed me, Mathias. Got me drunk, left me out there to freeze.

(Jim goes to the bar, pours them both drinks.)

MATHIAS: You did that yourself, Jim. You got greedy.

JIM: It was a gold rush! Greed was the reason for everything we did.

MATHIAS: Not me. Everything I did, I did for my child.

(Mathias pours himself another drink, vaguely desperate. Jim picks up the skull, looks at it.)

JIM: You're wrong. It don't look like nothing. It looks like a man. It looks like us.

(He holds up the skull.)

MATHIAS: You're a figment of my imagination. All of this. My mind running crazy, on a long winter night. The only real danger ever was that Canadian upstairs with all his dreams of justice and redemption. Took care of that, and I took care of you. It's over.

JIM: And your mind? You can take care of that too?

MATHIAS: My mind is my own. So is my will.

(Furious.)

My mind, and my will. I did it all. Myself. You'd all be dead if it weren't for me.

JIM: I am dead. So is the Chinaman.

MATHIAS: I'm sick of hearing about that Chinaman! He was nobody! You all didn't think what I did was so God-awful that winter when I saved your lives, I saved you —

(The sound of the bells comes up behind him.)

MATHIAS: *(Continuing.)* Those Goddamn bells!

(Annette, behind him, approaches Xuifei, who holds the bells.)

ANNETTE: Pa, look!

XUIFEI: Kuh-yi, kuh-yi.

(Xuifei holds the bells out.)

ANNETTE: What's he saying, Pa?

MATHIAS: I don't know, honey.

XUIFEI: Kuh-yi, hao.

(*Xuifei encourages her to come to him, holding out the bells, showing how they work.*)

ANNETTE: Can I do it?

MATHIAS: I can't do this again.

ANNETTE: Can I do it?

XUIFEI: Hao, hun hao.

JIM: I don't see why not.

MATHIAS: (*Reluctant.*) Can I get you a drink?

(*Friendly, Xuifei looks up at Mathias.*)

XUIFEI: Food?

MATHIAS: No, no food. Liquor's all we got.

XUIFEI: Food, I have food.

(*He searches through his gear, finds a tin of biscuits, offers it to Mathias.*)

MATHIAS: Look, you want a drink or not?

(*Xuifei turns to Annette, offers it to her.*)

XUIFEI: Bu-yau, bu-yau. Shr-ni-da. Na ba. Na ba.

ANNETTE: What's he saying, Pa?

JIM: Check his money.

MATHIAS: I can't look at this again! It's over and done with!

JIM: Listen to me, Mathias. I heard Stu Campbell's been up there, working a stake up by Fortymile, with some Chinaman. Word is they hit a vein.

(*Mathias looks over at Annette and Xuifei. Annette gets the bells to chime.*)

ANNETTE: Look, Pa, I'm doing it!

MATHIAS: Look, stranger, I got to ask to see your money. Don't like to do it but it's been a hard winter. Can't serve you unless I see you can pay.

JIM: Me and Charlie working like animals, we didn't end up with four dollars between us. And he comes in here, a Chinaman, he don't even speak English, and the gold just come out of the earth for him.

(*Xuifei dumps the gold on the table. Mathias backs away in horror.*)

MATHIAS: No!

ANNETTE: Pa, look!

XUIFEI: (*Offering Mathias a piece.*) Shr-ni-da. Na ba.

ANNETTE: What's he saying, Pa?

MATHIAS: How am I supposed to know?

XUIFEI: Such a beautiful girl. Will you take this for her? I see in your faces, you are hungry. The outpost up at Fortymile still has supplies. Take this, it is little enough, but it will help.

MATHIAS: That's not what he said.

XUIFEI: I am on my way home. Please take this, for the little girl.

(Annette gets the bells going again.)

ANNETTE: Look, Pa, I can do it!

MATHIAS: This isn't how it happened.

CHARLIE: There's an old story, about a prospector. And a bird! And horses committing suicide on the Dead Horse Trail!

XUIFEI: Do it.

(He holds out the axe.)

SALLY: Show me your palm, Mathias.

XUIFEI: Do it.

CHARLIE: You're all sons of bitches.

(Mathias takes the axe. Annette looks over.)

ANNETTE: What's that, Pa?

XUIFEI: You did it for her. Show her. Show them all.

CHARLIE: One day he wakes up, starts to make himself some coffee, turns around and there's another prospector, heading down the road, moving away from him.

MATHIAS: I am a good man.

XUIFEI: Show her what you did to me.

MATHIAS: What kind of a monster are you?

XUIFEI: You didn't do it for her.

SALLY: Show me your palm.

JIM: He's right, Mathias. I was there. I saw your face. When you saw the gold.

BAPTISTE: The price of the betrayal is not meant to give meaning to the act. The act itself renders the price meaningless.

ANNETTE: Pa?

MATHIAS: She was the price.

BAPTISTE: He was the price!

MATHIAS: Don't listen to them! I am a good man. One moment doesn't make a life!

ANNETTE: What did you do, Pa?

MATHIAS: Your children will be safe!

XUIFEI: My children will never be born.

MATHIAS: I can't care about that! I won't say it. I won't say it for any of you. None of you had the courage to look in your hearts and do what had to be done. You want me to confess! I won't confess!

SALLY: Show me your palm, Mathias! What is in your palm?

(The walls fly apart to reveal a lone campfire. The others disappear, leaving

Xuifei, Mathias and Baptiste on an empty plain, lit only by the light of the campfire.)

BAPTISTE: He gave you a gift as well, that night. To the child he gives the bells. But he sees starvation in her face. So, to you, he gives one piece of gold.

MATHIAS: It isn't enough.

BAPTISTE: No. It isn't. For having seen what you see, only the full amount will do. You see the future. You see ease. Comfort. The solution to all cares.

(Xuifei takes his pack and goes to sit by the fire.)

BAPTISTE: *(Continuing.)* You see happiness. You see fulfillment.

(Beat.)

You see gold.

(Mathias follows Xuifei, carrying the axe.)

MATHIAS: Chinaman.

(Xuifei turns, surprised, sees Mathias.)

MATHIAS: *(Continuing.)* I need the gold. You understand me? The gold in your pack. You're gonna have to give it to me now.

(Xuifei protests, confused.)

XUIFEI: Wo hwe Jung-guo chu. Jung-guo. Jung-guo.

(Mathias takes a step forward, with the axe.)

MATHIAS: I'm not arguing about this! You give it to me, or I'll take it. Give it to me now.

(Frightened, Xuifei takes the pack and tosses it to Mathias.)

XUIFEI: Wo chyou ni. Wo chyou ni.

(Mathias looks at it, at his feet.)

MATHIAS: Look away. Look away now.

XUIFEI: *(Protesting, frightened.)* Syansheng, wo chyou chyou ni.

(Mathias suddenly grabs him by the shoulder and pushes him down, face forward in the snow. Xuifei scrambles backwards, frightened.)

MATHIAS: It'll be easier for you if you just lay still.

XUIFEI: *(Begging.)* Wo chyou chyou ni! Bu yuah sha sz wo!

MATHIAS: I said look away!

(He raises the axe. Xuifei holds up his hand to protect his face. Mathias brings it down on him. Xuifei falls to the ground. Mathias hits him again, and again. He stops, finally, breathless.)

MATHIAS: *(Continuing.)* That wasn't so hard. Just wasn't so hard.

(He hears something in the silence, turns, startled.)

MATHIAS: *(Continuing.)* Who's there? No one's there.

BAPTISTE: This far down the trail, no one for miles.

MATHIAS: No one.

BAPTISTE: The prospector, Jim Lynch, he saw you leave the inn. He could, eventually, put the pieces together.

MATHIAS: He'll keep his mouth shut.

BAPTISTE: But what about the body?

MATHIAS: Burn it. Make it look like an abandoned claim. The land is littered with them. Men coming from all the world, looking for gold, finding only the blackened earth. They go home. But the earth is left behind. Just make it look like an abandoned claim.

(He drags the body back to the fire. Baptiste watches as he dumps the body, and rests.)

BAPTISTE: And so it is done. You have your heart's desire.

MATHIAS: Yes.

BAPTISTE: The gold. The axe. The fire. It is done. And you are at peace.

(Mathias crumples to the ground, wailing from the depths of his grief. Baptiste watches for a moment, as Xuifei rises and stares at Mathias.)

BAPTISTE: *(Continuing.)* You have your treasure.

(He turns upstage and walks away. Mathias and Xuifei consider each other as the earth begins to burn.)

(Blackout.)

END OF PLAY

THE WATER'S EDGE

ORIGINAL PRODUCTION

The Water's Edge was originally produced at Second Stage Theatre June 15, 2006. It was directed by Will Frears and had the following cast:

RICHARD . . . . Tony Goldwyn
HELEN . . . . Kate Burton
LUCY. . . . . Katherine Powell
ERICA . . . . Mamie Gummer
NATE. . . . . Austin Lysy

Set Design. . . . . Alexander Dodge
Costume Design . . . . Junghyun Georgia Lee
Lighting Design . . . . Frances Aronson
Sound Design . . . . Vincent Olivieri
Original Music. . . . . Michael Friedman
Production Stage Manager. . . . . Roy Harris
Stage Manager. . . . . Shanna Spinello
Artistic Director . . . . Carole Rothman

CHARACTERS

RICHARD: 46
HELEN: 46
LUCY: 26
ERICA: 24
NATE: 26

SET

The backyard of an aging, elegant country home. A wide porch. Trees. A bathtub has been placed some short distance from the house, with running water. In the distance, a lake.

ACT I
SCENE ONE

The back porch of a worn out but still elegant old home, in the country, near a lake. A small pile of junk rests against the baseboard of the porch. Prominent among the junk is an old claw-foot bathtub, covered with a tarp, and an old newel post. There are trees, and a path to a lake. While the place was once elegant, it has fallen in real disrepair.
Richard stands and stares. Behind him, Lucy.

RICHARD: The trees. Are like old men. Aren't they? The canopy. Is like a cathedral. I know this place so well. But it's not, it's unlike, like a dream, places you've been that are changed somehow by by the light of your mind, what you know or hope or yearn toward even, rivers running down city streets or or a mansion on a cliff, hovering over a beach you've never seen, the only way to get there is through an endless forest of beech trees . . . isn't it like that? Is it? I know all of it but I don't know — . *(Picking up the newel post, with growing excitement.)* My grandfather. Had a lathe. In the basement. And we would gather, amazed, while he, with his hands, it was a miracle, a piece of wood, so simple, turning, becoming . . . to be there at the birth of something so beautiful, and not understand, to a child's mind, how it could be, how could it be? I see his hands. It's the same moment. How can it be the same moment?

LUCY: Richard . . .

RICHARD: I'm sorry. But it is the same.

LUCY: There's someone here.

(She looks up at the porch. Someone is on the back of the porch, a shadow. Richard steps forward.)

RICHARD: Who is it?

(Erica enters, alert.)

ERICA: Who is it? Excuse me, I think the question is, who are you? I mean, who the fuck are you and you know, what the fuck are you doing here?

RICHARD: Erica.

ERICA: *(Continuing.)* Oh no no. *(Yelling.)* Nate! Hey Nate!

RICHARD: Erica.

ERICA: Don't — just — what — Who the fuck is she?

LUCY: I can wait in the car.

RICHARD: No —

ERICA: NATE!

RICHARD: Didn't you know I was coming?

ERICA: I don't even know who you are.

(Nate appears in the doorway. He steps out.)

NATE: What? What? (Beat.) Wait a minute. Wait —

ERICA: Yes. Yes!

NATE: Dad?

ERICA: Don't call him that!

RICHARD: Erica —

NATE: Oh my God.

RICHARD: Hello.

LUCY: Richard —

RICHARD: No. Stay here. I want you here. This is my friend Lucy.

NATE: Yes, um, really nice to meet you. Does Mom . . . does she . . .

RICHARD: I wrote and told her I was coming. Didn't she tell you? I swear. I
    didn't want to —

ERICA: Fuck you!

RICHARD: Erica —

ERICA: Get out of here!

NATE: Shut up, Erica.

ERICA: No! No! You can't — Nate —

NATE: It's OK!

ERICA: It's not OK! (To Richard.) You get out of here! Get out of here! Go!
    Go!

RICHARD: I told her —

ERICA: Fuck you! Just — fuck you, fuck you!

(She goes into the house, slamming the door. There is a tense pause.)

NATE: It's OK. She's just. I mean, it's . . . well.

RICHARD: I'm sorry.

NATE: No, no, it's good you're here. It's really good.

RICHARD: You're so tall.

NATE: Yeah. Well. You got, your hair is . . . different, is it a different color?

RICHARD: I don't think so. I mean, I'm vain, but I'm not foolish. I hope.

NATE: You look different, than I remember.

RICHARD: It's been a long time.

NATE: Yeah. (Off Erica's exit.) She's, you know — she kind of, just, you can't,
    because she —

ERICA: (Inside the house.) DON'T APOLOGIZE FOR ME!

NATE: I'm not, I'm just saying! (To Richard.) So, don't, because it's always —

and she's great, she's just — you know. *(Beat.)* Do you want some tea or something? Iced tea?

(Erica appears again.)

ERICA: Nate, stop it! You can't — *(To Richard.)* I'm sorry. But you can't, I just don't think —

RICHARD: I'd love some tea.

(Nate nods and goes inside. Erica looks at them. After a moment, she follows Nate inside.)

ERICA: Nate!

(Richard and Lucy, alone.)

LUCY: Are you all right?

RICHARD: Fine. I actually, that went better than I thought it would.

LUCY: It did?

RICHARD: *(A wonder.)* He's handsome, isn't he? To see your son, suddenly — it wasn't sudden, OK, but to me — I wasn't even sure they would be here — oh my God. Look at this — look at this.

(He pulls the tarp off the bathtub and during the following gets in.)

RICHARD: *(Continuing.)* My father put this out here when I was a little kid. We would take baths together, under the stars. It was incredible. He hooked the whole thing up to the plumbing in the kitchen, so you could run hot water out here, it was a whole production, and then the two of us would lie back and look up, through the branches, and pick out the stars. Every season. The winter nights. Watching the sky turn. Orion. Cassiopeia.

LUCY: Richard.

RICHARD: You probably can't see anything now, the trees are so overgrown, it's like a medieval forest, almost . . .

LUCY: Richard. *(Beat.)* Are you insane? I mean — are you nuts, here? You can't just show up like this. I mean, Jesus! Are you insane? These people don't know you!

RICHARD: These people are my children!

LUCY: Be that as it may. This clearly is not going to turn into *A Winter's Tale,* with everyone hugging and being so glad. I think we should go.

RICHARD: This is my house. It's my home.

LUCY: Look. Does your ex-wife know you're coming? I mean, at least she knows you're coming, right?

(Nate comes out again, with iced tea.)

NATE: *(Explaining.)* Mom is, somewhere, but I think she said, you know, errands and, so here's the tea. Do you like sugar? Or milk? Sometimes milk, in iced tea, most people don't but it can, or lemon, that's more, but I don't, the milk really seems more soothing. *(A breath.)* Not that we need to be soothed. But not that we don't either, I guess. I think, I could . . . I think I'll have milk. With the tea.

RICHARD: That sounds great.

NATE: OK. Here, you can, yourself, I . . . making tea for other people sometimes seems, I don't know. Too, almost, what we drink, is specific. So.

LUCY: I'll do it.

(She goes and pours tea for herself and Richard. Nate shifts on his feet, awkward.)

NATE: I've thought about . . . well, if you . . . you know. Ever. Of course I did. It's been a long time.

LUCY: *(Trying to be social.)* How long has it been, exactly?

RICHARD: Seventeen years.

LUCY: Whoa. *(Recovering.)* Really. Wow. Oh. That's not — wow. That is a long time. Isn't that funny, I had no idea. I mean, I knew it was — but I — . Since you've seen each other? Really?

NATE: It's a long time.

RICHARD: A very long time.

NATE: It's different than I thought it would be. Seeing you. It feels different. I don't know what it feels like.

(He looks at his father, trying to figure out what it feels like.)

RICHARD: I didn't want to stay away. I hope you knew that.

NATE: Oh, I don't — you don't have to say that. It's —

RICHARD: It's true. I asked. So many times. I hope she told you.

NATE: No no, she, uh — no. She didn't.

(Richard nods. After a moment, Nate starts to cry.)

RICHARD: Nate.

NATE: Sorry. I'm sorry. Sorry.

(But he continues to cry. Richard goes to him, tries to touch him. Nate takes a step backwards, confused. Erica comes out of the house, quick, and goes to Nate.)

ERICA: Come on. Come on.

(She takes him inside. They are gone. Lucy looks at Richard.)

LUCY: You're right. This is going so well.

RICHARD: Look. I'm not going to say anything against their mother. But this is not a situation of my making.

LUCY: I'm not criticizing.

RICHARD: You're not?

LUCY: I just, for heaven's sake, Richard, this is — aye yi yi. Seventeen years?

RICHARD: I told you —

LUCY: You said a long time —

RICHARD: Seventeen years is a long time.

LUCY: Seventeen years is a long long time. You haven't seen them ever? During that whole time? Your own children?

RICHARD: It was not a situation of my making!

LUCY: Be that as it may, I should not be here!

RICHARD: I want you here. I can't, anymore, I — . Seventeen years. That's not anything I could live with anymore. You understand that, don't you?

LUCY: I do. I do understand that, and I support, you know I — I'm just saying —

RICHARD: *(Upset.)* What was I supposed to do?

(Erica is there.)

LUCY: Richard.

RICHARD: *(Continuing.)* Is he all right?

ERICA: Yeah, he's just kind of in shock. That's all. I mean, there's nothing wrong with him. I don't want you thinking he's like screwed up or anything. Because that is so not the case. I mean, he's sensitive, obviously, and this is, you know . . . it's weird. That's all.

RICHARD: I did write.

ERICA: Yeah, OK. Good. I mean, I didn't understand that, and we're just a little, I mean, I'm sorry about before. Yelling like that. I am really sorry. *(Beat.)* You must think we're both freaks.

RICHARD: No.

ERICA: Well, yeah, but how would you know?

RICHARD: I would know.

ERICA: Anyway the point is, this is all a bit unexpected. The house, as you can see, has not even been painted. In years. I keep telling her, but she apparently likes it this way. I don't think it's been painted since you left, in fact. What's your name again?

LUCY: Lucy.

ERICA: Do you need to use the bathroom or anything? Did I say that yet? Did Nate offer?

LUCY: No, and I really would just love to maybe wash my face. We've been in that car for what, six hours?

ERICA: Six? Where did you drive from?

RICHARD: We just came up from Philly.

ERICA: Philadelphia? That's where you live?

RICHARD: Yes, why?

ERICA: I don't know, I . . . Philadelphia. That's . . . I thought New York, I guess. Didn't you live in New York at some point?

RICHARD: I have a place there too.

ERICA: You have "places" in New York and Philadelphia?

RICHARD: An apartment in New York and a townhouse in Philadelphia, yes. *(Beat.)* And, St. Bart's. There's a condo there. *(Beat.)* And Telluride.

ERICA: An apartment and a townhouse and a condo and Telluride! And a jet somewhere, probably. I mean, do you have like a yacht and a skimobile and and your own airplane, and —

RICHARD: No. No no, no — *(Beat.)* There is a share. In a Lear Jet.

ERICA: So you're, like, a gazillionaire, of course you are.

RICHARD: I sent money. All the time. To you and your brother, and your mother too, I wanted to send, anything you wanted, my hope was, Jesus, I'm sounding pathetic. If there's any way to say this without sounding pathetic, let me just say, I have money. Whatever you want.

ERICA: That doesn't sound pathetic.

RICHARD: Good.

ERICA: No, not good, fuck you, FUCK YOU, it sounds creepy, you fucking creep! Sorry sorry sorry. I'm sorry. Never mind. This is so fucked. Never mind. I was going to show you to the bathroom, wasn't I? Here, the bathroom is right inside, off the kitchen, here.
(She turns to show her. Helen stands just inside the doorway. Erica sees her first.)

ERICA: Mom! Hi! You're back from the store, I see. *(Beat.)* Look who's here.
(Helen steps out.)
(She and Richard consider each other.)

RICHARD: You got my letter.

HELEN: Yes, I got it. *(To Lucy.)* Hello. I'm Helen.

LUCY: Hi. Lucy. Snow, Lucy Snow.

HELEN: Erica, I think I heard Lucy say she'd like to wash up. Why don't you show her the bathroom?

ERICA: Yeah, I was about to do that.

HELEN: Good. Nate, you can show Lucy the bathroom, too.
(Erica takes Lucy inside. Helen looks at Richard.)

RICHARD: Helen.

HELEN: Hello, Richard.
(Pause. They consider each other for a long moment.)

HELEN: *(Continuing.)* Men age so well. It really is just enough to make you sick.

RICHARD: *(Taking her in, not condescending.)* You're still very beautiful, Helen.

HELEN: Oh I have no complaints, I'm perfectly content with my looks. Most women my age are not so lucky. Not that, I don't mean to say women don't age well, that's a terrible thing to say, just awful. We all age. And we're all frightened by it. Women get face-lifts. And men get cute little girlfriends. Now, I haven't had a face-lift, but apparently you've — how old is she? Don't tell me. The point being that rather puts me one up on you, doesn't it?

RICHARD: Does it?

HELEN: On the fear factor, I think it does.

RICHARD: I think you'll like her.

HELEN: Is that why you brought her? Because you thought we'd like each other?

RICHARD: I wanted you to know each other. I wanted Nate and Erica to meet her.

HELEN: *(Charming.)* You haven't seen your children in seventeen years, and you didn't think there would be enough going on to keep everyone entertained without adding a girlfriend into the mix? *(Then.)* Sorry. I promised myself I'd be civil. I mean to be civil.

RICHARD: So do I.

HELEN: Good! Let's go back. You look terrific.

RICHARD: So do you.

HELEN: I see Nate served the tea. Iced tea with milk. He started doing it when he was eleven. I'm still not sure why.

RICHARD: It's pretty good.

HELEN: Do you think so? I find it rather disgusting.

RICHARD: Are they living here?

HELEN: Is that a criticism?

RICHARD: Just a question. Most kids, in their twenties, want to see the world.

HELEN: They have time.

RICHARD: He did all right in college, then?

HELEN: He dropped out after his second year.

RICHARD: And he never went back?

HELEN: It didn't suit him.

RICHARD: So . . . what does he do with himself?

HELEN: He has a job, in town, at the bookstore. He's been there almost four years now, they love him.

RICHARD: And he's happy with that?

HELEN: He seems to be. Erica finished last spring, up at Brown. History.

RICHARD: History?

HELEN: She has a bent for facts, it seems. She did pretty well. A's and B's, that sort of thing.

RICHARD: And what's she doing now?

HELEN: Living.

RICHARD: Of course.

HELEN: It's not enough for you.

RICHARD: I didn't say that.

HELEN: It's all right. I understand, it must seem odd to someone like you.

RICHARD: You didn't push them, then.

HELEN: Well, Richard, quite frankly, I wanted them here with me. I think I earned that.

RICHARD: Do you think that?

HELEN: You don't get a vote.

RICHARD: You never told them. That I wanted to come back to see them. You never even mentioned —

HELEN: Don't you dare berate me.

RICHARD: I'm here now, Helen. We have to —

HELEN: To what? To be a family again? Is that why you brought your girl-friend?

RICHARD: I want a relationship with my children. You have to make room for that. It's time.

HELEN: Why? Because you say so?

RICHARD: Because it's necessary.

HELEN: I didn't invite you here, Richard. But I don't want to get into some sort of fight about it. I'm willing to be civil.

RICHARD: I'm glad to hear it.

HELEN: If you don't think this is civility, you clearly have forgotten a few things about human behavior.

RICHARD: I haven't forgotten.

HELEN: You've forgotten.

RICHARD: This is my house.

HELEN: What?

RICHARD: This is my house. I grew up here. It's my home. That's what's been forgotten.

HELEN: *(Beat.)* Yes, it has been forgotten, as far as we're concerned, that fact has completely evaporated. This is your house? Are you quite sure of that?

RICHARD: I grew up here. I slept in that bedroom, every morning of my life until I was eighteen years old I looked out onto the branches of that tree, I went fishing in the lake —

HELEN: The lake?

RICHARD: Helen.

HELEN: I can't believe you said that.

RICHARD: I never said you could have it forever.

HELEN: Oh, so forever only applies to certain things and certain people.

RICHARD: Helen.

HELEN: This is not your house.

RICHARD: I left you alone all these years. I gave you the children. I gave you everything you asked.

HELEN: And now what, you want it back? Which, the house or the children?

RICHARD: Helen. What happened is done. We both paid.

(Beat.)

HELEN: No, go on, please. This gets better and better.

RICHARD: It's time. *(Beat.)* I'll give you a place to live, that's not a problem, I'm happy to do that. And money, that's not a problem either. But, I do. I want my house back.

HELEN: I confess I am still perplexed by the workings of the male mind. You age well, it's true, but maybe that's because you don't seem to learn anything. Knowledge, life, wisdom, somehow you avoid the whole thing and time just passes you by. I'm not giving you the house back. You can't have the kids, either. You can have your tea. But that's pretty much it.

RICHARD: I don't want this to go to court. We've kept this out of the courts for so long. You don't want to go there, now.

HELEN: What are you even talking about?

RICHARD: This is not a joke.

HELEN: Am I laughing?

RICHARD: I don't — Helen. I don't want this to be hard. The last thing I want is to cause more pain, I'm trying not to live in pain anymore. I believe in atonement, I do, but I also believe it's possible to finally rest. To accept the solace of the earth. Being here, finally, I do feel that — that it is perhaps possible. In the air and the wind, the sound of the leaves moving in the dusk, that's not, I can't help but find something, in that, not God, I'm not talking about God or peace or meaning, not that. But

something something vivid and whole, sustaining. Larger than all of it. Larger than history. Larger than us.
(A beat.)

HELEN: It's hard to look at you.

RICHARD: I know.

HELEN: (Shaking her head, sad.) You want the house back.

RICHARD: We can talk about it later.
(There is a long moment of silence.)

HELEN: And now you want to come inside.

RICHARD: I would like to be asked.

HELEN: Oh, Richard. You already want too much. You always do.
(She turns and goes to the door. After a moment, she turns, looks at him, and holds open the door.)

HELEN: (Continuing.) Please.
(He slowly walks up the steps.)
(The lights fade.)

SCENE TWO

Erica, Nate, and Helen. Helen is shelling peas. Nate is looking at a fancy camera and reading the instruction manual. A beat.

ERICA: Why are you shelling peas? It's only nine in the morning.

HELEN: I thought I'd make a salad for lunch.

ERICA: Lunch is four hours away.

HELEN: Sometimes I like to be prepared.
(Beat.)

ERICA: Are we going to have to eat with them again? Because, to be frank, dinner last night was not exactly the most fun thing I've ever done in my life.

NATE: I'm glad he came. Sort of. But maybe that was enough. Maybe he should just go now. I mean, are you, do you —

ERICA: Glad? No. Glad is not actually the word I would have used. But I find it interesting that he came and I'm willing to be interested in this situation.

HELEN: Knock yourself out there, Erica.

ERICA: I'm just saying, you know, he wants the house back. I mean, how fucked up is that.

HELEN: How did you hear about that?

ERICA: Well, Mom. Listening at doors?

HELEN: He's not getting the house back.

ERICA: Mom, due respect. Did you ever get him to sign over the deed? I mean, did you? Is it in a document anywhere? In the divorce papers? Because you know, he could kick us out.

HELEN: He's not going to do that.

ERICA: You haven't seen him in seventeen years, how do you know what he's going to do?

HELEN: I just think it's better to be hopeful.

NATE: You — you do?

HELEN: Yes, I do.

ERICA: Well, I think this is war.

NATE: He's — it's not war. I mean — I — how is this war?

ERICA: He showed up with his girlfriend. How imperialistic can you get?

NATE: How is having a girlfriend imperialistic?

ERICA: It's the whole presumption of ownership.

NATE: He doesn't, you're insane.

HELEN: He's right. Erica, you need to calm down.

ERICA: Oh I do, do I? I mean, look at him. Nice camera, Nate.

NATE: What?

ERICA: Are you just going to let him buy you like that?

NATE: He's not buying me! I'm just — I — it looked kind of, I mean, I never, there are books, in the store about these things and I never, because . . .

ERICA: Beware of Greeks bearing gifts.

NATE: I didn't see you giving those earrings back.

ERICA: You don't see me wearing them. Gold fucking earrings. Give me a break.

NATE: Yeah, that sucks, somebody gave you gold earrings, your life really sucks. Those trust funds set up for us, that really sucks, too. Now we're both rich kids. Boy, life sucks.

ERICA: What sucks is he came here to take the house back! And you're just, you're both just —

HELEN: We're not doing anything, Erica.

ERICA: That's my point! The guy's got like six hundred houses all over the planet, and he's showing up here to kick us out. Six hundred houses, not enough, he wants this house, too! And you're just sitting there! Hellooooo —

(*Erica gets into the tub.*)

NATE: He won't kick us out. I mean, he just wouldn't.

ERICA: He wants to, Nate! I heard him.

HELEN: It's not you who would lose the house. I'm sure if you wanted to stay here, were he to move back, he would be happy to have you.

(Beat.)

ERICA: You didn't get the deed, did you?

HELEN: There were some details that were overlooked, over the years.

ERICA: The deed to the house is not a detail, Mom! What kind of a stupid divorce lawyer did you have, anyway?

HELEN: Well, sweetie — technically — there wasn't technically a divorce.

NATE: What?

ERICA: Wait a minute. You're not divorced?

HELEN: I'm afraid there was too much acrimony to pull off an actual divorce.

NATE: You're still married to him? You never told us that.

HELEN: It didn't seem relevant. Besides, you never asked.

NATE: Why would we ask?

ERICA: No no. That's OK. That's good, that's very good. So you divorce him now, and you say, I have to have the house. He abandoned us for seventeen years, no judge on the planet is going to give him the house after that.

HELEN: Every month, I got a check. He supported us the whole time.

ERICA: So? He should support us.

HELEN: You're still young, Erica. You believe in clarity. Which is fine, but not necessarily useful, in every situation.

ERICA: What does that mean? You keep saying all this stuff, I have no idea what you even mean! There's like no facts, here, Mom! Could you hand over a couple facts once in a while?

HELEN: The facts aren't necessarily relevant.

ERICA: I am going to scream.

HELEN: Please don't.

ERICA: Why are you being like this? Why aren't you mad?

HELEN: It's not that I'm not angry. It's maybe that I'm angry enough not to get too worked up about it.

ERICA: That makes no sense at all.

NATE: I think it does.

ERICA: Jesus Christ, Nate. Would you stop being such a patsy?

NATE: I'm not a patsy. You're — hysterical.

ERICA: This whole family is insane. Did he write and tell you he was coming?

Did he? Did he? He wrote and said I'm coming to take back the house? Huh?

HELEN: Yes, actually, he did.

ERICA: So why didn't you do anything?

HELEN: What could I do?

ERICA: You didn't even tell us.

HELEN: I was sort of hoping that he'd reconsider.

ERICA: Well, he didn't do that, did he!

HELEN: No. He didn't.

ERICA: *(Angry.)* How could you let him come in? How could you sit there and have dinner with him, and, and — what's her name —

NATE: Lucy.

ERICA: I know her name!

HELEN: I don't know, Erica. Maybe it wouldn't be so bad for you to know your father. As long as he's here anyway.

ERICA: Mom! That is so unbelievably lame I don't even — you have to protect yourself! I'm calling a lawyer. And, in addition, we are going to paint this place. It needs a coat of paint!

(She goes inside the house. Nate looks at Helen, moves closer to her.)

NATE: So they're still sleeping, huh?

HELEN: Richard is. He was always a night owl. I believe that Lucy is down at the lake.

(Nate turns to look, then —)

NATE: I think it'll be OK, Mom. He won't make you go. That would be just, you know. It won't happen. It would be too mean.

HELEN: *(Beat.)* I'm glad you think the world isn't mean.

NATE: No, I know it's mean. But people aren't. Necessarily. I don't think. It's, you know, everybody thinks they're right, and more like that, is what I think. I don't know what I think. But he can't, I don't think — what he said? Yesterday?

He said some things, I think, that, I know this is weird. But I just don't think he'll take the house.

(Lucy wet, in a bathing suit, comes up the path.)

LUCY: Good morning.

NATE: Morning.

LUCY: I just went and took a swim.

HELEN: Yes.

LUCY: Well, I guess that's obvious. Of course that's obvious. Anyway. It's

beautiful, the water. The way it moves from warm to cold, it's so mysterious, why does it do that?

HELEN: All lakes do that, I've been told.

LUCY: How far across is it?

HELEN: Three-quarters of a mile, straight across. If you swim it lengthwise, it
comes closer to two. There's only a few who do that regularly. Mr.
Samuels down the road, he's eighty-three. He's one of those old people
who doesn't have anything better to do than show off.

LUCY: He does up and back? That's four miles.

HELEN: It takes him all day.

LUCY: Still.

HELEN: Like I said, he's a big show-off.

LUCY: Do you ever do it? The . . .

HELEN: I'm not really much of a swimmer.

LUCY: Nate, you must.

NATE: Uh, no.

HELEN: None of us really. Are swimmers.

NATE: Once in a while.

HELEN: Don't lie. Never.

LUCY: God, I'd be down there all the time.

HELEN: Well. People are different, aren't they?

LUCY: No, no, I mean — I do understand why you might not. Swim. I mean,
when I was a kid, my parents would take me out to the country and you
know, it was always, get in the lake! But I was convinced, out in the middle? I was convinced there were monsters out there, ready to just drag
me down.

HELEN: Yes. I think that's the general feeling here.

LUCY: Or sharks.

NATE: *(Awkward.)* Sharks don't swim in fresh water.

LUCY: No, I know, but you think of, you know. What lurks. Sharks. Piranhas.

HELEN: *(Abrupt.)* Do you need another towel? Or coffee?

LUCY: I don't drink coffee.

HELEN: Of course you don't.

LUCY: No, well, I mean, I'm not some weirdo health freak, although swimming at the crack of dawn and no coffee, I guess it could seem like I'm
on my way to some holy land where you could just take a whole day to
do the whole lake. Like what's his name?

HELEN: *(Tight.)* Mr. Samuels?

LUCY: It's wild, if you think about that? That at the end of his life, he wants nothing more than to live in the water, day in day out . . . It's kind of beautiful. The water. Returning to the womb.

(Helen stands up, taking a breath.)

NATE: Are you OK, Mom?

HELEN: *(Fighting her anger, and losing.)* I'm just, I'm sorry, are you — I just — I'm finding this extremely difficult. What is your point. Could you tell me what your point is?

LUCY: *(Startled.)* I don't have a point. I just I think it's kind of beautiful. The water —

HELEN: Look. What happened here is really none of your business. I'm not interested in your youthful wisdom about water and wombs and childish versions of Nirvana.

(There is a silence. Lucy looks back and forth.)

NATE: What happened, with Lea, it's still kind of, even though it was a long time ago. That's true. So it's not like, but it is still. You know?

LUCY: *(Beat.)* Lea?

(Helen turns on her, appalled.)

HELEN: Our daughter. Lea. *(Beat.)* He hasn't told you anything, has he? Died. In the lake. He skipped that part? Well, isn't that convenient. Just skip right over it. Why not. Why not.

LUCY: I'm so sorry.

NATE: You don't just tell people. I mean, I don't, if a customer, oh by the way, my sister drowned in the lake, that'll be twenty-three fifty.

HELEN: I think this is a little different, Nate.

NATE: I know. I'm not saying — I know! I'm just, I wouldn't either. If I was him. What's the point?

LUCY: I'm so sorry.

NATE: It was an accident.

HELEN: No. You are not allowed to say that. An accident is you look away for one moment, half a moment, he didn't even know it had happened! How long was she in there?

NATE: I don't —

HELEN: *(To Lucy.)* I was the one who found her. He didn't even know.

NATE: Mom, maybe we should, maybe, maybe —

HELEN: If you go down, in the morning, the light on the water — it's quite extraordinary, really, everything moves. Because the reflection, on the trees, all those subtle greens, everything seems to be moving but nothing, it's a trick of the light.

NATE: Mom.

HELEN: On this side, not — the reflection of the trees across the lake, they're black, almost, the sun is behind them so the shadow cast across the lake, and then, the lily pads, on the shadow, they pick up the sun, all of them so flat and white, and — it was — because you go down, to look, and and you you you have no, no —

NATE: Mom, please —

HELEN: I'm explaining something —

NATE: I know, I just —

HELEN: To see that, in the water. So sure that it must be impossible. She's with Richard. That's not your child. It's a trick of the light.

(Beat. She shakes her head, and goes down the path, to the lake. After a moment, Nate clears his throat, speaks.)

NATE: It was pretty bad. That's why he didn't tell you.

LUCY: Is it?

NATE: I mean, I can't even — it was really bad. She kind of lost her mind, that's pretty much all I remember. I mean, I remember some of it, after, I can't remember the specific, how he left, because he, well. It kind of all goes white. When you look back and try to remember it. It's very white, in your head. There's stuff before and stuff after. But right around when it happened? It's all pretty white. *(Off Helen's exit.)* I wish I could make her brain go white. I think it would be better for her.

LUCY: *(Chagrined.)* I am the stupidest woman alive.

NATE: No, no. I mean, he didn't tell you. You didn't know.

LUCY: *(Upset.)* I went for a swim! I mean how — oh, God — that's just — oh, Jesus —

NATE: A lot of people swim in the lake.

LUCY: Yes, yes, I'm sure, but this is a little different! I mean, you know, I — oh, God. This is just — you know, oh, he just forgot to mention —

NATE: It's really hard to talk about. I mean, she acts like oh he should have told you, but we don't talk about it. We don't talk about anything! Get this. She just told us not ten minutes ago, they aren't even divorced. I mean, for how long, seventeen years, my own parents! And I didn't even know!

LUCY: They're not divorced?

NATE: No. But the thing is, I don't really think it's deliberate. Some things are just hard to talk about. You know, I mean, I'm trying not to sound, about, because it was awful, like I said, but it was seventeen years ago. You know, seriously — seriously, it was terrible, but what can you do about it now?

LUCY: So why talk about it.

NATE: That's right.

LUCY: So that's why he didn't say anything.

NATE: Well, yeah, I mean, especially since . . . never mind.

LUCY: There's more?

NATE: No! Not really. I mean — no. He just . . . I mean. *(Beat. She looks at him.)* He was kind of, there was some, at least she thinks — he may have been, meeting someone. Else.

LUCY: A woman? He was meeting another woman, when —

NATE: It's hard to say, for sure. I mean, he did — he had done, I mean.

LUCY: Had done what?

NATE: Other, um, women. That's what she says. But, you know. It was a long time ago. *(Beat.)* Really. It was such a long time ago.

LUCY: I fall for guys way too fast. It's like a disease, it just is. My therapist just about threw a fit when I told her I had hooked up with Richard, I was supposed to take a year off from men, ha ha. I mean, I totally get why I do it, I had a hideous father, really just nuts, and now I spend way too much time looking for approval from men, any one of them will do. If they're twenty years older and want to boss me around, so much the better.

NATE: I'm sorry.

LUCY: Please don't apologize. I mean, this is, the only thing that could make this situation any worse would be if people started apologizing to me. Because I'm the one, I just, what am I doing here?

NATE: You didn't know.

LUCY: I knew something! I knew something was up! You get that feeling, you know? That feeling? What good is it, having it, if you don't . . . whatever.

NATE: How did you meet him, anyway?

LUCY: Oh, waiting tables. He sat at one of my tables and flirted with me. Therapy is wasted on me, it just is.

NATE: You're a waitress?

LUCY: No, I'm a highly educated person who is temporarily between things. And then Richard . . . I mean, I'm not just attaching myself to men. I've studied. I studied journalism, for a while, that just depressed the hell out of me. Everybody was so mean, I just couldn't figure out — I said to this one professor, he was like this major genius, and he was just a mother-fucker, and I finally said, why do you think the truth is just the meanest thing you can think of to say? And he told me I was naïve and then he

said a bunch of other shitty things, I was actually sleeping with the guy, so he felt he had license, I guess. Anyway, that was it for me and journalism. So that's not, that wasn't a good choice, obviously, something else will show up and until then . . . I'm sorry. I'm really sorry.
(Beat.)

NATE: I think you're right. About people being mean. I don't believe in that either.

LUCY: No no, well, please, I'm ridiculous, really. I can't believe I even say things like that.
(She looks at him. Richard appears in the doorway with his cell phone.)

RICHARD: Goddamn it, isn't there a fucking signal anywhere?

NATE: Cell phones don't work here.

RICHARD: *(Continuing.)* Nor should they on a morning like this. It's amazing, being here, after all this time, you'll have have to forgive me for turning into a babbling lunatic for a day or two, but it's truly so overwhelming just to be here. I forgot — or I didn't forget, I just didn't let myself fully remember. How much a place, a specific place — this place — can fill you or . . . forget it. I am babbling. Oh hey, Nate, you try this thing out yet?
(He picks up the camera, starts to fiddle with it.)

RICHARD: *(Continuing.)* I got one of these for myself last year; the technology is amazing. They can do everything except cook dinner for you. Except yours is a newer model, so maybe it can do even that now. Here, let me show you . . .

LUCY: Richard. You have told me nothing. You piece of shit.
(There is a moment, then —)

NATE: I'm going to go see how Mom is.
(He heads down the path, to the lake.)

RICHARD: What . . . OK. What . . .

LUCY: *(Angry.)* You brought me here. You told me nothing. You knew I would find out, how could I not find out, in the most humiliating way possible.

RICHARD: *(Beat.)* They told you about Lea.

LUCY: Yes they did.

RICHARD: I was going to tell you.

LUCY: Oh when? Around the time you filled me in on how you're still married to another woman —

RICHARD: You wouldn't have come.

LUCY: No, I would not have come! You, that was why it all, yes? Why they made you leave? Because you let your own child drown in this lake that you now think is so fucking BEAUTIFUL —

RICHARD: We both lost our daughter! And then I lost everything else. She, couldn't, and so I — she insisted I go — no visitation, nothing, just — I sent them money, all these years, I paid for anything they, and I didn't ask for anything. There was no way back in but just to come. You see that. You must see that.

LUCY: You were meeting another woman.

RICHARD: *(A beat, then.)* That's between me and Helen.

LUCY: Oh, fuck you.

RICHARD: You think there's a reason! There's no reason! When children die, there is no reason! She needs my guilt. And I gave it to her. I let her have it so that she had a story, everybody, we all have to think something, there has to be a story, doesn't there, otherwise it's too — *(Beat.)* There is no story. And I don't want this to sound cold, but I have moved on. I lived in grief for a long time, and I'm not living there anymore. And I wanted you here. I'm not apologizing for that, either. I need a witness. That I am living in the present. While I face all of it.

LUCY: *(A beat, then very plain.)* This idea, this whole, coming here, this is a disaster, Richard.

RICHARD: I don't believe that. This is my home. This is where I belong.

(He goes into the house. Lucy stands, still. Lights fade.)

SCENE THREE

Late afternoon. Nate is moving a small table out from the side of the house, while Helen counts and cleans silverware in a basket.

NATE: I'm not sure the legs still work. They're pretty rusted.

HELEN: I tried one of them this morning. It seemed all right.

(Nate starts to set up the legs)

HELEN: *(Continuing.)* This will be nice, having dinner out here. We used to do it, when you were little, we'd set up that very table and have a party, don't you remember?

NATE: No.

HELEN: It wasn't that often. Your father always enjoyed it more than I did. I found it buggy. But tonight there's a breeze, it should be fine.

NATE: Is Lucy coming?

HELEN: I don't know.

NATE: I can't figure out why she's with him.

HELEN: He's handsome. Like you. And he's rich.

NATE: So?

HELEN: Well, that's not everything, but it's not nothing.

NATE: You think he's handsome?

HELEN: Not as handsome as you, but handsome. Is he still down there? With Erica?

NATE: I think so.

HELEN: I can't imagine what they have to talk about, for all this time.

NATE: Yeah but you told her. You said — maybe she should get to know him. Since he's here anyway.

HELEN: I know what I said, Nate, you don't have to repeat it back to me. I'm just saying. Down at the lake? You'd think he'd have the decency, if he wanted to take a walk with his daughter — the one that's actually alive, I mean — to take a stroll into town. But he was never the most sensitive of men, even given all that poetry he takes to spouting. Does he actually think we buy that, do you think? I'm not criticizing. What would be the point? It's not like he's staying. But it does make you wonder. If he buys it himself. Given reality, such as it is. Back in town for a couple days, just thought I'd drop by, maybe I'll take my daughter for a walk around the lake.

NATE: They're probably on their way back right now.

HELEN: And what about her? This girlfriend? Let's take a lovely swim.

NATE: It wasn't her fault, Mom.

HELEN: *(Snapping.)* Don't tell me whose fault it was!

(She looses control of the silverware, which goes flying. She looks at it. Nate starts over, to help clean it.)

HELEN: *(Continuing.)* I'm sorry. Leave it, Nate, would you leave it? You're not my slave for God's sake.

NATE: I know, I —

HELEN: I'm upset. *(Beat.)* Him showing up. I'm not going to lie, why should I? Even the sight of him. The comfort of thinking him dead. Always ruined once a month, he had to keep sending those checks, his gesture of remorse, money, every month here comes the money, I'm still out here, look how successful I am. That's not enough. Now he has to show up, in the flesh. Here I am. The flesh of me is still in the world. Flesh and money. LEAVE IT NATE.

(For Nate has reached over, and he is trying to clean up the silverware.)

HELEN: *(Continuing.)* I'm not incapable! I can do this!

NATE: I know you can —

HELEN: No matter how much has been asked of me, I can do it! That is the one thing I think I can say. After all this time. After everything? I do what is asked of me.

NATE: Why don't you tell him to go?

HELEN: *(Beat.)* I know, I know. It's what I should do.

NATE: He doesn't need the house —

HELEN: That's not why he's here.

NATE: It's not?

HELEN: You're so naïve. I love you so much, sweetheart, but you are NAIVE.
  (Nate flinches.)

HELEN: *(Continuing.)* Every gesture is a — I want the house. Here's my girl-friend! I want my kids. What else do you think he wants?

NATE: I don't know. I just think you should tell him, you should tell him —

HELEN: *(Flaring again.)* I don't have to tell him anything! This isn't a conversation! He's not "talking" about anything. He's just taking. You think I don't know him by now? I had three children with that man. And now he's here again, and even after all this time, after all this time, do you think I don't know who he is, and what he wants?

NATE: I don't know, Mom. I don't — I don't —
  (Lucy comes out on the porch.)

LUCY: Hi.

NATE: *(Upset.)* Hi.

LUCY: We're having dinner out here. How lovely.

HELEN: *(Cool.)* It was Richard's idea. Nate was just getting the candles. And the napkins. Don't forget the napkins, sweetie, you always forget.
  (Nate goes.)

LUCY: Is there anything I can do?

HELEN: No. Thank you.
  (Helen opens a tablecloth, which is on a chair, brushes the leaves off of it, and drapes it over the card table, as Lucy continues to speak.)

LUCY: I'm sorry.

HELEN: Excuse me?

LUCY: I just wanted to say I'm sorry. For . . . well . . . I mean I I I think it's obvious I'm a little out of the loop here.

HELEN: Yes, well. He's here now, that part is done. The rest, we'll just have to get through.

LUCY: Well. I know that's what he wants. He's been talking for so long about coming. As long as I've known him. So I thought it would be a kindness, to help him get here.

HELEN: You helped him?

LUCY: I told him, when he said he wanted to come, that I thought it was a good idea, I thought — I just wish I had known more. But he really, when he spoke to me, about what this might mean to him — he's very eloquent.

HELEN: Eloquent. Yes. I'm sure. About everything. The air. The trees. The universe. He always did that.

LUCY: Did he?

HELEN: Doesn't he?

LUCY: I don't, I never thought of it as something he "does," I guess I just think of it as who he is or something.

HELEN: Well. I'm glad he found someone who can live out there on a wider philosophical plane with him.

LUCY: No. Oh. No, I actually, normally, I guess I would consider myself much more of a realist. Sort of.

HELEN: Then philosophy isn't realistic?

LUCY: Is it? I mean, mostly it always struck me as completely crazy.

HELEN: How so?

LUCY: Well, you know — like, nobody can even prove that we exist. Which, I mean, what would be the point, then?

HELEN: Of what?

LUCY: Of everything. People, you know. Planets. What would be the point, if we didn't exist?

HELEN: What is the point if we do?

LUCY: Oh. I don't — I don't know. I'm sorry, this is making me a little uncomfortable. Maybe if I could help set the table or something . . .

HELEN: No no. You know what, though? If you want to help. There is something you could do.

LUCY: Sure, anything.

HELEN: If we could have the evening.

LUCY: Have the evening?

HELEN: Richard and I. And the children.

LUCY: Oh.

HELEN: I hope you don't mind.

LUCY: You want me to leave.

HELEN: Just for tonight.

LUCY: Uh. Well.

HELEN: I know why you're here.

LUCY: *(Surprised, unsure.)* You do?

HELEN: And I appreciate, why you're here. I do, I appreciate that.

LUCY: Well, I, I, I —

HELEN: It just might give us a little room. To understand each other. There are a couple terrific restaurants over in Neponset. And the drive is beautiful, especially this time of year.

LUCY: OK. I see. Sure. *(Beat.)* You don't mind, do you mind if I talk to Richard about this?

HELEN: I don't know what your relationship with Richard is like. Is that how you work things out?

LUCY: No. I mean —

HELEN: You do whatever you need. I just ask you, as a favor.

(Nate comes out with napkins, candles, and glasses. His arms are much too full.)

NATE: I couldn't, there weren't enough in the kitchen so I had to go to the closet, upstairs. Are these the ones you meant?

HELEN: They're fine.

(She heads up the steps.)

NATE: It's such a little table. I guess we should just put people around. Like on corners.

HELEN: No no, sweetie. Lucy's not staying. Only four places. I need to go check on that roast.

(She goes inside before Lucy can say anything. Nate looks at her.)

NATE: You're not going to be here.

LUCY: Yeah, I might not be here, I guess.

NATE: Where are you going?

LUCY: I guess I might go to Neponset, for dinner. And the drive.

(He continues to set the table.)

NATE: Oh great. I mean, that is just — you're just going to leave? You're kidding! So we're, what, we're expected to have some sort of family dinner? Why?

LUCY: I don't know. I —

NATE: *(Upset.)* Why does she want this? Why? Why do we have to do this? Why?

LUCY: I think she —

NATE: You don't know! How could, because why? I don't want it! I thought I did, but you know, I just, everything was fine! It was fine. I want to go back. This is just, there's nothing that can, we need to go back, just back, you know. Back. Not back. Not all the way back, that's not, oh, God, you know, I just — I'm just insane. Obviously. I'm sorry.

LUCY: You're not insane.

NATE: No, of course not. I don't really think that. But like, dinner! I mean. Dinner.

(Erica and Richard arrive, coming up from the lake.)

RICHARD: This path has gotten so overgrown, you don't keep it up?

ERICA: Sadly, it is not a priority, no.

RICHARD: My father would throw a fit at the state of this place. He . . .

(Lucy takes a step back from Nate, who quickly turns away. Somehow, Lucy manages to look a little guilty.)

RICHARD: *(Continuing.)* Everything OK?

LUCY: Sure.

RICHARD: Nate?

NATE: Yeah. We're just getting ready for dinner. I'll go help Mom.

(He hurries into the house. Richard looks at Lucy.)

RICHARD: What's that about?

LUCY: Nothing.

ERICA: Well, maybe I'll see if I can help with dinner, too.

(She heads after him.)

RICHARD: No, no stay! Erica and I were just walking down to the pier, to see my old dingy, it's still there, if you can believe that.

ERICA: *(Cool.)* Yep. Pretty amazing.

RICHARD: You mentioned you had some plans to paint the house!

ERICA: It's not actually plans.

RICHARD: OK, so what are you thoughts?

ERICA: My "thoughts" are, the house could use a coat of paint.

RICHARD: You thinking about changing the color?

ERICA: I'm not thinking about anything other than it needs a coat of fucking paint!

(She heads into the house.)

RICHARD: Do not just walk away from me. Please. I want to talk about this; that's why I'm here. I'm your father.

ERICA: *(Turning, pissed, taking up the gauntlet.)* OK then. *(To Lucy.)* Due respect to you, which I know this is none of your business — *(To Richard.)* But like, are you going to take the house? Is that really your plan here?

RICHARD: Your mother and I —

ERICA: Don't change the subject. You just said right now, right here in front of witnesses, that you want to talk to me, you're my dad, well, the elephant in the room, Dad, is the house and what you think you mean when you say you want it back. Because you wanna know what I did today, I called a lawyer to find out what kind of rights you do have in this situation, and the fact is, you have quite a few. Quite a few, and we have none. So I want to know what you're going to do about that. Because it's kind of hard to "get to know you," Dad, when we all have a fucking gun to our heads.

RICHARD: I don't have a gun to your head, and you don't hate me, even though you want to. This isn't about tearing things down.

ERICA: But you still want the house.

(Richard looks around, unable to answer this.)

ERICA: *(Continuing.)* Cut it out and just admit it! You want the house! So I want to know what does that mean, are you going to kick us out? Is that what it means? The irony being of course that you have six thousand other places you could live, what the FUCK do you need our house for?

RICHARD: If I offered you one of the six thousand other houses, free and clear, would you take it?

ERICA: Why should I? This is my house!

RICHARD: Ah, then I'm not the only one capable of being irrational about this place. Thanks, I was just checking.

ERICA: Yeah, that's hilarious. So you honestly expect to just come back here, and and make us LEAVE —

RICHARD: Cut it out, you know that's not what's going on.

ERICA: I don't know that; I don't know anything of the —

RICHARD: *(Overlap.)* All right then let me tell you that is not my intention

ERICA: *(Overlap, cutting him off.)* But you can't tell me. You can't tell me anything. Because I don't know you AT ALL, I don't know you and what's more I don't believe a word out of your fucking mouth.

RICHARD: Fine. You don't know me. I'm a total stranger. Get your lawyer. Get, whoever you want, to come out here and tell me to leave. Do it.

ERICA: I will.

RICHARD: *(Needling her.)* Do it! What's the matter, you can't do it? Why not?

ERICA: *(Overlap, trying to regain her ground.)* Why, you know — you, you could have, almost any time up to this point! Who are you supposed to be, now? Some creepy rich guy who's going to hang around and just give everybody trust funds —

RICHARD: That money is for your future — OK — all right — all —

ERICA: *(Continuing, overlap.)* Have a camera, let's forget everything that ever happened here, how about some gold earrings?

RICHARD: I just wanted to bring something! All those birthdays and Christmases, all those years I never got to give you anything —

ERICA: And whose fault was that?

RICHARD: It's no one's fault!

ERICA: That's a very convenient position.

RICHARD: Can we stay on the subject?

ERICA: I think we are right on subject. This is exactly —

RICHARD: We were talking about whether or not I am trying to buy your affections with a pair of earrings.

ERICA: It's the same point! The same point! You have not been here, and you don't know me! Do I look like the kind of person who would give a shit about a pair of earrings? Do I?

LUCY: Richard. Maybe I should —

RICHARD: She wouldn't send me any pictures of you. So I had to imagine everything. And you were so — sweet when you were seven. You liked all that makeup, and pink clothing. You always wanted to wear pink.

ERICA: I never wore pink.

RICHARD: You wore pink all the time. I have a little shirt, I . . .

ERICA: You have one of my shirts from when I was seven?

RICHARD: I just wanted to bring something. A pair of earrings, seemed . . . I'm sorry if it was foolish. You don't like earrings, you're right, I didn't know. I don't know you. *(Beat.)* You can exchange them.

ERICA: That's not the point! Oh, never mind. This is a nightmare.

RICHARD: Tell me how to help. Tell me what I could do, to make this easier. *(Beat.)* Look. I was wrong before, when I said it was no one's fault. I did fail you. I should have come back before this, I should have . . . I'm sorry. I can go. Do you want me to leave?

(Erica looks at him, looks away. For a long moment, she tries to think of something to say.)

ERICA: You — that was your boat? I mean, that boat down there? Was really your boat?

RICHARD: My father gave it to me. When I was twelve. We'd take it down to the far end of the lake, where the bass run.

ERICA: Did you ever catch any?

RICHARD: Bass? *(Beat.)* Yeah. Trout, too. Once, not a lot, just once.

(There is another moment of silence. Erica sighs, finally.)

ERICA: I've never been fishing in the lake. It's sort of the unspoken rule here. No one goes on the lake.

RICHARD: I'll take you fishing.

ERICA: Are you kidding? Oh please. That would be, I don't . . .

RICHARD: Times change. I'll take you fishing.

(She looks at him, not trusting this, more and more upset.)

ERICA: I'm sorry. I can't do this. I can't, I just, I'm really, I'm sorry — .

(He goes to her, concerned now.)

RICHARD: Erica, please.

(He touches her arm. He holds her for a moment. Then she puts her arms around him. Behind them, Helen watches from the doorway.)

HELEN: Oh. I'm sorry.

(Erica pulls away, sudden.)

ERICA: No, it's fine. I was just coming in. To help with dinner.

(She shakes her head at the lameness of this, then goes inside, leaving Lucy and Richard and Helen.)

HELEN: Lucy, maybe you could give me a hand with these.

LUCY: Sure.

(Helen hands her glasses, and they continue to set the table in silence for a moment.)

LUCY: *(Continuing.)* Richard, um . . . I have to . . . uh, Helen has mentioned that maybe I might want to, I guess, take off for the evening. She seems to think it might be a good idea for me to have dinner in someplace called Neponset.

RICHARD: Helen asked you to go . . . somewhere else to dinner?

LUCY: Yes.

RICHARD: Why?

HELEN: I thought she might like to see it, as long as she's up here. You remember, it's a terrific little town, and the drive is sensational. You just take a left, out of the drive, and then right when you get to route twelve. It's a straight shot from there. The trees are magnificent.

RICHARD: I'm sorry, I'm just — catching up here. Run this by me again. You asked my girlfriend to leave?

(It's a direct challenge. Helen sighs and looks at him.)

HELEN: Actually, Richard, I didn't ask her to leave. I asked you to leave.

RICHARD: Yeah, OK —

HELEN: You were the one who came without invitation. I was just making an attempt to be a good sport about it.

RICHARD: So asking Lucy to leave is being a good sport.

HELEN: Since — you are not leaving — and since you claim you're here to get to know your children — in addition to taking our house from us —

RICHARD: This is classic.

HELEN: How so, Richard? Since that is what you claim to be here for, and since I apparently have very little choice in the matter, I thought I would make an attempt to actually help you out. She can stay. I told her, it was up to her. If it makes you both uncomfortable, we'll just set an extra place. It's not a big deal. You've both already made much too much of it.
(She goes back to the table. Richard watches her, eyes narrowed.)

LUCY: Well, that's good. I mean, thank you, Helen, because I was feeling, a bit —

HELEN: I didn't mean for it to cause even a moment's insecurity on anyone's part. I'm sorry it did.

LUCY: No, it's not that —

HELEN: Say no more about it. It's done!
(Richard grabs her arm.)

RICHARD: Would you just stand still for a minute? And stop this?

HELEN: Richard.

RICHARD: Helen. Stop it.
(She looks at him. After a moment, he lets go of her arm.)

HELEN: Sorry. Let me just get an extra place setting.
(She heads for the house.)

RICHARD: *(Sudden.)* No. No, it's fine. I'm sorry. It's fine, Lucy. Helen's right. I need to spend some time with the kids.

LUCY: Richard, for heaven's sake —

RICHARD: You've been such a trooper, you should take the night off.

LUCY: Richard, could you and I please, just can we have a moment of privacy to discuss this?

HELEN: Of course.

RICHARD: No, it's fine, Helen. We don't have to talk about it. It's already way too big a deal.
(Beat.)

HELEN: So . . . we're OK about this?

RICHARD: We're fine.

HELEN: Good. Oh good, the brussel sprouts. Nate, did you remember the mint jelly?
(Erica comes out, carrying a bowl of vegetables. Nate, behind her, carries a lamb roast.)

NATE: Yes, you told me eight times.

HELEN: Well, sometimes you're a little light-headed, sweetheart.
   (Nate turns and looks at Lucy.)
NATE: Are you going?
LUCY: I don't know. I guess I am.
HELEN: Who's got the wine?
ERICA: I'll get it.
   (She goes.)
HELEN: *(Before Lucy can answer.)* What about the orzo? Nate!
NATE: OK!
   (He turns to go inside.)
RICHARD: *(Handing her the keys.)* Here.
LUCY: Richard, maybe —
RICHARD: You're worrying about nothing. It's fine, Lucy.
ERICA: *(Coming out, with wine.)* Does anyone want white?
HELEN: It's a lamb roast, sweetie.
ERICA: I know the red meat rule, Mom. But some people like white anyway.
RICHARD: Red's great. Here, let me help you with that.
HELEN: Thank you.
LUCY: *(A beat, then.)* Yeah. OK. Good-bye.
RICHARD: Bye. This looks sensational. When I suggested we eat outside, I didn't expect you to go to so much trouble.
   (After a moment, Lucy goes around the side of the house, while the others sit down to dinner.)
   (The lights fade.)

END OF ACT I

ACT II
SCENE FOUR

An hour later. Nate, Erica, Helen, and Richard are under the stars, eating dinner. Richard looks up at the sky.

RICHARD: Cassiopeia. Orion's belt, is that Orion?

HELEN: It's amazing you can pick that out, the trees block most of it.

RICHARD: The trees weren't so full forty years ago. I can still see the sky, plain, in full view. It's there, and not there. Memory. You know what we should do? We should take the boat out. My brother and I used to do that. Middle of the night, from the center of the lake, the night sky is beyond imagining.

ERICA: We could go fishing.

NATE: Now?

ERICA: It's night. That's when fish come out.

NATE: Fish sleep. I mean, don't they? Sleep? Because — never mind.

RICHARD: No, she's right, right at dusk, as the stars are coming out, that's when they feed. We could do it. I went down to the basement and took a look at the tackle just before, it's in pretty good shape, all things considered.

HELEN: You went downstairs and checked the fishing tackle? Why did you do that?

RICHARD: I mean — I'm sorry. It's not such a good idea. We'll try it another night.

ERICA: Is there going to be another night?

RICHARD: Of course there is.

(There is a pause. Helen pours wine.)

RICHARD: *(Continuing.)* Thank you. *(Beat.)* So, Nate. You're working in a bookstore. How is that?

NATE: How is it?

RICHARD: Do you enjoy it?

NATE: Yes.

RICHARD: What do you do down there?

NATE: You know, you — help people find the books they want to buy and then you go to the cash register and you ring it up, and then you take their credit card and run it through the slot, and wait for the approval, and then you get them to sign the slip, and then you put their books in a bag, most people actually don't want a bag, up here people are environmentally conscious, but sometimes you give a bag and a little bookmark that has the logo of the store, and then it's like that.

RICHARD: Sounds terrific.

NATE: I also unpack the books out of the boxes, and figure out where to put them on the shelves. Sometimes that's not, like, easy, because you have something like you know, Primo Levi, *Survival at Auschwitz*? Where do you put that, under biography or history? You have to make a decision, about stuff like that.

RICHARD: So there is some challenge to it, that's good.

NATE: Well, that's — I don't, you know, I, it's not brain surgery or anything, obviously —

RICHARD: No, no, I — I just meant —

NATE: I don't think it's — because people come in, some new people, all the time, or there are a lot of people in the, around the, who read a lot, and want to know, mysteries are, when they come in, there's always a few people waiting and you talk to them and, or there's one guy who used to teach, not at a big college or anything, but he still, it's like he's, last week he came in and he was looking for *War and Peace*, because he never — and I, because he read *Moby Dick*, which he also never, and he thought — you know, how did he ever get to this place. Where he's like seventy or something. Without reading *War and Peace*. So we talked about that, and I found it for him. *(Beat.)* Sometimes I think, you know, he doesn't have a lot of people to talk to, so when he comes into the bookstore, that's, you know. Anyway. *(Beat.)* I need to get some water.
(He stands up and goes into the house.)

ERICA: *(Defensive.)* Look. It's not like he's a freak or anything.

RICHARD: I know that.
(Erica stands and goes into the house after him. After a moment, Richard looks at Helen.)

RICHARD: *(Continuing.)* All I said was —

HELEN: What you said was, "So there is some challenge to it, that's good."

RICHARD: I didn't say it like that.

HELEN: You didn't have to.

RICHARD: Well, it sounds like he's given up. He's twenty-six years old. Why has he given up?

HELEN: Maybe he wants other things out of life.

RICHARD: You won't always be here to take care of him.

HELEN: You are really something. You haven't learned anything in seventeen years. Have you? You're exactly the same person. Of course, why wouldn't you be.

(She starts to clear the table.)

RICHARD: That's not exactly helpful.

HELEN: *(Hissing.)* Oh, now I'm supposed to be helpful? You want help now? From me? You want me to help you — help you —

RICHARD: Hey. Hey, hey.

(He reaches over and takes her hand.)

RICHARD: *(Continuing.)* I'm sorry. I'm sorry this is so hard.

(They look at each other for a moment. Richard's hand stays on hers. She finally moves, goes to finish cleaning the table. He watches her in silence. Finally, Nate comes back out onto the porch, with Erica.)

NATE: I can — I can do that, Mom.

HELEN: *(Subdued.)* It's OK, I've got it.

(She picks up some plates and goes into the house.)

NATE: Maybe, I can just start on the dishes with you, that way —

ERICA: Mom can do that, Nate. She's fine.

HELEN: Of course I am.

ERICA: Come on, you're freaking out over nothing. Richard just wants to talk about, like, what we've been doing our whole lives. That's all.

NATE: I'm not freaking out! I was just getting a drink of water!

ERICA: No, I know. But Mom can start on the dishes herself.

(She pushes Nate a little. He goes down the steps.)

RICHARD: I am interested in what you're doing. *(Beat.)* I mean, I love bookstores. Working in a bookstore. That seems to be a very elegant occupation.

NATE: *(Beat.)* I like the books.

RICHARD: Do you read a lot?

ERICA: Constantly. You should see his room, there are like piles of books around his bed. He reads like a book a day, it's ridiculous.

RICHARD: A book a day! Come on.

NATE: What?

RICHARD: Well, a book a day, that's — That's impressive. I mean, that's more than impressive, that's — spectacular.

NATE: *(Abashed, but pleased.)* Well, they're not all, some of them are kind of stupid —

RICHARD: They don't all have to be Tolstoy to still be worth reading —

NATE: *(Explaining.)* Yeah but some of them are kind of, I mean, like mysteries. Some of them are really dumb. Not dumb, you don't want to judge, I'm not judging, because it's still a book, and books are —

RICHARD: Yes.

NATE: And people! Because people come in, some — they hope, or yearn even, that the person in the bookstore will know, the books will be inside you, and you can tell them, because reading is very, almost to some people, even a dumb mystery is something they hold onto like a chalice, or — I don't know. I'm sorry.

RICHARD: No. No. You're right. Books are holy. I feel that.

NATE: You do?

RICHARD: Yes. Of course. When I'm surrounded by books, it's —

NATE: I know!

RICHARD: I didn't mean, before, that I thought there was something wrong, with working in a bookstore.

NATE: Oh, no.

RICHARD: Because it might have sounded like that. It sounds like something I wish I knew how to do. How to just live so simply, give everything else up, just for the chance to be surrounded by something you think is holy.

NATE: Well. I mean — you're right, I guess I — because that's the best part. I mean, when you're surrounded. By how much love people have in their hearts, when they're looking at books. It's very hopeful. They think, all of them, that the next book they find is just going to be amazing. Even if it's a dumb mystery. And it's so great. Getting to help them find that. *(He smiles at his father.)*

RICHARD: What are your favorite ones?

NATE: Oh, I like them all.

RICHARD: All of them?

NATE: *(Excited.)* I really do! I like all books. The little kids books, the pictures are so — and the art books and the photography books are always, just — they're easier to just get a sense of than, the history and the biography and the novels of course you have to read the whole thing, or what would be the point? And OK, the literary criticism, or philosophy, that can get a little dense, but —

RICHARD: You read everything?

NATE: What?

(Richard is laughing, admiring. Nate laughs as well, happy.)

RICHARD: And you like them all?

NATE: Well, yeah —

ERICA: Even coffee table books? Like, even books about beading? *(She laughs.)*

That was my favorite, one time I stuck my head in his room, he was trying to figure out this workbook about how to make a beaded purse.

NATE: I thought it was interesting!

(*They laugh. Helen steps out onto the porch, carrying a bottle of liquor and
two glasses on a tray. She watches this.*)

ERICA: Yeah, but that Feng Shui book, Nate. He's in there, reading *Clear Your
Clutter with Feng Shui* and he's like surrounded by these piles and piles
of books.

NATE: So what's your point?

(*They all laugh at this. Helen watches for a moment before speaking.*)

HELEN: Well, this is lovely.

(*They look over at her, their laughter fading.*)

HELEN: *(Continuing.)* So what was that all about?

NATE: Nothing.

HELEN: Don't be ridiculous, you were all laughing, what was so funny?

RICHARD: Nate was telling me about his work.

HELEN: And that's funny?

NATE: *(Embarrassed.)* It wasn't anything. Really. It, I didn't, it wasn't anything.

HELEN: You don't want to tell me?

NATE: It was about, it was stupid. About this book I read on Feng Shui. It was
stupid.

(*A beat.*)

HELEN: Maybe you could start on those dishes, Nate. I'd really appreciate
that.

NATE: Yeah, OK.

HELEN: Erica, could you help him?

ERICA: Well —

HELEN: Your father and I have a lot to talk about.

NATE: Yeah, no, of course. Come on, Erica.

ERICA: OK. Would you not rip my shirt, I said OK!

(*She snaps at Nate, as he tugs at her sleeve, but she goes with him.*)

RICHARD: *(As she goes.)* Those earrings look beautiful, Erica. They suit you.

ERICA: Thanks. I think they're pretty.

(*She goes. After a moment, Helen hands Richard the bottle of liquor.*)

HELEN: I remember you liked the occasional after-dinner drink.

RICHARD: Yeah, thanks. You want some?

HELEN: No.

(*He pours.*)

RICHARD: You can't just send them off the instant we start getting along. It's not right, Helen.

HELEN: We have things to talk about, Richard. There's no point in putting it off.

RICHARD: I'm not putting it off. I'm just making an observation. You didn't seem too terribly interested in actually talking to me about anything, until I started hitting it off with them. I'm just asking you to consider what that might mean to me, after all this time —

HELEN: Why, because you're so considerate of my feelings, showing up out of nowhere —

RICHARD: I wrote and told you I was coming.

HELEN: With your girlfriend. A particularly considerate touch.

RICHARD: She's not here now. I let you get away with that.

HELEN: You "let me"?

RICHARD: For God's sake, Helen, you were so transparent. Quite frankly, I think you've lost your touch over the years.

HELEN: And yet, I did manage to get rid of her.

RICHARD: Yes you did.

HELEN: My motives being what, might I ask?

RICHARD: Your motives I'm sure will reveal themselves, as they always did.

HELEN: As do yours.

RICHARD: My motives aren't secret. I've told you what I want.

HELEN: Not all of it, Richard. You never show your full hand.

RICHARD: You know what? Maybe you don't know me as well as you think you do. After all this time. I mean, I'm trying, here, and as a matter of fact, I think I'm doing pretty well.

HELEN: Of course you do. After seventeen years, you manage to have a two-minute conversation with your grown children, and that means everything's going to work out for you and them, you can just come back and reclaim all of it, and it will all be perfect, is that how it's supposed to be?

RICHARD: I don't know how it's supposed to be. I just know, you can't keep fighting me, because I'm not going away.

HELEN: I'm not fighting! *(Beat.)* I don't want to fight. *(Beat, calling.)* Erica, get away from the door!

(Erica steps from behind the door.)

ERICA: OK, but don't forget to ask about the house!

RICHARD: *(Laughing.)* She's really something.

HELEN: At least one of them meets with your approval. But you always had a soft spot for her.

RICHARD: They're both wonderful. You've done a wonderful job. *(Beat.)* And the meal was terrific.

HELEN: Richard, please stop complimenting me, you sound almost insane, and it's not helping.

RICHARD: I thought you didn't want to fight.

HELEN: This isn't fighting. When we're fighting, you'll know it.

RICHARD: This is just the foreplay, then.

HELEN: What did you say?

RICHARD: Helen, relax, I was kidding. I know it's hard for you. That I'm here. I was just trying to keep things light.

HELEN: Yes, I guess you would prefer that. To keep things light. To act as if that's what our lives were. Full of light.

RICHARD: Who wouldn't prefer that? You should try it sometime.

HELEN: Guess what, we're about to start fighting.

RICHARD: No, we're not. I'm sorry, I'm just, honestly, I know this is hard, impossible, even, but I can't seem to feel anything except happy. Just, really happy to be here. Remember the first time I brought you here? During college, Mom and Dad were gone visiting someone, I don't remember who, and we had the whole place to ourselves. We just made a wreck out of every room, remember? Leaving our clothes everywhere, eating whatever we wanted, making love in the bathtub —

HELEN: Richard.

RICHARD: I can't help it. I don't just remember what went wrong. I remember all of it. How good it was. I should have made you leave with me. It was a mistake, letting you stay here.

HELEN: You "let" me —

RICHARD: It just might have given you some room —

HELEN: Like you?

RICHARD: Yeah, like me. To move on.

HELEN: If you've moved on, then why are you here now?

RICHARD: *(Frustrated.)* Look, would you just look around you? It's so beautiful, the trees, the water, the air, it's so — impersonal. Serene. Yes, I have moved on. But you know what, so has this place. The trees don't care anymore. The earth — it doesn't care.

HELEN: Well. That's pretty convenient for you, then, isn't it?

RICHARD: Helen, you know, the fact is, you need to let me help you.

HELEN: Help me.

RICHARD: You're just stuck here —

HELEN: Yes, I am, and I didn't ask you to come back and "help" me. You just remember that. I told you to stay away.

RICHARD: That was not going to work forever! It never would, and you knew that, all along! You and I both know, it wasn't that I didn't love you.

HELEN: You know what, Erica's right, we should just talk about the house. If we just keep it on the house, and off the universe —

RICHARD: I don't agree to that.

HELEN: I'm not asking you to agree.

RICHARD: *(Firm, getting to it.)* It was an accident!

HELEN: Don't you fucking tell me it was an accident, there is no such thing as accidents, when my child is dead —

RICHARD: She was my child too —

HELEN: A month. Every summer. I'll clear out, the kids can do what they want, and you can have the house a whole month out of every year. That's what I'll give you. Do you accept my offer?

RICHARD: I want to talk about it. We never talked about it, we just screamed and ripped each other up like animals —

HELEN: Do you accept my offer?

RICHARD: No, I don't!

HELEN: It's all I have to give. If you want more I cannot help you.

RICHARD: It wasn't my fault. It really was just an accident, a terrible, tragic accident, and the way it happened was different, so different than what you —

HELEN: *(Overlap.)* Oh, that's what you want. You want history back, you want to change it all, in memory, say it never happened.

RICHARD: I'm not saying it never happened. But what you thought happened wasn't what happened.

HELEN: It happened as I know it happened and you can't change that now, after all this time you can't suddenly make it all different! You show up saying, nonsense, it's nonsense that you're even here —

RICHARD: It's not.

HELEN: Saying it was different, it was not what I thought, it was only what I thought, every day, it's in my head, you think I don't wish that — you think I didn't want to move on, be impersonal as your fucking trees, you think I don't wish she was never born — but it can't, so don't you — you can't — you —

(He stands, goes to her, and puts his arms around her. She tries to push him away. He won't let her.)

RICHARD: Don't push me away. You need to let me help.

HELEN: There's no help.

(He holds her.)

RICHARD: We should have been able to comfort each other, Helen. It didn't have to end the way it ended. And it doesn't have to keep going.

HELEN: If it doesn't have to, then why does it?

(She struggles.)

RICHARD: Shhh. It's me. It's me.

(This somehow reaches her, and she slumps. She lets him hold her for a moment. Finally, he takes a step back, looks at her, and kisses her. She pushes him away. He backs away, unswayed.)

RICHARD: *(Continuing.)* You don't have to. I'm the same as you. Neither one of us survived it. For so long I just . . . I'm no different from you.

(There is a long moment of silence. Helen stares at him.)

HELEN: It's so strange, to see you, and to not . . . merely hate you.

RICHARD: That's good.

HELEN: Is it?

RICHARD: Of course it is.

HELEN: I remember that time you brought me here. That first time. How happy we were, just to . . . we couldn't stop, that whole week, we just . . . we were so alive. I miss being that person.

RICHARD: You are still that person.

HELEN: I don't know.

RICHARD: You are all of it. Who you were when we met, who you were after it happened. The last time I saw you, you were so —

HELEN: I know what I was.

RICHARD: All of that — and your younger self, too —

HELEN: I can't do this. I have to go in. I have to, Richard, I CANNOT DO THIS.

RICHARD: Helen. Listen. You have to just let me tell you this one thing, please. It will make a difference. It didn't happen, the way you think it did. There was no one else there. I know you thought that. But it wasn't true.

HELEN: You were meeting someone.

RICHARD: I wasn't.

HELEN: That woman. Renting the house at the end of the, she was flirting with you all summer, and I saw her, Richard. I saw her going down there, to the lake, you were meeting —

RICHARD: *(Overlap.)* That woman flirted with everyone, I don't even remember her name —

HELEN: She, I saw her going to the lake —

RICHARD: I don't know what you saw, but she wasn't there. I wasn't cheating, Helen.

HELEN: You were —

RICHARD: I wasn't cheating. I know you thought that because I had, I don't deny I — . But that was over, and you were what I wanted, we were so clear on that, both of us, when —

HELEN: You were, Richard —

RICHARD: No. You think something so untrue, all these years. I wasn't meeting anyone; it really was just an accident. I was worried about work. Some investments the firm had made, this huge account, something had gone wrong and someone was blaming it on me, it was all — I got this phone call from one of the partners. On our way out the door.

HELEN: A phone call?

RICHARD: You remember, the phone call.

HELEN: No, I don't remember a phone call —

RICHARD: And Lea — had already run, up ahead of me, but the call came in, I went back. Just for a minute. I thought she was just ahead of me. How many times did we take that path. Where you let them run, just ahead, around the next tree, you let them just get out of sight for a second, it wasn't like anything we hadn't done before. And then she wasn't there.

HELEN: It was more than a minute, Richard. She was gone. You didn't even know — how long, she was, at least as long as — you didn't even know, she was gone —

RICHARD: Helen —

HELEN: It was —

RICHARD: Don't go back there, please. This is meant to help you —

HELEN: Help me? How can you — it was ten minutes, at least —

RICHARD: Listen to me. Helen. Listen. I'm trying to tell you, the truth.

(She stops, hears this, looks at him, bewildered.)

HELEN: It was business? Just business?

RICHARD: *(Trying to keep her on track.)* I didn't betray you. There was no other woman. You were what I wanted. You were always what I wanted.

(She looks at him, taking this in, confused, then looks away.)

HELEN: If I could just drown in your return. If I could drown in the present. Maybe all the rest would make sense. Maybe all the moments could just be this moment.

(She looks at him. After a moment, she goes to him, and kisses him. The door to the house swings open, Nate appears.)

NATE: Mom?

(He sees them kissing and stops, startled. Helen takes a step backwards, and turns. They stare at each other.)

HELEN: Yes?

NATE: Oh I'm sorry, I, I — the last of the dishes are still, so I thought — to bring the rest, in inside so we could —

HELEN: It's all right, Nate. We can get them in the morning.

NATE: I can get them.

HELEN: You should go to bed. Where's Erica?

NATE: She's watching TV, in her room.

HELEN: You don't need to worry about the rest of the dishes. I'll take care of it, all right?

(He doesn't answer.)

HELEN: (Continuing.) It's fine, Nate. You go to bed.

(Nate stands in the doorway, for a moment. He goes, shutting the door behind him. Helen kisses Richard again, then, suddenly laughing like a girl, takes his hand and goes to the bathtub, and Richard turns on the water.)

RICHARD: What if they come out?

HELEN: I don't care if they do.

(He kisses her. She helps him to undress and get in, then goes to the table.)

HELEN: (Continuing.) Do you want a drink?

RICHARD: Yeah.

(She pours him a drink.)

RICHARD: (Beat.) Hey, are you coming?

HELEN: Yes.

(She turns and looks at Richard, who lies in the rising water, his eyes closed. She crosses, bringing him the drink, kisses him, and begins to get into the tub, as the lights fade.)

SCENE FIVE

The following morning. The air is bright. There is a large tarp covering the tub. The dinner table, now cleared of all dishes, remains in place. Lucy is there, alone. She looks around, confused. Nate comes out. He stops, when he sees her.

NATE: You're here.

LUCY: I got back last night, after midnight. Everyone seemed to be asleep. But the door was open, so I just — came in. And — went to bed.

(Nate starts to collapse the table and put it away.)

LUCY: *(Continuing.)* Have you seen Richard?

NATE: Oh, I, he left.

LUCY: Oh. Well, do you, do you know when he's coming back?

NATE: No, I don't know.

LUCY: Is he down at the lake?

NATE: I don't, I don't think so.

LUCY: He didn't sleep in our room last night.

NATE: *(Beat.)* Oh.

LUCY: And his stuff is gone. I mean, it's not in my room anymore, so I guess that's just, well, no surprise, huh. Anyway. I just wanted to tell him I'm going home, I don't know why I even bother, it seems polite. To say good-bye. Don't you think? Whatever. Did he say where he was going? *(Nate continues to move the table, and the chairs.)*

NATE: No. I I I don't know where Richard is. I maybe, may may — maybe Mom — I — I don't —

LUCY: It's OK, Nate. Serves me right, I should have known better than to get involved with any guy that fast, especially an older guy.

NATE: You couldn't know. What was going to happen. You just couldn't know.

LUCY: *(A beat.)* They're back together, aren't they?

NATE: *(Looks away.)* I don't know.

LUCY: I don't care. I mean, I just feel stupid. When things go like that, everything just gets so messy and hideous when it's not necessary! To drag me all the way up here, so he could get back together with his ex-wife? I mean, that's twisted, right? That's twisted!

NATE: Yes!

LUCY: I shouldn't have left last night. You kept telling me not to go, and I knew — I mean I knew, at that point, what the score was. And why hang around, right? That's what I thought, I don't need to hang around for this! But I still — I just —

NATE: I know.

LUCY: I know you do, I know.

(The back door opens, and Helen comes out.)

HELEN: Lucy. Good morning!

LUCY: Good morning. Um — do you know where Richard is?

HELEN: Has Nate told you about what happened last night?

LUCY: No, we just, I was looking for Richard.

HELEN: Oh, you didn't tell her? He left.

NATE: I told her.

LUCY: No, I mean, yes, he did say that. I just wondered if you knew when he'd be back. I would like to say good-bye to him.

HELEN: I'm sorry. You misunderstand me. He actually left. He decided this, coming here, was just too upsetting for everyone, at least for now. So he left.

LUCY: He left? You mean — left? Without his car?

HELEN: He caught a train back to Philadelphia. I assumed he tried to get hold of you, didn't he call?

LUCY: No.

HELEN: Maybe he tried and couldn't get through. The cell phones are awful up here. Anyway, I think he assumed you would need the car to drive back. I think that's fine, Nate. It is dirt, after all.

(Nate nods, and sets down the broom.)

LUCY: So —

HELEN: This has been, as you know, so complicated and difficult for all of us. Just overwhelming. So when he decided to go, so suddenly, I frankly understood it. I think he wanted to give everyone a little room. Including himself.

LUCY: So, he — he left.

HELEN: Yes.

LUCY: When Nate said he left, I just, I didn't understand that. OK. Well, um, can I, can I use your phone?

HELEN: Of course.

(Helen steps aside, as Lucy goes into the house. Nate watches, then looks at Helen.)

NATE: It's cold this morning.

HELEN: It is a little brisk. Here, let me warm you up.

(She goes and hugs him. He pushes her away. She looks at him. Erica comes out, still in pajamas, carrying a cup of coffee and a piece of toast.)

ERICA: Hey.

HELEN: Good morning.

ERICA: Is something going on?

HELEN: What do you mean?

ERICA: Well, that Lucy person's in the kitchen, she looks kind of bent out of shape.

(Lucy comes out, carrying a phone.)

LUCY: He's not answering his phone.

HELEN: Perhaps he turned it off.

LUCY: Well, what time did he leave?

HELEN: Eleven, eleven-thirty?

ERICA: Dad left? Where'd he go?

HELEN: I don't know.

ERICA: He left? Without saying good-bye?

HELEN: Back to Philadelphia, at least that's what he said.

ERICA: He left? Without saying good-bye?

HELEN: He didn't want to wake you up.

ERICA: *(Sudden.)* Oh, fuck him. Fucking asshole.

    (She goes into the house.)

LUCY: He left without saying good-bye?

HELEN: He said good-bye to Nate.

LUCY: He did?

    (She turns to Nate. There is a beat.)

NATE: Yes.

LUCY: Oh. 'Cause you didn't — I'm sorry. I'm just confused. Because before, you didn't —

NATE: *(Looking away.)* Mom took him to the train station.

LUCY: OK. Sure.

HELEN: I know, it's disorienting.

LUCY: It is, a bit.

HELEN: I told him — well what does it matter what I told him, he never did what I asked anyway. Is there anything I can do for you? Before you go?

LUCY: No, I'm sorry. This has just been — *(Beat.)* I'll go get my stuff.

    (She goes into the house, sudden. Helen looks at Nate.)

HELEN: It's all right, sweetheart.

    (Nate starts to cry. She goes to him. He pushes her away.)

NATE: Don't, don't.

HELEN: I know. It's so upsetting. Him coming at all has been hard on all of us. But listen to me, Nate. It's going to be alright again. It's going to be just like it was.

NATE: Is it?

HELEN: Yes, it is. Everything is fine.

    (Lucy enters, more upset, with the phone. Erica enters behind her, curious now.)

LUCY: You know, I just checked my messages and he didn't call.

HELEN: Didn't he?

LUCY: No he didn't, and I hope you don't think I'm nuts — but this just doesn't make sense.

ERICA: Nothing makes sense. Welcome to our lives. When you see Richard, please tell him to go fuck himself.

HELEN: Erica.

ERICA: No. It's fine. Who needs him. But I'll tell you, if he comes back and tries to take the house again, we are going to hammer him in court. Hammer him.

LUCY: What train did he take? I'm calling the station.

(She starts to dial. Helen crosses, quick, and takes the phone from her in an abrupt gesture. Lucy looks at her.)

HELEN: Look. You're working yourself up, over nothing. Everybody knows this was an extraordinary situation. Richard felt that he had pushed it as far as he could, and he needed to go. I'm sorry if you can't understand that. Other than that, I don't know what to say to you. I don't know you, and I don't care what you think.

ERICA: OK? Is that good enough for you?

LUCY: No, it's not.

ERICA: You've been dumped. You'll survive.

LUCY: This isn't about being dumped!

ERICA: I'm sure.

NATE: Leave her alone! She's not stupid, she's just — leave her alone!

(There is a momentary silence at this.)

ERICA: *(A dawning doubt.)* What are you so bent out of shape about?

NATE: Nothing happened! It's what Mom said! He's just gone! That's all, he's gone! I mean, just stop it! Everybody, just, God, this is, all of you — I can't, this is, please! It's done, you can't make it go back! It's, all of it is done. *(Beat.)* My head is all white.

(Helen looks at Lucy, then goes to Nate.)

HELEN: Come on, sweetheart, let me take you inside.

NATE: *(Yelling at her.)* Stay away from me! *(Beat.)* I'm sorry. I'm sorry. But God, you just can't touch me now, don't you see that?

ERICA: Mom?

HELEN: He's fine, Erica.

ERICA: What — what —

NATE: I didn't do it. You know that. I wouldn't. I just helped, after. It was too late, it was just too late. What else could I do? It wasn't her fault.

ERICA: *(Harsh.)* What wasn't?

HELEN: Erica, I think you should take your brother inside.

NATE: She knows, anyway! It wouldn't matter, Mom, she would know anyway.

(There is a terrible pause at this.)

ERICA: Know what? *(Quiet.)* Where is he?

NATE: *(Simple.)* What was I supposed to do? Mom? You were asleep. You fall asleep with the TV on. But someone had to help her, after. What else was I supposed to do? It was too late anyway. It was just too late.

ERICA: *(A beat.)* You helped her what?

NATE: It was too late!

(Erica sits, silent. There is a moment of silence.)

ERICA: Mom?

(Nate pulls the tarp off the bathtub; it is drenched in blood.)

HELEN: It didn't have to happen, Erica. I mean, it's not like I went looking for him. And believe me, he knew it would be a mistake to come back. But he couldn't let it go. You don't understand, you're too young, and frankly, I've tried to protect you from all of this. So many things you didn't know. My silence, everything you blame me for, that was protection, so no, you can't understand. He said, last night, that he wanted to step back into the center of his nature. That meant, all of it. All of us. Forgiving him, moving on. He wanted everything, so many men do. They want their crime and their forgiveness too, more than forgiveness, they want the earth itself to rise up and erase the worst of everything they do, no responsibility, action without consequence, everything is still theirs, that's what they want! And I'm not going to lie to you. Most of them get it. And it's a sin. The erasure of justice? We can't survive it. As a people. It has deformed us, this insistence that men, with their power and their selfishness and their cruelty can crawl the Earth and destroy everything, everything, and no one holds them to account. Justice? Do you know what kind of justice I was offered when he murdered my child? The police came, then, and ruled it an accident. To be told endlessly it was no one's fault. Last night I heard it all again, he wasn't responsible, he simply went into his head and that's why it happened. Because he was absorbed in the intricacies of his endlessly fascinating mind, his child disappeared in the wood, and then into the water, she disappeared from this Earth and he was not responsible. How could he help going into his head and worrying about nothing? It wasn't even nothing, to him, even now, it was still important to him, these things in his head, he was telling me, there was someone, at his work, looking to blame him for some loss of revenue, do these words mean anything? To anyone? *(Laughing.)* To him, they still did. He had justification. It wasn't his fault. He offered this to me — seriously — as something that might heal me! He was all concerned, at one time, in my rage I accused him of betraying me, I was hungry, for some absurd meaning, if he had fallen in love, perhaps, his passion led him and all of us astray, that was something, I thought, for a moment, years ago, that might have been a reality, something to explain the inexplicable, how can you let your child drown, before your eyes? How can you do it? And he took that lame hope from me, as a gift, no, there was no other woman! If there was any blame, it was mine. We should have gone through it together. I was somehow not womanly enough, the failure was mine, I should have risen from the tragedy like an angel and wiped his crime away from his brow. Like a mother. Well, I am a mother. Over time, all this time, that is what I have been, and there has been too much time given to me. You don't know how hard I prayed, year in and year out, for the rage and the bitterness to leave me, for it to grow into some larger meaning, I begged whatever is out there to reveal to me how to move on, I lived with nature, I cared for the children who were left to me as if they were life itself, I held them to me as protection against all of it and still there was nothing! You pray for justice and the gods laugh. You pray for peace and they abandon you. A moment's peace. He had it. That is what he brought here, to me. The sight of his peace. The yearning to be together. Again. To move forward. To leave it behind. Well, I gave him what he wanted. We finished it, together, the only way it could be finished. And I have no remorse. *(Then, to Lucy.)* Call the police. I don't care. I have my peace now, and God knows I've earned it.

(She goes into the house.)

ERICA: Nate? You helped her?

NATE: Yeah. I did. She came up to my room and she was covered in — and I went down, and he, he was —

ERICA: Oh my God.

NATE: We had to. Because Lea. You remember. How wild she was? She would like throw herself off the furniture, you had to follow her, she was always throwing herself into into the lake.

ERICA: What are you talking about?

NATE: *(Overlap.)* You and me, you didn't have to watch you and me! The lake scared me to, and you were born knowing how to swim but Lea — and he just let her run down the path! Like it was oh, we did it all the time, but only a fucking moron would let that kid run down to the lake, she was the one you didn't take your eyes off! And he, ten minutes, at least —

ERICA: Did Mom tell you this? That makes it OK to kill him? Is that what she said?

NATE: It's just true. Fuck it. We have to finish cleaning it up, now.

LUCY: We have to call the police.

ERICA: I'll do it. Nate don't. Don't touch anything. Don't clean anything.

LUCY: We have to do it now, Erica, right now!

ERICA: *(Overlap.)* I'm doing it! *(To Nate.)* If you try to cover it up it'll just be worse. This can't get any worse. But the cops will just think it's worse, everybody will think it's worse. So just don't, just don't clean anymore, OK?

NATE: You're going to call the cops?

ERICA: Of course we're calling the cops!

NATE: What are you going to tell them?

ERICA: I'm gonna tell them — you have to tell them what, happened —

NATE: I'm not talking to them. I'm not talking to anybody. I have to clean this.

(Nate pushes by them and goes to the hose.)

ERICA: I don't think that's a good idea!

LUCY: Just dial the phone, Erica, what are you waiting for?

ERICA: Would you give me a minute?

LUCY: We don't have a minute, this is murder!

ERICA: I'm aware of that! THERE'S BLOOD ALL OVER MY BACKYARD. This sucks. This is a nightmare.

NATE: You didn't even have to do it! You didn't have to do anything! I don't know what you're complaining about!

ERICA: What am I COMPLAINING ABOUT? Nate, I know you're only half with us most of the time, but I mean, you're kidding, right? You are just fucking KIDDING ME.

NATE: I'm not. You didn't have to do it. I mean, you might think about that.

ERICA: I DON'T WANT TO THINK.

NATE: Yeah, me neither, but then what you're left with? Is what you do. You can sit there, go ahead and sit there, you never had to do anything —

ERICA: Don't you fucking defend yourself —

NATE: *(Overlap.)* He was here. Naked. Covered in — and I did it. She said, and I just, I went down to the basement and got the garbage bags, and the twine, and the bricks —

ERICA: *(Overlap.)* Stop it, I don't want to know!

NATE: *(Overlap.)* His blood. Everywhere. My own — father — and I — drenched. Drenched! I had to pick him up, she couldn't even so I dragged him. To his own boat. And we, out there, on the lake. I did it. You didn't.

ERICA: What's your point, Nate? Are you fucking proud of yourself?

NATE: I'm just saying what happened. What I did, that you didn't. It makes us different now.

LUCY: Nate. It wasn't your fault.

NATE: *(Furious at her.)* I know it wasn't my fault! It happened because it had to happen! Because she — . And I did it. Because I'm such a good boy, I'm such a, whatever she said, I just, if she told me to chop him into little pieces, cook him up and have him for dinner, I would have done it! Why? Because I love her? No! He deserved it! They both deserve it! That's the next thing, isn't it?

LUCY: What?

NATE: I don't want to hurt anybody. But that's what, that's what —

LUCY: No no no —

NATE: Isn't it? Erica?

ERICA: You're crazy.

NATE: Am I?

LUCY: No, come on —

(Nate is focused on Erica, watching her figure it out.)

NATE: She showed me how to do it.

LUCY: *(Overlap.)* Nate. You don't want to hurt anybody.

NATE: She said, you have to help me. And the thing is, it's horrible, and there's so much, but once you say, I'm doing this, it's just something you're doing.

LUCY: *(Overlap.)* No no, it's not, you're not —

NATE: *(Overlap.)* It's not as hard as you think.

LUCY: *(Overlap.)* Listen to me, please, both of you —

NATE: *(Overlap.)* She's the same. She's just as bad, she's worse! She's like one of those animals who eats her young.

LUCY: Nate.

NATE: Shut up! That's the way it is, in nature. There isn't any justice. There's just the thing that comes next.

LUCY: Nobody thinks —

NATE: I said, shut the fuck up!

ERICA: I'm calling the police.

NATE: *(Grabs the phone from her.)* Why? This doesn't have anything to do with them. It doesn't mean anything if they do it. It's just television then. They think they know things out there, they don't know anything.

There's no justice, not even in their world. Is that what you want? A trial? Because I don't want that. I want this. It may not mean anything? But it's true. Don't you? Want to?

LUCY: Nate, come on. You don't know what you're saying now, we can we — *(She grabs his arm, to talk to him. He shoves her aside and turns back to Erica.)*

NATE: Both of them. It was always about, who was going to win. They took our lives from us! To satisfy their own, all of it, they were supposed to, our parents! And neither one of us ever even existed. Well, I exist now. It has to be both of them.

ERICA: No. No! I didn't want him to come back, it was too hard, but he — he wanted me. He came back. For me. She never, it was always you —

NATE: No —

ERICA: And now I don't have anyone. Fuck this! Just fuck it.
(She starts to go away from him. He suddenly grabs her.)

NATE: You have me.

ERICA: I know.

NATE: I love you more than anybody. More than her. I do.

ERICA: I know, Nate.

NATE: She was the one who took him from you.

ERICA: I know.

NATE: *(Quiet.)* I would do it, for you.

LUCY: Nate, stop it. Both of you. It doesn't have to keep going!

NATE: If it doesn't have to, then why does it?

LUCY: No no, listen to me —

NATE: We could do it. Together. We could finish it. It would be over.

LUCY: Listen — we can go. Now, right now, before something . . .

NATE: *(Laughing.)* Before something happens?

LUCY: Nate. Come on. Please. You don't have to do anything that you don't, in your heart you —
(He turns, furious, hits her in the stomach, hard. She hits the ground. He cocks his arm, about to strike her again.)

ERICA: Chill out, Nate. *(Then, to Lucy.)* You know, people been telling you for days that you don't belong here. What exactly is it gonna take for you to get the message?
(Lucy scrambles to her feet, then turns, and suddenly goes.)

NATE: Is she gone?

ERICA: Yeah.

NATE: Good.

(He looks out at the trees.)

NATE: *(Continuing.)* You know all those books?

ERICA: What books?

NATE: All those books people write. And then other people read.

ERICA: Oh, those books.

NATE: They're all full of shit. I mean, look at the trees!

ERICA: What about them?

NATE: They're red.

(Helen stands in the doorway. She steps out.)

HELEN: Is that person gone?

NATE: Yes. She's gone.

HELEN: Thank God. Now maybe we can have a little peace. Nate?

(She looks at the bathtub.)

NATE: I'll finish it, Mom.

HELEN: Thank you, sweetheart. You're such a good boy. Oh, I feel so much better! Your father suggested last night he should have made me leave long ago and I had to completely resist the urge to laugh in his face. I just mean. How could you leave a place like this? The earth is so beautiful here. How could you ever leave?

(She looks up at the trees, happy. Nate and Erica sit beside her on the steps of the porch.)

(The lights fade.)

END OF PLAY

THE SCENE

ORIGINAL PRODUCTION

The Scene was originally produced at Actors Theatre of Louisville, 30th Anniversary Humana Festival of New American Plays, made possible by a generous grant from The Humana Foundation, March 11 – April 2, 2006. It was directed by Rebecca Bayla Taichman and had the following cast:

CHARLIE . . . . Stephen Barker Turner*
LEWIS . . . . David Wilson Barnes*
CLEA . . . . Anna Camp*
STELLA . . . . Carla Harting*

Scenic Design . . . . Paul Owen
Costume Design . . . . Catherine F. Norgren
Lighting Design . . . . Tony Penna
Sound Design . . . . Matt Callahan
Properties Design . . . . Jennifer Dums
Fight Director . . . . Cliff Williams III
Stage Manager . . . . Brady Ellen Poole*
Production Assistant . . . . Danielle Teague-Daniels
Dramaturg . . . . Mervin P. Antonio
Casting . . . . Vince Liebhart
Directing Assistant . . . . Shirley Serotsky

* Member of Actors' Equity Association, the union of professional actors and stage managers of the United States.

Presented by special arrangement with The Gersh Agency.
Director underwritten by Ed Seigenfeld and Sharon Sparrow.

NEW YORK PRODUCTION

The Scene was originally produced at Second Stage Theatre. It was directed by Rebecca Bayla Taichman and had the following cast:

CHARLIE . . . . Tony Shalhoub
LEWIS . . . . Christopher Even Welch
CLEA . . . . Anna Camp
STELLA . . . . Patricia Heaton

Scenic Design . . . . Derek McLane
Costume Design . . . . Jeff Mahshie

Lighting Design . . . . Natasha Katz
Sound Design . . . . Martin Desjardins
Press . . . . Barlow Hartman
Casting . . . . Tara Rubin
Production Stage Manager. . . . . Kelly Hance
Stage Manager . . . . Shanna Spinello
Associate Artistic Director . . . . Christopher Burney
Production Manager . . . . Jeff Wild

Media sponsor: WNYC

CHARACTERS:
  CLEA, early 20s, a voracious party girl
  CHARLIE, 40s, a bitterly funny, out-of-work actor
  LEWIS, 40s, his best friend, shrewd and wry
  STELLA, 40s, Charlie's wife, funny, loving and capable

SET
Several locations around New York: a party, Charlie's apartment, Lewis's
apartment, Clea's apartment.

ACT I
SCENE ONE

Charlie, Lewis, and Clea. A corner of a party, loud music, talk, laughter. Charlie and Lewis hold drinks in their hands. Lewis is clearly interested in Clea; Charlie is not.

CLEA: I love the view here.

LEWIS: *(Surreptitiously checking out her butt.)* Awesome.

CLEA: I mean, mind-blowing, right, it's just so surreal, the lights and the water, it's like unbelievable. I love this loft! Do you know the guy who lives here? He must be incredible. Because I have just no idea, I came with a friend, who knows, like, everybody and I know she told me it was somebody in the fashion industry who I just so had never heard of, my bad. 'Cause he's like, what, like clearly so talented, this place is so beautiful. The water, the air. It's just so surreal.

CHARLIE: How is that surreal?

CLEA: What?

CHARLIE: The air and the water, you said that before, that you found it surreal. How is air and water surreal?

CLEA: Oh you know, it's — just — wow! You know.

CHARLIE: *(To Lewis, annoyed now.)* You want a refill? What is that, a mojito?

LEWIS: Yeah, great.

CHARLIE: How about you, I'm sorry, what's your name again?

CLEA: Clea.

CHARLIE: Would you like a mojita, Clea?

CLEA: No no, I don't drink. My mother was an alcoholic. I mean, she was a wonderful woman and she really loved me but it's like alcohol is so deadly, I mean at these parties sometimes when I'm at a party like this? To stand around and watch everyone turn into zombies around me? It just really triggers me, you know? You go ahead. I mean, that's just for me, I don't impose that on people or anything.

LEWIS: I mean, it's not like, I'm not like a huge drinker, or —

CLEA: Oh good, because you know, I was at this party last week it was such a scene, there were so many people there. You know it was this young director, he's got like seven things going at once, Off Broadway. Can you imagine, the energy level of someone like that? Anyway, it was his birthday party, and they rented out the top two floors of this loft in Chelsea, it was this wild party, like surreal, and then at one point in the evening? I just realized, that everyone was just totally shit-faced. I mean I don't want to be reactive in situations like that, I don't like to judge people on a really superficial level or anything but it was kind of horrifying. I mean, not that I — you know, drink, you should drink! Enjoy yourselves!

(Lewis and Charlie look at their drinks.)

CHARLIE: Yeah, well, I think I'm gonna head out. Nice to meet you. "Clea."

CLEA: Oh. Whoa. I mean — what does that mean?

CHARLIE: *(Annoyed now.)* What does what mean?

CLEA: "Clea." I mean, "Clea." I mean, whoa —

CHARLIE: Is there a problem?

CLEA: You tell me. You're the one who's all like, "Clea." "Nice to meet you."

CHARLIE: What are you even talking about?

CLEA: Nothing. It just struck me as a little edgy, that's all.

LEWIS: You want me to get those drinks? Why don't I do that? I mean you got to at least talk to Nick, he's gonna show up.

CHARLIE: I'm not talking to Nick. I'm leaving. *(To Clea.)* "Nice to meet you — " is "edgy — "

CLEA: Well, you're totally giving off a vibe here, I'm not making that up. And that is so fine, I mean I do not judge.

LEWIS: Look, Nick's here. Hey Nick —

CHARLIE: I'm not talking to — "A vibe?"

CLEA: Oh is "vibe" like a totally uncool word, in your little tribe —

LEWIS: Hey, Nick!

CHARLIE: No no, it's got a real seventies charm that I find particularly captivating in someone who wasn't born until nineteen eighty-two —

CLEA: Oh, I'm young, well, I guess you're not, huh, that's really the problem isn't it? *(A beat.)*

LEWIS: Whoa.

CHARLIE: There's no problem, Clea. I don't know you. I came by my friend's loft — his name is Edward, by the way, and he's an actor, he's not in "the fashion industry," he's a very fine stage actor even though he's not doing seven Off-Broadway shows at once —

LEWIS: Look, look, look —

CLEA: Yeah, whatever —

CHARLIE: I'm here because my friend asked me to come by, and I did that and now I'm going. Nice to meet you.

CLEA: If there isn't a problem, what are you so bent out of shape about?

CHARLIE: You're really a fucking piece of work.

LEWIS: Charlie.

CHARLIE: What? She's a fucking idiot!

LEWIS: Hey, whoa, are you —

CLEA: No. It's OK. There were, obviously, there were some things said here, that maybe rubbed you the wrong way and I am totally willing to talk about that. I mean I apologize for that. But you were like jumping all over me because I said "surreal," and I just started to feel stupid. So I apologize. If I was edgy or something.

LEWIS: Look, it's OK.

CLEA: Maybe I should get some vodka or something.

CHARLIE: I thought you didn't drink.

CLEA: I don't! I mean, I really don't. Hardly ever.

LEWIS: You want me to get you a vodka?

CLEA: Would you?

LEWIS: Sure. *(He goes. After a minute, Charlie sighs, makes another move to desert her.)*

CHARLIE: Listen, I really do have to . . .

CLEA: I totally understand. This is your friend's party, you should go, go, you know a ton of people here probably. You need to talk to Nick, that's clearly a big thing, or something.

CHARLIE: Nick's an asshole.

CLEA: Whatever.

CHARLIE: Look — are you here alone?

CLEA: No! God, no, I came with a friend, I don't know where she is. She's like the total scene-machine.

CHARLIE: Can I ask — I mean — Why do you talk like that?

CLEA: *(Defensive but firm.)* I talk the way I talk. I'm not apologizing for that. I mean, I apologize for before, acting like a little edgy, but language is a totally idiosyncratic and very personal, very organic function of you know, someone's humanity, so I'm not apologizing for my language.

CHARLIE: OK.

CLEA: OK what?

CHARLIE: OK nothing. That's actually a fairly coherent and legitimate point.
(Lewis returns with three drinks. He hands them around.)

CLEA: *(Continuing.)* Thanks.
(She downs the drink. Lewis and Charlie watch her.)

CLEA: *(Continuing.)* Wow! That is . . . good. Ah. Wow. Mmmm.

LEWIS: *(Cautious.)* Should I get you another?

CLEA: No, I just want to feel this one first. I never drink. My mother was an alcoholic so I have to be like totally careful.

LEWIS: So where are you from, Clea?

CLEA: Ohio. Isn't that hilarious? Plus I just got here, like, what, six months ago? It's a lot, I mean, to get used to. But it's so alive, just walking down the street, the energy. I'm like from, you know, the middle of nowhere, and I land here and it's so much more intense than even you think. Not like I'm some sort of cornball. But more like I'm alert, you know, really on fire with how amazing it is to be here. Because my experience, already, and don't take this personally, but people here are like not awake. To what — I don't want to sound judgmental because that is so not what I'm about but like what I mean is, I had this job interview yesterday, or the day be — no yesterday, I'm pretty sure, I had this amazing opportunity to work on this talk show, not that I think television is really a good place for anyone but I'm like trying to be open, really open, and anyway the agency sends me in to talk to this person who is like, she does something, I can't even tell what it is, for this talk show, like these people go on the television and interview movie stars or you know important people. She's the person who books, you know, she books people.

LEWIS: Really? 'Cause —

CHARLIE: Yeah, so you went in —

CLEA: Yeah, so I'm walking around this television studio, and there's like lights and you know "people" and everyone is so phony and intense, you just want to puke, like, what is supposed to be going on in a place like that? It's just like a void, with a lot of color in it. Totally bizarre. And this woman is so into it. Her name is like "Stella." And everything is just do this, be perfect.

LEWIS: Stella?

CLEA: Right? Right? And she could not be more like a Nazi priestess or something, she is so worked up over these phone lists and highlighting in blue and mint green who needs to get returned, who hasn't returned, just utter crap — oh and on top of it all, she's in the middle of one of those adoptions, she's one of those infertile women who is like adopting an abandoned baby from China and those calls go on the special list, like lists are the Holy Grail to this total Nazi, like the lists and the movie stars and this invisible baby in the middle of China is like, you know, life to her. And I'm like — look around you! This city is so alive and you're just like — I don't know. Wow I think that vodka just hit, I so don't drink. Do you know what I mean? About being alive, I mean?

LEWIS: Uh — you're alive, but Stella —

CLEA: Was totally not.

LEWIS: You know, I should tell you that I think I know that person

CLEA: Stella? You know like, Stella the Nazi priestess from TV Land? Really?

LEWIS: Yeah, I, I think I do.

CLEA: Come on. Like, that is so wild. How do you know her?

CHARLIE: I'm married to her.

(There is a pause while Clea takes this in. Blackout.)

SCENE TWO

Stella, Charlie and Lewis, doing shots of tequila in Stella and Charlie's apartment. They trade off the bottle, and speak on top of each other.

STELLA: *(Pouring a shot.)* What did she call me? A "Nazi priestess"?

CHARLIE: A frigid Nazi priestess —

LEWIS: Infertile. An infertile —

CHARLIE: It was "frigid."

STELLA: Stop it, God, you guys — Why didn't you tell me about this last night?

CHARLIE: You were asleep. Did you want me to wake you up and tell you I met some girl at a party who said you were a frigid Nazi priestess?

LEWIS: It wasn't frigid!

STELLA: Why are you defending her?

LEWIS: I'm not! I'm just striving for a shred of accuracy or something —

CHARLIE: Frigid.

LEWIS: Infertile.

CHARLIE: Frigid —

LEWIS: Infertile!

CHARLIE: Frigid —

STELLA: *(Overlap.)* Stop it, stop it! What a bitch. I mean, I was incredibly nice to this stupid person, I mean she was patently stupid and I was so nice, and now I find out she's what, offended, she's morally offended by my phone lists and my highlighters? Everyone in New York has phone lists, how are you supposed to remember who you have to call back? And excuse me but having blue and green highlighters makes me a Nazi, and the fact that I don't kill Jews is irrelevant? She sounds like a genius. She can hardly speak, as I recall. She looks great in black and she can't speak the English language, she'll do just fine in New York.

CHARLIE: I shouldn't have told you.

STELLA: Why shouldn't you tell me? Why didn't you tell me when you got home, you met someone who called me a frigid —

LEWIS: Infertile! Infertile!

STELLA: Why were you even talking to this stupid person —

CHARLIE: She was interesting, in a vapid way.

STELLA: She was a moron who looks good in black.

LEWIS: She wasn't a moron. She's pretty.

STELLA: Oh, for heaven's sake. I've had such a shitty day. With my highlighters, me and my highlighters trying to take over the world and buy Chinese babies for some sinister fertility ritual. Like it's better to leave them in orphanages. Children all over the world who need homes and if you decide to take one in, it must be because you're some frigid crazy workaholic bitch who wasn't woman enough to, you know, have her own.

CHARLIE: Stop! Stella. Just stop, OK?

STELLA: Sorry. Sorry, Lewis.

LEWIS: It's OK.

STELLA: Are there chips? Maybe some chips would cheer me up. Did you go to the grocery store?

CHARLIE: No.

STELLA: Oh, Charlie, come on — I have to work all day, trying to take over the world with my highlighters, couldn't you at least go to the grocery store?

LEWIS: I'll go to the corner and get some chips.

STELLA: Would you?

LEWIS: Absolutely.

STELLA: Thank you, Lewis. You are so nice to me.

LEWIS: I'll get the chips. (*He stands grabs his coat and goes. There is a moment of silence.*)

STELLA: I had a horrible day.

CHARLIE: I know.

STELLA: That idiot not showing. Not your idiot. I'm moving onto my idiot. Who didn't show. All the shit I had to go through to get her to do us, six dozen white lilies in her dressing room, do you know what that many lilies smells like? It's enough to truly knock you out, like a disease, that many flowers. And I'm not even talking about all the stupid candy we had to buy. M&Ms. Reese's Cups. Twix. Why do these people think it's so cool to eat bad chocolate? Could someone, and I mean, I literally had to turn her fucking dressing room into a kind of physical representation of a complete psychotic break, lilies and bad chocolate and an EXERCISE MACHINE — she was only supposed to be in there for an hour and a half, and she needed her own STAIRMASTER, with the chocolate, what's the plan, to eat the mounds of chocolate, while you're ON the stairmaster? Turns out there was no plan, because — she didn't show.

CHARLIE: You told me. A couple times.

STELLA: I told you eight times. I'm turning into one of those people who say things over and over and then you have to tell them so kindly, yes you told me, like they've gone senile — this happened to my mother, after she turned fifty, she told the same story over and over and over again, it was so dreary — it was like oh, and now Mom's gone insane, she's not just a pathetic nut, now she's a boring pathetic nut, telling the same story, over and over and over again —

CHARLIE: Stella. Have a drink.

STELLA: I'm half smashed already. That idiot didn't show. She did not show!

CHARLIE: You told me this morning she wasn't going to show. I mean, there's no real surprise here, is there? This is the fourth time —

STELLA: Yes, it is the fourth time, it is the fourth time she's fucked us and they insist that I book her anyway! And then it's my fucking fault we have a hole in the schedule. And there's not even a hole, I back us up every time with that idiot who makes the low-carb pasta dishes, why do people believe that? Low-carb pasta? Why do they —

CHARLIE: Stella —

STELLA: But it's so, demeaning, to put that on television, it's just demeaning. These people are all such liars. Low-carb pasta? And it's pathetic, these women sitting out there, so hungry for this specific lie, you can eat pasta and still lose weight, that's like pathetic, it's not pathetic, it's sad, if you think about it too long, it is so sad all those women sitting out there in the house, their yearning for life to be just that little bit easier. It's probably one of the few things they have to look forward to, a nice plate of pasta with a little red sauce — only most of them, they don't go for the sensible red sauce, they go for the alfredo, or the carbonnara, I actually had to do a low-fat carbonnara show once.

CHARLIE: I know.

STELLA: Oh God. I want to have compassion for these people, I feel bad —

CHARLIE: Stella —

STELLA: That they think this is a cool thing to do with their time, go and be the studio audience for a stupid talk show!

CHARLIE: Honey —

STELLA: Because they think it means something, to be on television — Only you weren't, really, you just sat there while someone else got to be on television. It's so sad. It's so so sad.

CHARLIE: No more tequila for you.

STELLA: I'm fine.

CHARLIE: Well, I'm suicidal.

STELLA: But I don't really feel sorry for them.

CHARLIE: You shouldn't!

STELLA: Oh my God of course I should. These are people who deserve compassion, these fat people who feel terrible about themselves because we're the ones, we're constantly putting on television things like low-fat carbonnara, low-fat foie gras, like this is some kind of good idea, to rip the pleasure and essence out of everything, that's how horrible it is to be fat. I mean these people didn't ask to be fat! And they're just surrounded by a culture — everything, everything — tells them they're worthless because they're fat! If that's not worthy of compassion, what is?

CHARLIE: Stupid people are destroying this planet. I don't have to have compassion for that.

STELLA: Low-fat foie gras. You know that's coming. That's just, out there somewhere, someone's going to try to stuff some poor duck full of low-fat corn, and tofu. You just know it.

(Charlie laughs. Stella laughs. He kisses her.)

CHARLIE: You need to take a day off.

STELLA: Oh, God, you think?

(They continue kissing. It starts to heat up. Charlie tries to take off Stella's shirt. Laughing, she pushes him away.)

STELLA: (Continuing.) Stop it, Charlie! Lewis is going to come back any minute. Good heavens.

CHARLIE: What did you say? "Good heavens?"

STELLA: I said let go of my shirt!

CHARLIE: I'm sure Lewis would love to see you without your shirt on —

STELLA: Oh my God. No more tequila for you.

(She takes the bottle from him.)

CHARLIE: You should have come to that party with us last night. I mean, it was horrible, and boring and a complete waste of time, there was no one to talk to other than a bunch of feckless drunks and this idiot girl, plus everyone was about fifteen years younger than me, so I felt like a freak —

STELLA: Yes, I should have come, it sounds terrific.

CHARLIE: I know! It's ridiculous. But rich people's apartments are so strangely comforting. This guy Edward's hooked up with is some sort of gazillionaire, this place is freakishly opulent. Heated tiles in the bathroom, a fucking Picasso on the wall. Not a good one, but it was a real Picasso, why is it that real art makes real people feel phony? Real clothes, too. This guy knows how to dress. Edward's taken to wearing silk.

STELLA: Edward?

CHARLIE: Right? It looked good on him. He looked good. He looked rich. The whole place was so, we were so high up. I mean, really, in the stars. I love that about New York, when you get to go to one of those parties way above the rest of the city, there's something so surreal about it. Not surreal. Oh God. I did not mean surreal.

STELLA: It actually does sound kind of surreal.

CHARLIE: No no. No. Let's be precise. What's surreal, if anything, is one's internal state in a situation like that. Everyone acts like surreal is some sort of definition, an image can be surreal, water or or or air, how can that be surreal? Water and air, that's the definition of real. Surreal is more the connection. Or not.

STELLA: What are you talking about?

CHARLIE: *(Laughing at himself.)* I have nooo idea.

STELLA: So, did you talk to Nick?

CHARLIE: I haven't been to a party like that since I did that sit com. Remember, when we were stuck out in L.A., and we had to keep going to all those parties in the hills —

STELLA: Those parties were hideous. You hated those parties.

CHARLIE: The food was great at those parties. And the flowers, also great, and the pools —

STELLA: All those people constantly sucking up —

CHARLIE: But they were sucking up to me.

STELLA: Oh my God. You hated every second of that —

CHARLIE: I did not hate everything.

STELLA: So tell me what Nick said.

CHARLIE: You know what we should do, Stell? We should take a trip. We should blow out the bank account and go somewhere great, Paris, or Saint Petersburg, Florence, stay at the Four Seasons, eat incredible food, wallow in bed, buy you expensive earrings, drink wine on some gorgeous town square somewhere —

STELLA: What's the matter, Charlie?

CHARLIE: Nothing's the matter! People take vacations, Stell. Come on. It would be so great to get out of this place for just a week. It would just be fun. Couldn't you use a little fun? Not thinking about all those lunatics for a whole week. Una Settamana a Firenze. A week in Florence. The Uffizi. Wine on the Piazza.

STELLA: Stop it.

CHARLIE: I'm not going to stop it. The Medici Chapel.

STELLA: Charlie, we can't just —

CHARLIE: Sure we can. We could go for two weeks. Possiamo andare per due settimane Leather gloves. Gorgeous earrings. Joilli, sono mola costosi Botticelli.

STELLA: *(Laughing.)* This is not — it's just not —

CHARLIE: Yes it is. It is. Say yes. Say yes. Say "si." Say, "si, Charlie . . ."

(He starts to kiss her. She laughs and kisses him back. It starts to heat up. Lewis calls from the hallway.)

LEWIS: *(Calling.)* Can I come back now?

CHARLIE: Vada Via! Go away!

STELLA: Charlie . . .

CHARLIE: Go away! Go away!

STELLA: It's fine, I'm done melting down. I need some food, I have to eat something.

(She stands, goes to the door, and opens it. Lewis brings in chips.)

LEWIS: I didn't know what kind. They had all these different flavor nachos. Like, fake guacamole and fake ranch, and fake chili something, fake onion something . . .

(He hands them all out.)

STELLA: Oh God this is so nice, and horrifying at the same time. You are so nice to just buy all these chips for me.

(She smiles at him.)

CHARLIE: I'm starving. We should order something real.

STELLA: *(Eating chips.)* So did Nick even show up at Ed's stupid party?

LEWIS: Yeah, he was there.

STELLA: Nick was there? So what did he say, how did it go?

CHARLIE: *(Slight beat.)* I didn't talk to him.

STELLA: What?

CHARLIE: I didn't get a chance.

STELLA: You didn't talk to him?

CHARLIE: I didn't stay that long.

STELLA: But that's why you went.

CHARLIE: I wasn't in the right mood.

STELLA: What kind of "mood" do you have to be in to —

CHARLIE: Oh for God's sake —

STELLA: Oh for God's sake, what? *(Beat.)* Charlie?

CHARLIE: I didn't talk to him. I didn't want to talk to him, so I didn't talk to him.

STELLA: Well, that's just brilliant.

LEWIS: Are you hungry? Maybe I should get some like real food.

STELLA: Yeah maybe you should.

CHARLIE: No, don't go, you don't have to —

STELLA: Yes, go, Lewis —

CHARLIE: We're not getting into this.

STELLA: We're not?

LEWIS: It wasn't the right moment, Stella, it really wasn't. Nick was like surrounded by all these people and to even get to him was just —

CHARLIE: *(To Lewis.)* Do not excuse me to my own wife!

STELLA: Well that's really nice.

CHARLIE: We are not talking about this, Stella!

STELLA: You can tell me about the person who called me a frigid Nazi priestess but you can't —

CHARLIE: There's nothing to tell. He showed up. I was in a bad mood, so I didn't talk to him.

STELLA: Well then you have to call him —

CHARLIE: I'm not calling Nick —

STELLA: He's got a pilot, Charlie —

CHARLIE: I know all about that, Stella. You've told me about —

STELLA: Oh don't do that —

LEWIS: Listen, you guys, maybe —

STELLA: He loves you. You have to remind him —

CHARLIE: Nick does not —

STELLA: You went to high school with him! You were best friends for —

CHARLIE: Oh my God. We were never, ever —

STELLA: Yes you were and you're a terrific actor, he knows how good you are, he knew you when you were —

CHARLIE: *(Bitter.)* When I was working?

STELLA: *(Unflinching.)* Yes. When you were working. A lot. You're a wonderful actor, Charlie, come on, you have to fight for yourself —

CHARLIE: Talking to Nick at a party is not going to get him to give me a part on his pilot!

STELLA: Well, if you don't talk to him he's certainly not going to give you a part, I can guarantee you —

CHARLIE: Oh yeah he really is desperate to have people he knew in a previous life suck up to him at parties —

STELLA: *(Firm.)* People like that, Charlie. These people, these TV people like it when you suck up — they like it —

CHARLIE: Oh. That's why I should do it —

STELLA: You should do it because you need a fucking job —

CHARLIE: *(Overlap.)* Because sucking up to assholes so that you can work in television is clearly something that's worked out so well for you —

STELLA: It's certainly worked out well for you, since I pay all the bills around here.

(Beat.)

LEWIS: You guys want some chips? These Cool Ranch chips are surprisingly . . .

CHARLIE: Shut up, Lewis!

STELLA: Could you please stop taking this out on Lewis? He is not the problem here.

CHARLIE: I'm well aware.

STELLA: *(Beat, then.)* Nick —

CHARLIE: *(Strained.)* Nick doesn't have a pilot. They just say that, people run around this fucking city saying things like "he has a pilot," "he has a go picture," "it's got a green light," when it's all just crap, it's just not even, it's lying taken to it's natural conclusion, these people are lying to make themselves feel better and they don't even know that they're lying and then everybody else around starts to tell the same lie and it's never true. That's the fucking punch line. Everybody's running around like psychotic sheep, bleating, "He has a pilot! He has a pilot — "

STELLA: He does have a pilot.

CHARLIE: Oh, God —

STELLA: You need a job!

CHARLIE: I know I need a job!

STELLA: Why would it kill you —

CHARLIE: I don't know, Stella!

STELLA: You just have to talk to him at a party —

CHARLIE: *(Furious.)* I am not talking to Nick! I'm not talking to that asshole! Do you understand me? I am not talking to Nick.
(He goes. Stella and Lewis look at each other, stunned. Blackout.)

SCENE THREE

Clea and Lewis, in Lewis' apartment. There is a cheese plate on a table.

LEWIS: Can I get you a drink? Vodka, you're a vodka girl, right?

CLEA: Water would be fantastic. Just a glass of water. I really don't drink.

LEWIS: Oh I know, I just, at Edward's party the other night you were like, you know —

CLEA: I was not drunk. At all. I hope you don't think that. Because I totally —

LEWIS: No no. I just meant you had one or two, so I thought that "no drinking" thing was not like a hard-and-fast rule or anything.

CLEA: *(Indignant.)* Is this a problem for you? Is it like important to you that I drink? Because that is so not something I feel comfortable with.

LEWIS: *(Alarmed.)* No! Oh my God of course not!

CLEA: I mean I asked for a glass of water and you're turning this into some major moral crisis here.

LEWIS: No —

CLEA: And I completely object to being called a "Vodka Girl." I mean, I told you before, my mother is an alcoholic so it's just not something I can be casual about, and for you to like insinuate, whatever, that I was drunk or something at that party —

LEWIS: No no, that's not what I meant at all. It's just, when you said "water," I just — it doesn't seem . . .

CLEA: Doesn't seem what, like you could get me drunk on water? Do you find like, drunk women attractive?

LEWIS: *(Sad.)* I was just, no! — I was just going to say that water doesn't seem festive. It seems so plain. I know everybody drinks it now, out of bottles and everything, but it just always to me it just seems so — plain.

CLEA: Plain is good. Plain is strong. Water is the strength of the earth. I don't find that "plain." I find that inspiring.

LEWIS: I know. I know! *(Beat.)* Let me get you a glass of water.
(He goes, to get her water.)

CLEA: Wait a minute. I'm sorry. I'm sorry, I'm a little, reactive. You're right, I said I'd come over for a drink and water, it's just not nice or something, I apologize. I know you're trying to be real nice and I'd love a vodka. I had a real ridiculous day, vodka is actually an excellent idea. Maybe put some ice in it.

LEWIS: OK.

(He goes off. She looks around the apartment, calls after him.)

CLEA: So. How's your friend the Nazi priestess?

LEWIS: *(Calling back.)* Oh, she's, you know, she's really not that bad.

(Lewis reenters with a glass of vodka, and ice. He hands it to her.)

CLEA: I know! I feel so terrible, I was totally exaggerating that interview I had and the whole thing was like, you know, just the sort of thing you say when you're not thinking!

LEWIS: Well, you didn't know —

CLEA: *(Sparkling now.)* No, but your friend did! And he just let me keep going! It was just like a little hostile, you know. To let me go on like that. I was like, ouch! Got a little problem in the sack with the old wife, maybe?

LEWIS: No, no — not at all — they're really tight, they've been together —

CLEA: Oh totally, I didn't mean —

LEWIS: Forever! Fourteen years or something. And they're adopting this baby. They're great.

CLEA: Hey, what do I know. *(She downs her drink.)* Oh. Wow. Mmm. That is so — wow.

LEWIS: *(Disturbed now.)* He was just tense, that night. About other stuff.

CLEA: Look — don't treat me like I'm stupid. I mean, I think I know the difference between tension and hostility. So it's not like I'm stupid.

LEWIS: I don't think you're stupid!

CLEA: Well, you're acting kind of —

LEWIS: No, no —

CLEA: Because I really object to that. A lot of people treat me like I'm some sort of flake because I look a certain way, and that is just, I don't want to sound like some hideous feminist, but I will not be treated like a stupid person. I want to be clear on that.

LEWIS: God, no! I wouldn't have asked you to come over, if I thought —

CLEA: Well, good. Because I respect what you are saying, but I'm just, you know, your friend has like a lot of angry energy. Which I like! I mean, it's not like I'm saying that's a bad thing, if he's married to a screaming woman who is like obsessed with phone lists and highlighters —

LEWIS: She's really nice —

CLEA: Oh totally. I so totally get that. I'm just saying. I don't judge him if he's hostile about it.

(There is an awkward pause.)

LEWIS: I'm gonna get myself a drink. Can I refresh that for you? You know what, I'm just going to bring the bottle.

(He goes. Clea considers the cheese plate for a moment. Lewis reenters, pouring himself a stiff drink, and watches her.)

LEWIS: *(Continuing.)* Would you like a piece of cheese, or —

CLEA: Oh God no. I am totally on a diet. Food is like disgusting to me.

LEWIS: It is?

CLEA: Oh my God, are you kidding? Most of the things people put in their mouths are like totally just like eating death. That's how bad our food is for us. Do you not know this? They proved, somebody proved that eating is killing people. And that if you eat like hardly anything? Just like lettuce and maybe a few vegetables or something, every day, that could make you live to be like a hundred and fifty years old. This is true, I read about it in *The New York Times*.

LEWIS: Eating —

CLEA: Is terrible for you. Don't do it.

LEWIS: Wow.

CLEA: Isn't it?

LEWIS: Yeah, that's — 'cause everything I've heard before this, you know, food is considered to be life-sustaining.

CLEA: Well, except didn't you suspect that it was probably bad for you? All those people getting fat, all over America, just like buying food from grocery stores or going into restaurants where they give you these portions, and everything has chemicals in it, or who knows what, who knows what they put in our food anymore.

LEWIS: Wow. Not eating makes you live forever. Who, uh, knew.

CLEA: Well, I know it sounds weird but . . . *(Suddenly spooked.)* You know what? Forget it. I'm sorry. This is, I should go —

LEWIS: No! Why?

CLEA: I don't feel right, this just doesn't feel right.

LEWIS: Come on, you just got here! Have another drink —

CLEA: I don't really drink. I'm feeling embarrassed now, that I have to keep telling you that.

LEWIS: Please. I really like you. I, I want you to stay. Please.

CLEA: You just want to sleep with me.

LEWIS: What — that is — no!

CLEA: You don't want to sleep with me?

LEWIS: I didn't say that —

CLEA: See? This just happens to me all the time. Just, everyone just wants to sleep with me. Every guy I meet, it's just, I don't know what to do about it — because I am like, a very sensitive person —

LEWIS: I didn't just — invite you over here for sex, if that's what you think —

CLEA: It is what I think! It is!

LEWIS: No, no. No, no no — no —

CLEA: Oh, please —

LEWIS: No! I really like you. I think you're really interesting. I do.

CLEA: It's just, everybody just falls in love with me all the time. So many guys are just obsessed, and I — I mean, I'm just overwhelmed. I'm from Ohio, it's different there. I feel very out of control here.

(There is a long pause while Lewis tries to figure out what to do next.)

LEWIS: Would you like a glass of water, or something?

CLEA: Maybe some vodka, I don't know. I'm kind of tense.

(He nods, and pours her a drink. He hands it to her. She holds it.)

LEWIS: Here, sit down. Come on, sit down.

CLEA: It's just been a very confusing day.

LEWIS: What happened?

CLEA: I don't want to talk about it.

LEWIS: *(Nice.)* Come on. I'm interested.

CLEA: *(Sudden.)* Would you like to kiss me?

LEWIS: *(A beat.)* Is this a trick question?

CLEA: You just, you seem like a really nice person, and I would really like it. If you would kiss me. If you're interested.

LEWIS: Yes, I'm interested! But I don't want to — you know —

CLEA: Do you think I'm a freak, or something? Because I've been freaking out here?

LEWIS: No, you just said that you were overwhelmed by men showing too much sexual interest in you, so I —

CLEA: I know, I know, I did just say that. But I would really like it if you would kiss me. I just think it might make me feel better, or — forget it —

LEWIS: No! No. No! It's OK. Really.

(He takes a long drink, sets his drink down, leans in carefully, and kisses her.)

LEWIS: *(Continuing.)* How's that?

CLEA: It's nice.

(She kisses him again. They start making out. There is a knock at the door. They ignore it for a while, but the knocking continues.)

LEWIS: Go away!

CHARLIE: Hey Lewis! You in there?

CLEA: Oh my God, is that your friend?

CHARLIE: Come on, you got to let me in, man —

LEWIS: Go away, Charlie —

(She pushes away from him.)

CLEA: No, it's fine, it's fine — you have to let him in, please, he's your friend! I'm fine! Let him in.

(Lewis goes to the door, and opens it. Charlie enters, carrying a script.)

CHARLIE: I saw that shit head Nick. I went and had fucking lunch with that fucking shit head.

(He sees Clea.)

CLEA: Hi.

CHARLIE: Oh. Hi!

(He is not happy to see her.)

LEWIS: Clea just came over for a —

(Lewis tips his head toward the open door, indicating that he would like Charlie to leave. Charlie railroads over him, not noticing.)

CHARLIE: That fuck head. I said, did I not say, he is a fuck head? I told her that this would be a waste of my fucking time. I told everyone. Did I not? Did I not? What is this, vodka?

(He picks it up and uncorks it, then proceeds to drink from the bottle as he rants.)

CHARLIE: *(Continuing.)* Because he is a fuck. You know this to be true. I mean, in high school he was a fuck, and in college, he was a fuck, and time is not a friend to people like that. I mean, it's not like they mellow. It's not like they ripen, like a good bottle of wine! No no no, Nick is still Nick, only more so. And now someone has actually told him that they are going to make his fucking pilot, which was just what Nick needed to really put the final touches on his complete lack of character! Give him a shred of power over hopeless and desperate people, that'll really make him shine! Not that I even believe it. I don't give a shit how many people say it. I do not believe that they are going to make his fucking pilot! Which by the way, he gave to me, to read, so on the sidewalk, outside the restaurant, after our cappuccinos, he took off and I opened it up and I read it, and I'm sure you'll be stunned to hear that it is utter mindless, soulless, uninspired, unoriginal, bereft, soul-sucking crap. Which is the only thing that makes me think he might actually be telling the truth. The fact that his fucking pilot is so irredeemably awful, such a complete expression of the bankruptcy of the American character, that alone argues for the shred of a possibility that he is flirting with the truth for once in his life, with his assertion that they are going to make his astonishingly shitty pilot. It is so bad, there actually is a possibility that they're going to make it. Against all my better judgment, I truly have to concede that.

CLEA: Wow.

CHARLIE: Oh you have no idea. This is the tip of the iceberg. This day was, I actually had lunch with that asshole at a place called "Grind". "Grind." Next thing you know they're going to be calling restaurants things like "Hot," "Wet," "Fuck Me," someday we are all going to be forced to have lunch with assholes at some restaurant called "Fuck Me." Nick of course is on his cell phone for a full five minutes before he can even say hello. Five minutes of the finger in the air, twitching — *(He sticks his finger in the air, twitches it.)* While I sit there grinning, like a SCHMUCK, it's OK, man, I know you got to hang on this endless phone call 'cause you're so fucking important, you're a completely essential piece of the whole mind-numbing motor that keeps capitalism itself running, you're the guy, you're the guy, and I'm just some stupid SHIT HEAD who needs to lick your ass —

LEWIS: Hey, Charlie —

CHARLIE: C'mon I'm not making this up! I'm not even exaggerating! It was like a scene out of some bad nineteenth century novel, or a good one, even, *War and Peace,* he's Prince Somebody and I'm the bastard son of Somebody Else, who remembers, except for the licking of the ass part. Except if we were in Russia, in the nineteenth century, there would be a form for it all, a ritual, a way to keep your dignity while you said, please your highness, save my fucking worthless piece of shit self. Give me some money. I'm fucking broke, I'm not a man, GIVE ME SOME MONEY. And if you do, I will go to Siberia for you, I will face Bonaparte with my bare hands, I will fling myself into the abyss, just give me some fucking money so that I don't have to — Plus he's thin! Did I tell you this? You remember Nick, he was just like a normal guy, right? Aside from being a fuck? He's lost like forty pounds. And I mean, he was normal, before, it's not like he was fat, he was just normal so now he's like — it's like his face is just sitting right on his skull. You're like talking to a really skinny skull version of who Nick used to be. And he's dressed all in black, this bizarre black suit with a black silk T-shirt under it, so he actually does look like one of those freaks from a vampire movie, do they honestly think that looks good, in Hollywood? They must! I don't know. I don't know. So then he orders like a huge slab of red meat, because that's all he can eat, apparently. That's how he got so thin, by eating only raw meat. I swear to you, I am not making ONE WORD of this up. And I'm completely, I am just trying to stay focused on the sucking up end of the conversation, trying not say anything truthful, just stay in the conversation, let him know that I'm a total failure of a human being, but I also know and appreciate that fact that he is not.

LEWIS: Charlie —

CHARLIE: Oh, stop it, don't even, that is completely what those conversations are about! That is what they are about! And I'm doing it, I am absolutely humiliating myself so that I can get Nick to give me an audition for a teeny-tiny part in a pilot I don't even believe exists, when he looks at my plate and says, "I could never eat that. That is just too rich." I mean, he's got a slab of red meat the size of Nebraska sitting on his plate, and I've got a plate of mushroom puree, sitting in front of me. Mushroom puree, with about five or six itty-bitty scallops on top of it, I got so fucking self-conscious about how fucking thin he was, that I ordered a completely girly meal, scallops in mushroom puree, just so I wouldn't have to think about that crap while I castrated myself for this — this — skull-person — and then he — he — *(He stops himself. Sits. Takes a big hit off the vodka bottle.)*

CHARLIE: *(Continuing.)* Sorry. Forget about it. I don't even know what I'm saying.

CLEA: No. Are you kidding? That was incredible. What you just said. That was — wow. I'm like tingling.

CHARLIE: Oh, good. *(Then.)* Am I interrupting?

CLEA: No!

LEWIS: Well, kind of —

CHARLIE: Oh, shit —

CLEA: No, it's fine —

CHARLIE: You're, like, having a drink here —

LEWIS: Yes.

CHARLIE: I'm sorry. I'll take off.

CLEA: God no, that was horrible what you just went through! You have to stay with your friends and just like, at least stay, and and and stay, until you feel like a human being again!

CHARLIE: Thanks, but —

CLEA: *(To Lewis.)* He should stay, right? You can't send him back to the Nazi priestess at least until he just relaxes or —

LEWIS: She's really not that bad —

CHARLIE: No, she's great. She's great.

CLEA: Oh I know. I totally know. But come on. Should I get you a glass? So that you don't have to keep —

(She gestures, drinking from the bottle.)

CHARLIE: Maybe that's a good idea.

CLEA: Totally. They're like in here, right? I'll get another glass.

(She goes. There is a long moment of silence. Charlie tries hard not to laugh. Lewis looks at him, not amused.)

CHARLIE: *(Laughing at this.)* You said you asked her for drinks, I didn't know that meant today.

LEWIS: Yes! Today! Today!

CHARLIE: Come on, you're not actually getting anywhere are you?

LEWIS: Yes, I am, I was, at least, I don't seem to be anymore —

CHARLIE: She's a fucking moron, Lewis —

LEWIS: I don't care!

CHARLIE: You want me to take off?

LEWIS: Yes! No. I don't — she's very — sensitive. If you left, I don't think — I don't know —

CHARLIE: I'm sorry, man —

CLEA: *(Reentering.)* What are you sorry about?

(She takes the vodka bottle from Charlie and pours him a drink.)

CHARLIE: Just about coming over here and losing it.

CLEA: Don't apologize! Are you kidding! You are so in touch with your feelings.

CHARLIE: That's not actually something you want to say to a guy, to make him feel better. That's not actually considered a compliment, on our planet.

CLEA: Well, you are so just wrong about that. Because if you lose, like, knowing who you are? If you lose that? You're lost. And then the bastards like Nick, they just rule the world.

CHARLIE: They already rule the world, Clea.

CLEA: They don't rule you.

(She hands him his drink.)

CHARLIE: Yeah, uh, thanks.

CLEA: Besides, it's so great you came by because I totally need to apologize. That stuff I said the other night? I mean, whoa. My bad, my total bad.

CHARLIE: It's OK.

CLEA: That's very very decent of you to say. Because I felt terrible afterwards, I was being so rude about everybody. Especially your wife! The things I said! Here —

(She pours him more vodka.)

CHARLIE: Look, forget it, would you? We all say shitty things about people we don't know. It's the only true pleasure left in the world, trashing other people. Especially when they have something you want: money. Or power. Or just, coherence —

LEWIS: Hey, Charlie maybe we should —

CHARLIE: *(Complete overlap, revving again.)* Not that I think Nick is coherent in any way, any larger cosmic truth has evaded Nick altogether —

LEWIS: Yeah, but I just don't know that —

CHARLIE: *(Complete overlap.)* But he's still the object of desire, isn't he? Him and that fucking pilot. He could be shooting kiddie porn as far as anyone's concerned and I still have to suck up, don't I, that's how degraded this whole fucking planet has gotten, SUCK UP to assholes like Nick because they have something you must want even though you don't, you don't want it, everyone just thinks, God, it's like we don't even know how to have a real DESIRE anymore! It's all the opposite of enlightenment, remember when that was a goal? Nowadays if someone said to you, what you want out of life? And you said, I don't know, enlightenment, what do you think would happen? WHAT DO YOU THINK WOULD HAPPEN? These are the fucking end times. The entire fucking culture has devolved to such a point that what we WANT, what we DESIRE isn't love or passion or sex or money, it's MEANINGLESSNESS. And that's what I'm supposed to sell myself for. Time to sell it, my heart, my soul, my common sense, my hope, my dreams, my pride, anything that means anything at all to my little preconscious, subconscious self, all of it goes on the auction block for what? That's what I want to know. What am I supposed to get? To give up everything? What do I get? *(Beat.)* I have a feeling we're gonna need more vodka. You got another bottle back there?

LEWIS: Sorry.

CLEA: Can you, can you go get some?

LEWIS: Oh —

CHARLIE: No, no — God, I'm sorry — I got to get out of here, I'm just —

CLEA: No no please. Don't be ridiculous. I'll go —

LEWIS/CHARLIE: No — no — no —

(Beat.)

CLEA: Just I mean, for vodka.

CHARLIE: I'll go, it's fine. Really. There's a liquor store just a couple blocks, besides, I'm the one sucking it down.

CLEA: You're in crisis! You just got here, and you're wrecked! Lewis, can you go?

(Beat.)

LEWIS: Maybe we should go to dinner.

CLEA: All three of us? Do you want to?

CHARLIE: *(Slight beat.)* You know what? I'm going to take off — I really —

CLEA: Stop it! That is insane. Besides, I totally want to hear about all of this. I mean, you have no idea how inspiring it is to hear you just talk! To someone like me? Because I am so new here, I mean, I just came like minutes ago from Ohio and the whole world seems so — just insane, you know — I am so confused like all the time — and then I listen to you, and I know I'm not crazy. *(To Lewis, gushing.)* Doesn't he make you feel like that? Just less crazy?

CHARLIE: Actually, Clea, I am being alarmingly self-indulgent, and I need to go home.

CLEA: If you wanted to go home, wouldn't you have been there by now? And you are not being self-indulgent. I think it's sad that you think that. Because you're like on fire. They don't deserve you.

LEWIS: They, who?

CLEA: None of them.

LEWIS: Maybe we could all go. For the booze, I mean.

CLEA: Do you need money?

LEWIS: No!

CHARLIE: That's a good idea, we'll all go.

CLEA: But that doesn't make any sense. Besides, you must be starving! All you had for lunch was a couple of scallops and some mushrooms. Aren't you hungry?

CHARLIE: Yeah, but —

CLEA: *(To Lewis.)* Could you pick up some pizza, too? There's like a stand down there someplace, right?

LEWIS: I thought you only ate vegetables.

CLEA: Not for me! I can't eat a thing, I am so totally bloated right now. But I would have another drink. I mean, I don't drink, I really don't? But sometimes it clearly is just what has to happen. It'll only take you like a minute, right?

LEWIS: Yeah. *(Beat.)* Yes! Sure!

CLEA: Great!

LEWIS: Yeah, OK. I'll be right back.

(He grabs his jacket and goes to the door, where he turns and looks at them.)

LEWIS: *(Continuing.)* I'll — be right back!

(He goes, shutting the door behind him. Clea turns to Charlie, smiling.)

CLEA: That is incredible, the way you define things with so much fire. I really can't even, I mean, it's totally overwhelming.

CHARLIE: Yeah.

(He smiles at her, brief, looks away, at the cheese plate, then stands, moves away from her.)

CLEA: You knew I was going to be here, didn't you?

CHARLIE: What? No.

CLEA: I could tell. When you walked in.

CHARLIE: No, that's —

CLEA: You're lying.

CHARLIE: You know what? I'm taking off.

CLEA: That's not what you want to do.

CHARLIE: Actually, it is. Just tell Lewis — you don't have to tell him anything, he will be so relieved I'm gone, he won't care.

(He heads for the door.)

CLEA: You spent the whole day doing things that made you feel shitty about yourself. Why don't you just do something you want to do?

(She gets close to him. He takes a step back.)

CHARLIE: You're on a date with my best friend.

CLEA: So?

CHARLIE: So I think I'd like to pretend that I still have a shred of integrity —

CLEA: Why?

CHARLIE: Because — you know — because I don't have much else left.

CLEA: You don't know what you have. Because nobody has been telling you. They've just been telling you what you're not. Why don't you try being what you are?

(She starts to kiss him. He pushes her away for a moment. Then, he leans in and kisses her, pushing her back to the couch. They land on the couch and start to make out in earnest. Blackout.)

ACT II
SCENE FOUR

Charlie's apartment. Clea and Charlie are having sex on the couch, and else-where. They are both in a half state of undress, as if they hit the ground run-ning. It is quite athletic. After an extended and quite vocal climax, they col-lapse.

CLEA: Oh, God. Don't stop. No, don't stop. Don't stop!

CHARLIE: You got to give me a minute here, Clea.

CLEA: No, don't stop —

CHARLIE: How old did you say you were?

(He means it half as a joke, but it does stop her.)

CLEA: No no don't do that. Don't categorize me.

CHARLIE: *(Still breathless.)* Asking you how old you are is categorizing?

CLEA: You're trying to define age as a life characteristic. As like, something
that says something about a person.

CHARLIE: It does say, how old you are.

CLEA: No, it doesn't. It really doesn't. You say, "how old are you" like I'm
young and you're old, like that's some joke, because you think you're old?
But you're timeless. You're like this incredible lion who's been stalking
the Earth since the dawn of nature, or something.

CHARLIE: Tell me, do you actually believe all this crap that you keep spouting?

CLEA: Of course I believe it. Maybe you should try believing it, too. Why
wouldn't you want to believe that you're a timeless lion? Isn't that better
than thinking you're some old loser who can't get a job?

*(She climbs on him and starts to kiss him. He pushes her away, sudden,
stands and puts his pants on.)*

CLEA: *(Continuing.)* No no. Don't do that. That's what I'm saying, that's not
who you are!

CHARLIE: We have to get you out of here.

(He starts to dress, and straighten out the room again.)

CLEA: We just got here.

CHARLIE: And now we have to go.

CLEA: You said she was going to be at work, all afternoon, she's off screaming
somewhere, come on, you said, we have all afternoon. Be a lion.

CHARLIE: I think we've had enough of the lion, Clea.

CLEA: I haven't. I mean it. I can go all day, and all night, I could go a whole weekend. Have you ever done that? Just, spent a whole weekend inside, doing things . . .

CHARLIE: Don't you get sore?

CLEA: You want to find out?

CHARLIE: Jesus! You're like, it's like talking to a porno movie —

CLEA: You are so hung up about the way I talk all the time!

CHARLIE: Well, it's very unusual, Clea, to find someone so remarkably uninhibited in so many ways —

CLEA: Yeah but you always turn it around, like you don't like it. You make it sound like it's maybe not so great, the way I am. That I'm sort of stupid, or just stupid or something —

CHARLIE: *Voracious* is actually the word I was thinking of.

CLEA: Yeah, like that's a bad thing. But you know what? You like it. It's actually driving you crazy how much you like it. Why can't you just say it? If I'm voracious then you're something that wants voracious more than anything it ever saw before.

CHARLIE: How can you know so much and so little at the same time?

CLEA: You have no idea, how much I know. Come on. You said we have all afternoon.

(She kisses him. He is increasingly a lost man. He tries to push her away.)

CHARLIE: We do have all afternoon. Just, not here.

CLEA: Ohhh please . . .

CHARLIE: Listen to me. This is my apartment.

CLEA: I know. I love it that you brought me here. It's so hostile.

CHARLIE: You are really something.

CLEA: Yes, I am. And you're the one who brought me here, to have sex in your apartment.

CHARLIE: Stella could just walk in on us —

CLEA: *(Laughing.)* That would be hilarious.

CHARLIE: Yeah, no, it wouldn't.

(He pushes her away, firm. Looks at her, suddenly simple and clear and a little desperate.)

CHARLIE: *(Continuing.)* I mean, you understand what this is. We're clear on what this is, right?

CLEA: Relax. I know what this is. You're at a place, so am I. This is that place.

CHARLIE: Yes.

CLEA: It's what you need and I want, and that's why it's so hot. Trust me. I understand what this is.

CHARLIE: Good.

(Unsure, hoping that was clear, he leaves the room. She watches him go, goes to her purse, and takes out an apple, starts to eat, and calls to him in the next room.)

CLEA: *(Yelling.)* You know what we should do tonight? My friend can get me into this party. It's up on the Upper West Side so it is totally not like a really hip scene or anything, but there's going to be some movie stars there, she wouldn't tell me who, but they also have this hot tub there? On the roof. She went to a party at this place a couple weeks ago, and everyone takes their clothes off and gets in the hot tub. And then they have these cater waiters come around, I'm not kidding, with sushi. So you sit in the hot tub and like talk and eat sushi naked. It sounds so nineties, doesn't it? Movie stars and sushi in a hot tub? Maybe they'll play R.E.M. on the "record player." Or do lines of cocaine. It's so unbe-lievably retro, a hot tub on the roof. I soo want to go.

CHARLIE: *(Entering.)* I've been to this party.

CLEA: Get out.

CHARLIE: I swear to God, I went to that party twenty years ago. Riverside Drive, ninety-six or seven and Riverside.

CLEA: I don't know.

CHARLIE: Sushi and cocaine in the hot tub on the roof? I went to that party. No kidding. I was doing this play Off-Broadway, and one of the other actors knew somebody who was going to this party, on the Upper West Side. This rich guy, nobody knew his name, and the place is like a man-sion, right, he owns the whole building and it's got Art Deco everything, completely tasteless. The place was huge, like five floors, people screw-ing in corners of the den and the living room, there was a three-way going on in one room, I'm not kidding, real hedonistic shit. And then there's that hot tub up there on the roof with the greenhouse. *(Laughing now.)* He's got a fucking greenhouse up there, growing cactuses and hibiscus, something, I can't believe I remember this, everybody was com-pletely coked out of their minds, like all night, till five, six in the morn-ing. That's how stupid we all were. It's amazing most of us are still alive. I was such hot shit. That play was unintelligible but I got amazing reviews, and I was . . . the world was on fire for me, boy. Sushi and cocaine and whatever I wanted. God that was fun. That was really fun.

CLEA: Well, guess what, it's your lucky night. Because you can go to that party again. With me.

CHARLIE: *(Reality check.)* I can't go to a party with you.

CLEA: Why not?

CHARLIE: Because I can't.

CLEA: It'll be realllly fun. That's what you said, it was reallly fun.

CHARLIE: I'm not going to a party with you, Clea!

CLEA: No one will see us! That's the whole point, that scene is completely over, so it won't matter!

CHARLIE: Great.

CLEA: You said yourself, the guy who owns this place is so nobody on Earth that is important, just some rich guy with a lot of money and a house with a hot tub, we can totally just go together. I mean, with my friend, we can dump her when we get there, which will be fine with her, she dumps me all the time.

CHARLIE: Look, I have — a life, Clea.

CLEA: Don't you mean, a "wife"?

CHARLIE: Yeah. That's what I mean. And like you said that scene is over. I'm not going to a party with you.

(He continues straightening the apartment.)

CLEA: No, come on, forget about her! You should see how much happier you are when you forget about her. We don't have to go to any party. Let's just pretend we're at a party. We're in the hot tub right now. No. No. Let's skip the hot tub. I like the sound of those rooms, where people are just doing things, in the middle of somebody's house, who they don't even know whose house it is. Let's just think about doing it in front of everybody, in somebody else's room. . . .

(She reaches up and kisses him. He kisses her back. As things are heating up again, the door opens. Stella enters, and sees them. She stops. After a moment, she speaks.)

STELLA: Charlie. I'm here.

(This is the first Charlie and Clea are aware of her entrance.)

CLEA: Shit.

CHARLIE: Stella.

STELLA: What are you doing, Charlie?

CHARLIE: Nothing. No — this isn't —

STELLA: What, what it looks like? It isn't what it looks like?

CHARLIE: Stella —

STELLA: In my home? You brought, to my home?

(Clea starts to laugh, embarrassed. She tries to stop herself, but simply can't.)

CLEA: I'm sorry. Oh, I am so sorry. But this is just hideous. Oh my God. Wow. It's just so, horrible, and embarrassing.

STELLA: What is she doing here? Don't tell me what she's doing here, I can see what she's doing here. Get out of my house. GET HER OUT OF HERE.

CHARLIE: You have to go.

CLEA: Oh, look. I mean, this is horrible, right, but there's no reason to get all, like, rude. Things have happened here, obviously, but it's not like that's somebody's fault. I mean, I am so not interested in some kind of a ridiculous scene.

(She stands and looks for her clothes.)

STELLA: Oh she's a brain surgeon isn't she? Yeah, this makes complete sense now. I can see why this happened.

CLEA: See this is what I'm talking about! People getting all insulting in a situation like this, why? Is that supposed to help? Because I don't think that is in the least bit helpful.

STELLA: Charlie, get her out of here!

CHARLIE: Clea. Just go.

CLEA: Why should I go? I mean, I was invited here. You and I are doing something here. You made a choice, Charlie, that involved me and not her, and that choice made you happy for the first time in whatever, I mean, you were like fucking miserable until I showed up.

STELLA: Why are you talking?

CLEA: I'm talking because I have something to say!

STELLA: You don't have anything to say! You don't know anything! And you're in my house! This is my house, I pay the rent here, that is my husband, you don't have any rights here!

CLEA: I've been fucking him all afternoon and you haven't. That doesn't exactly give me no rights.

(She sits on the couch, defiant. Stella looks at Charlie, stunned.)

CHARLIE: I'm sorry. Clea. You have to go. We have things, Stella and I have things we need to — this shouldn't have happened, this way, at all, and, and —

CLEA: But it did happen. And you were the one who made it happen. So "should," I think *should* is a very useless word in a situation like this.

STELLA: Charlie?

CHARLIE: I'm sorry. I'm completely in the wrong.

CLEA: Stop. Just stop, already. "In the wrong"?

CHARLIE: *(Furious.)* Clea, do not interfere in this!

CLEA: She's the one who's interfering! Come on, things were fine until she showed up!

CHARLIE: Stop acting like an idiot!

CLEA: You're the one who's being an idiot! "In the wrong"? You're just going to give away your power like that? To her? That's what she wants, that's what she's been about this whole time, "I pay the rent, I want a baby, go suck up to stupid crazy Nick because me and my highlighters rule the world," what about what you want?

STELLA: Is that what you told her? This person, this, you told her — what did you tell her? Why do I care what you told her, that's clearly the least of, we're married, we've been married for —

CHARLIE: *(Overlap.)* No. No, I did not tell her — this is not, this was not meant to be anything, Stella, this was a mistake —

STELLA: A mistake is forgetting my birthday, Charlie. I don't know what this is. *(She sits, desolate.)*

CLEA: Charlie, are you coming?

CHARLIE: What?

CLEA: Look, we're doing something. Right? We were doing something, before she barged in.

STELLA: I live here! Are you insane? Because you sound insane. You're having an affair with an insane person. Maybe I'm the insane person, I can't, I don't even know, I have, there are — I don't, was your life that bad that you had to let this into it?

CHARLIE: No.

STELLA: Fourteen years, fourteen! You can just, for this? This thing, this isn't a person, even, I don't know what she is —

CLEA: OK —

STELLA: You shut up! You've ruined my life, I don't have to take care of your feelings! Charlie, say something, please! What happened? Why did you do this? Was there some other way I should have been taking care of you?

CLEA: He's a man, he doesn't need a mommy.

STELLA: You know, I will hurt you. I will find some sort of weapon, there's got to be something somewhere, a knife or a vase, anything really is starting to look good, and I will hurt you and we will all end up in the *Daily News.* I promise you, I am not kidding. You need to get out of my house, right now. RIGHT NOW.

CLEA: Look at you, you don't even get it yet! You're just acting like a man, threatening violence and oh you're in charge of everything, why don't you just start waving your highlighters and screaming "Heil Hitler"? If you knew how to keep him, you would've. Look at him! He's just like totally silent around you. He's nobody with you. Let me tell you something, he isn't like that with me. With me, he's a lion, roaming the Earth. With me, he's a god!

STELLA: You have got to be fucking kidding me.

CLEA: You don't make him feel the way I do. You don't even begin to know how. So you can go ahead and hit me, or hurt me, or whatever, be violent, just like a man? But that's what your problem is. I'm going, Charlie. You know where to find me.

(She goes. There is a long moment of silence.)

STELLA: Why?

CHARLIE: Don't ask why.

STELLA: *(Suddenly furious.)* Don't ask — why? "Why" is off the table? You just completely — that was the most humiliating — I'm humiliated, Charlie! I'm, I'm everything is, my whole life is suddenly not even — and for that? And I'm not allowed to ask WHY?

CHARLIE: This is just, I can't — I can't . . .

STELLA: Stop being such a fucking coward and say something!

CHARLIE: You're too competent. *(There is a silence at this.)*

STELLA: What?

CHARLIE: Everything. Gets done. Even when you hate what you're doing, you get it done. You're like a machine. Everything gets done.

STELLA: *(Almost in tears, suddenly.)* I'm not a machine. That's a lie.

CHARLIE: You're coherent. Everything coheres, and I, I can't — anymore — because I'm — and you're perfect. Your feelings are perfect. Your work is perfect. You hold down a job you think is stupid and it frustrates you in the perfect way. Even in how you're not perfect, even in how things get to you, you're just, even your neurosis is perfect. You're so fucking competent, you don't ever expect too much out of life. You handle all of it. Even this. Even this! I'm watching you — you're handling it. You're already going to forgive this. THAT WAS A FOREGONE CONCLUSION. And then I'll have that, too. Your competence, and your forgiveness. Oh and your money, let's not forget that.

STELLA: So this is my fault?

CHARLIE: *(Snarling.)* No! It's my fault! It's my crime! And I own it! It's the only thing you left me, the ability to fuck up, and I want it! It's mine! This fucking disaster is mine, and you can just keep your fucking hands off of it!

STELLA: I don't understand why this is happening. Why are you talking to me like this?

CHARLIE: I'm talking to you like this because this is who I am! And I'm sick of pretending to be perfect, like you, because that is not the person I want to be!

STELLA: This is some sort of fucking midlife crisis. You want to fuck idiotic twenty somethings because that's what everybody else does, there isn't even a shred of originality in this —

CHARLIE: I wasn't looking for originality, Stella. I was looking to feel like someone who still had a shred of life in him!

STELLA: And fucking great-looking idiots is the only way you can do that? Are you kidding me? I mean it. You don't like your life so you honestly think that screwing that girl — that girl who can hardly speak — who has no character or substance or anything — that that is going to do something, for you, make you whole, make you understand who you are in the world —

CHARLIE: I don't want that. Don't you understand?

STELLA: This is just, it's just self-loathing, Charlie! You're projecting your self-loathing all over the rest of us and destroying everything so you can destroy yourself —

CHARLIE: Thanks, Stell, that's really, this is a thrilling moment to be psycho-analyzed —

STELLA: What else am I supposed to do?

CHARLIE: Nothing! Don't do anything! And don't explain this because I don't want to understand it! I just want to feel something. Remember when you felt things?

STELLA: I feel things!

CHARLIE: You feel unhappy. You feel competent. You feel like a wall.

STELLA: Don't you tell me what I feel. I feel disgust!

CHARLIE: You know what? She's right about one thing. If you want me to stay, you really don't know the first thing about how to make that happen.

(He heads for the door.)

STELLA: Where are you going?

CHARLIE: I'm going to a party.

(He slams the door. Blackout.)

SCENE FIVE

Stella and Lewis, in Lewis' apartment.

STELLA: Thanks for letting me come over, I . . .

LEWIS: No, sure, thanks for calling. You look great.

STELLA: I look like shit.

LEWIS: Well, no. You feel like shit. But you look, great. Come on in, come on in.

STELLA: Have you heard from him?

LEWIS: No.

STELLA: Do you know where he is?

LEWIS: Stella . . .

STELLA: Is he living with her?

LEWIS: I don't know. That seems . . .

STELLA: I know, but where else would he be?

LEWIS: I don't know.

STELLA: How did this happen? So fast? Didn't it happen so fast?

LEWIS: Yes. It did.

STELLA: Did you know it was going on?

LEWIS: I . . .

STELLA: You did.

LEWIS: I thought, there was one night, here, a couple weeks ago. I thought something might . . .

STELLA: How long ago?

LEWIS: A couple weeks. Three weeks?

STELLA: Was it going on, then, is that what you mean? He was already, three weeks ago?

LEWIS: I don't know. Maybe it started that night, I don't — do you really want to —

STELLA: Yes. Yes! I want to, I can't — there's so much, you go, we had a good marriage. I thought. There was so much bile, when he, I'm too competent. That's what he told me. With so much hatred, I didn't . . . I thought he loved me.

LEWIS: He does love you.

STELLA: He's gone, Lewis! I called his cell phone, a bunch of times. I left utterly humiliating messages, please call, please come home, we have to talk, and and and nothing. I don't even know where he is. Do you think he's with her? Why would he be with that person?

LEWIS: I don't know.

STELLA: I mean I guess she's pretty. She's just so — but she is pretty. Is that enough?

LEWIS: No.

STELLA: Do you think she's pretty?

LEWIS: No.

STELLA: But she's attractive. She's sexy.

LEWIS: No.

STELLA: I walked in on them. Did he tell you?

LEWIS: I haven't spoken to him.

STELLA: Then how do you know where he is?

LEWIS: I don't, Stella. Sweetie. I don't know.

STELLA: I know, I'm sorry, I'm sorry, I shouldn't be dumping this on you.

LEWIS: That's not —

STELLA: I should go. I should go home. I'm afraid to go home. I don't know where my husband is.

(She starts to cry. Lewis goes to her, puts his arm around her. She sobs into his shirt.)

LEWIS: I would like to kill him.

STELLA: No. It's OK. It's not OK, it's so confusing. I'm sorry, I don't want to get snot on your sweater.

LEWIS: It's OK. I'm going to get you a glass of wine.

(He goes. Stella sits alone for a moment. She starts to cry again, then dries her eyes, shakes herself. She reaches into her purse and pulls out a manila envelope. She sets it on the coffee table, then takes it back and holds it to her chest. Lewis returns, carrying two glasses. He sees her, takes a moment, then proceeds.)

LEWIS: *(Continuing.)* Hey.

STELLA: Oh. Thank you. I'm sorry about all this, Lewis. I just didn't, I needed to see you and think about how normal my life was, when something like this happens, all of a sudden everything you thought you knew, it's all, I'm too competent. Did you know? I didn't know. I'm too —

LEWIS: Sweetie, there's nothing wrong with you. He's going through something, it doesn't have anything to do with you. You're perfect.

STELLA: That's what he said. That's why he hates me now.

LEWIS: He doesn't hate you.

STELLA: Oh God I'm sorry I'm being such a, oh, I don't want to drown in self-pity, that's so repulsive, I hate it when people do that. I'm just very confused.

LEWIS: Have some wine.

STELLA: *(With a shred of irony.)* Yes, that will help, won't it. Alcohol is so useful when you just want to clear your head.

(She takes a drink.)

LEWIS: *(Cautious.)* What's that?

(He points to the envelope.)

STELLA: It's the baby.

LEWIS: What?

STELLA: My baby. They sent me, when you do these international adoptions, they send you pictures, when they've picked out your baby. So. They sent me pictures of my baby.

(Upset, but trying to stay on top of it now, she tries to open the envelope. She can't manage it.)

LEWIS: Here. Let me.

STELLA: I'm sorry.

(Lewis opens the envelope and takes out several photographs, and a document of several pages.)

LEWIS: She's beautiful.

STELLA: Isn't she beautiful?

LEWIS: Beautiful.

STELLA: She's, they send you that packet, when they pick your baby — I just told you this already, I'm sorry, I started doing that — repeating myself all the time — like my mother, my crazy mother does that —

LEWIS: Does Charlie know . . .

STELLA: I told him. I mean, I called him, and I told him. That we have to let them know. If we want her or not. I left a message on his cell phone.

LEWIS: And he didn't . . .

STELLA: No. Nothing. *(Beat.)* I don't know what's happened. To my life.

LEWIS: You can do it anyway. Can't you? You went through the whole process. They approved you.

STELLA: They approved both of us, and I don't know where he is! I don't know where that girl lives, I even tried to track her down through the stupid temp agency and they wouldn't give me the information and I told them off and canceled our contract with them. I did. Without consulting anyone, I just — I'm acting like a crazy person and I don't care. I would go over there and beg him, just — how can I, I would anyway, my pride is, I don't care. Do think this is why? That he didn't want the baby?

LEWIS: I don't know why, Stella. You want my opinion, he's completely lost his mind, leaving you for anybody for any length of time is just about the most insane thing I've ever heard of. Ever.

STELLA: I'm not going to be able to get her. Am I. They won't give her to me, now. And all I'll have, ever, is that stupid job that I hate, I hate that job —

LEWIS: You'll get her.

STELLA: Nothing. All I'll ever have, is nothing.

(She is utterly bewildered with grief. Lewis sits there, bereft for a moment.)

LEWIS: *(Blurting.)* It's my fault.

STELLA: Oh, Lewis, don't be ridiculous.

LEWIS: It's true. All of this, with Charlie, he didn't even — when he met her, he couldn't stand her. I was the one who brought her into our lives —

STELLA: No — she was just there —

LEWIS: I did, I asked her over. Because I didn't care, I knew that she was, some kind of succubus, and I wanted her anyway, that's why he even saw her again, he wouldn't have, if it wasn't for me. He wouldn't have.

STELLA: *(Beat.)* You asked her . . . what did you ask her?

LEWIS: *(Beat.)* Nothing.

STELLA: Your apartment? You said that before. She was in your apartment. Because you were on a date with her?

LEWIS: No. I mean, it doesn't matter. It doesn't . . .

STELLA: Well, what was she doing here, then? If you weren't on a date with her?

LEWIS: I was just, you know, I invited her over for a drink.

STELLA: And Charlie, you invited him over —

LEWIS: No, he just came by. And . . . she was there.

STELLA: Because you invited her.

LEWIS: Yes.

STELLA: Why did you invite her?

LEWIS: I know, it was stupid, I just —

STELLA: You wanted to, to fuck her.

LEWIS: No! Well, of course I — Stella, this isn't — useful —

STELLA: Useful! And being useful has worked so fucking well for me up to this point! She was here because you, you wanted her too, that monster, I mean, she is just a fucking nightmare — of a human being — and that didn't matter, did it —

LEWIS: Stella, this isn't, there's no point to this —

STELLA: THERE'S NO POINT TO ANYTHING, LEWIS, HAVEN'T

YOU NOTICED? I'm sorry. I know, I'm being, I don't have to apologize, to you, you ruined my life —

LEWIS: I didn't, you know I —

STELLA: Fucking men, you fucks, you always stick together —

LEWIS: That is not —

STELLA: Not what, not useful? Christ. My head is going to explode. You and Charlie. Want her. Want her. That's what men want.

LEWIS: It isn't! You are what I wanted, but I couldn't have you because you're married to my best friend!

STELLA: *(Reeling.)* Stop it, you liar, you're a fucking liar!

LEWIS: *(Furious.)* It's true, you know it is, that's why I invited her —

STELLA: You invited her because — fuck you, who cares why you did it. You just did it —

LEWIS: Stella — *(Overlap.)* OK, you have to — Stella —

STELLA: Fuck you, fuck you, you invited her in, why, why was she here for him to see again, why was she here, it was because you — you were the one —

LEWIS: No —

STELLA: You just said it yourself! I have to get out of here. I have to go. I can't . . . I can't . . .

LEWIS: Stella —

STELLA: Shut up. Shut up. Don't talk to me. Don't ever talk to me again.
(She takes her pictures and papers, clutches them to herself, and goes. Blackout.)

SCENE SIX

Clea's apartment. It is a mess. Charlie lies on the bed, a big bottle of vodka in his hands. He pours himself a very stiff drink — a huge drink — which finishes off the bottle.

CHARLIE: *(Calling.)* We need more vodka!

CLEA: What?

CHARLIE: *(To himself.)* We need more vodka.
(He drinks, then — .)

CHARLIE: *(Continuing; calling.)* So what'd you think of Nick?

CLEA: *(Offstage.)* What?

CHARLIE: *(Yelling.)* Nick. I saw you talking to him. At that party last night.

(Clea enters, dressed in black, to go out. She is jazzed, happy.)

CLEA: I thought he was fine.

CHARLIE: He's an asshole.

CLEA: Well, that's a little reductive.

CHARLIE: Reductive?

CLEA: *(Friendly.)* Yeah, you know, like, reductive. Reductive. Like, judgmentally reductive.

CHARLIE: It's judgmentally reductive to call an asshole an asshole?

CLEA: *(Cheerful.)* Look I don't even know the guy. I just think defining any human being by one word, one demeaning sort of reducing word is something I don't want to be involved with.
(She hunts under the couch for shoes.)

CHARLIE: Yes, you have very high moral standards.

CLEA: I'm not trying to be judgmental! That's what I'm saying!

CHARLIE: Do you even know what reductive means?

CLEA: Somebody's in a bad mood . . . .
(She leans over and kisses him. He starts to drag her back onto the couch, but she pulls away.)

CLEA: *(Continuing.)* Oooooooh, I can't, Charlie. I have this thing I have to do.
(She slips on her heels, then goes to the wall, picks up makeup and jewelry off a bookcase there and finishes getting ready to go out.)

CHARLIE: What thing?

CLEA: It's like a dinner thing, with one of my girlfriends. I told you about it.

CHARLIE: Yeah, but all you say is it's a "thing." It's not exactly specific. It's like the opposite of specific. The only way you could say less is to say nothing at all.

CLEA: Which I know you would think was just fabulous since you think the way I talk is so stupid.
(He grabs her.)

CHARLIE: You look like a spider tonight. Getting ready to go out and sting some poor unsuspecting but delicious victim —
(He starts to kiss her. She pulls away.)

CLEA: Charlie, wow, you know, this is, you are acting, I think you have had a little too much vodka or something.

CHARLIE: We're out of vodka.

CLEA: That's not exactly a surprise. I mean, the way you've been sucking it down lately is a little —
(Beat.)

CHARLIE: No, go on.

CLEA: I am not criticizing. I mean, obviously you were in a very wrong place with the Nazi priestess and that was totally sucking you dry for how many years, I think it is obvious that I have had a lot of sympathy for you coming out of that situation, and I have been very supportive even through all this self-undermining behavior because of what you've been through.

CHARLIE: You never liked Stella, did you. Met her for fifteen minutes and you just couldn't stand her.

CLEA: Need I point out, neither can you.

CHARLIE: You don't know anything about anything.

CLEA: Oh brother. This is exactly what I mean about the vodka. No one made you do anything. You were very clear about what you wanted from this situation! Do you not recall saying to me, you just wanted to be clear?

CHARLIE: Yes I recall that.

CLEA: Well.

(She finds her purse and starts to go.)

CHARLIE: Can I borrow twenty bucks?

(She turns at this, startled.)

CHARLIE: *(Continuing.)* We need more vodka.

CLEA: You want to borrow money? From me? For vodka? Like, I don't have a job.

CHARLIE: Neither do I.

CLEA: So use a credit card. *(She starts to go again.)*

CHARLIE: She cut them off. None of them work anymore.

(Clea turns on this, startled.)

CLEA: I just — wait a minute. All of your credit cards? You have like six.

CHARLIE: All of them. None of them. Work.

CLEA: The Nazi priestess —

CHARLIE: Stopped them.

CLEA: So you don't have any money.

CHARLIE: Nope.

CLEA: Well, what does she expect you to live on?

CHARLIE: Not her, apparently.

CLEA: What a bitch.

CHARLIE: What did you say?

CLEA: Well, it's just so passive-aggressive.

CHARLIE: I think cutting off all my credit cards would be considered aggressive-aggressive, Clea.

CLEA: Which is why you're not with her. So, look — *(Digs in her purse.)* I don't have a lot of money because as you know I just came here a few months ago, from Ohio —

CHARLIE: *(Overlap.)* Ohio, you don't say.

CLEA: — and I have not yet found a job that I think is something I could really get excited about but I do have some money. My mom sends me a check once in a while. Here. I mean, that is terrible, what she did.
(She holds out a bill. Charlie stares at it, takes a breath, then takes it, looks at it.)

CHARLIE: This is a ten.

CLEA: Well, I don't have a ton of money, Charlie, I think that's obvious. And due respect, given what I've gone through with my mother, I don't really want to just give you all my money, to just get drunk with.

CHARLIE: Not that you're judging.

CLEA: Well — you don't — like — expect me to support you now? You don't expect that, do you?

CHARLIE: No. I don't.
(He pockets the bill, and downs the rest of the vodka. She watches him, uncomfortable.)

CLEA: So, like — where are you going to live, now?

CHARLIE: *(A beat.)* Are you kicking me out?

CLEA: Well, I think it's obvious that you can't stay here forever.

CHARLIE: Not to argue semantics, because that is in fact a dicey proposition with the likes of you, Clea — but there is a rather large difference between "forever" and "now."

CLEA: You're so drunk, I can't even talk to you.

CHARLIE: I'm not drunk. I wish I was drunk but unfortunately *(Yelling, suddenly.)* WE ARE OUT OF VODKA.
(She stares at him, shocked.)

CLEA: Did you just raise your voice to me?

CHARLIE: Why, yes I did.

CLEA: *(Hushed and pious.)* Because that is — unacceptable. I do not yell. No one in my family ever yells. That is not something I can accept in any way.

CHARLIE: Soooo. . . . stealing other people's husbands for the sheer fun of being a bitch is OK, but RAISING YOUR VOICE is pretty much crossing the line.

CLEA: *(High and mighty.)* I am asking you to leave.

CHARLIE: Yeah, we'll get to that in good time, I'm sure, but I have a question first. Who you going out with? Are you going out with Nick?

CLEA: *(Caught, tossed.)* That is just — I'm going out with friends! I told you!

CHARLIE: *(Yelling now.)* So cheating on me with that shit head NICK is all right, but YELLING IS OFF THE TABLE.

CLEA: Cheating on you? CHEATING? This exclusive and, and proprietary
   language is really so retro —
CHARLIE: Call it whatever you want —
CLEA: You were the one who wanted to be clear!
CHARLIE: *(Furious, yelling.)* All right then, as long as we're arguing semantics,
   why don't we just call it lying? Is that OK? Lying to my face while you
   go off to fuck my total nemesis?
CLEA: Like you even care —
CHARLIE: MEN ACTUALLY DO CARE ABOUT THAT SHIT, CLEA.
CLEA: You have to leave! This yelling is terrible! I am not a violent person and
   I do not accept it in the people I care about!
CHARLIE: That's easy enough to pull off, because you don't care about any-
   body! Do you? It's fantastic! You look like that, you screw like a bunny,
   and you have no soul! Seriously. It is awe inspiring. That no soul thing?
   You make it quite, it's very seductive. Letting go. Forgetting that you
   ever wanted anything else. Because what else is there? Except looking
   like that. Being hot shit. At a really great party. Inside the void. *(Stands
   on the bed, lost inside himself.)*
CLEA: I don't know what the fuck you are talking about.
CHARLIE: What are the odds?
CLEA: Well, I cannot have insane people living in my apartment and just
   yelling at me, whenever they feel like it. Here's another ten.
   (She reaches into her purse, holds out another bill. Charlie stares at it.)
CLEA: *(Continuing.)* Take it.
   (Charlie does not take it. She finally throws it on the ground.)
CLEA: *(Continuing.)* I don't care if you take it or not, you crazy loser. But you
   better not be here when I get back. Or I'm calling the cops.
   *(She goes. After a moment, Charlie reaches down and takes the money, pock-
   ets it. Blackout.)*

SCENE SEVEN

*A remote corner of a party. Stella is there, with Charlie. He is a mess. They
stare at each other for a long moment of silence.*

CHARLIE: Hi.
STELLA: Charlie, wow. Edward didn't tell me he had invited you. I didn't
   think, we asked so many people if they knew where you, where you —
CHARLIE: No. I just heard from someone, you know, I bumped into a friend

of his on the street, and he mentioned that Edward was, you know . . . you know, you look great. How have you been?

STELLA: How have I been? Terrific. Being abandoned by my husband was a trial at first but over time it forced me to do some real soul searching and I think I've grown as a result.

CHARLIE: You're still working for that talk show.

STELLA: Oh for heavens's sake. It's been months, Charlie. You disappear for months, and now you just show up like like like — did you get my messages at all? I left like, a hundred messages, maybe, on your cell phone. Didn't you—did —

CHARLIE: Yeah. I got them. For a while. I mean, my cell doesn't work anymore. They cut it off, when I stopped paying. When you stopped paying.

STELLA: Well, what was I supposed to do? I didn't know if you were dead or alive, or if, or if —

CHARLIE: (Overlap.) No, you did the right thing. You should have cut me off, long before you did. You did the right thing.

STELLA: You look like shit.

CHARLIE: Yeah, right. Right? (Beat.) Look, can I borrow a few bucks?

STELLA: What?

CHARLIE: I'm really broke. I mean, it's temporary, but a few bucks would really help right now. There's a kind of housing situation . . .

STELLA: A housing — where are you living, Charlie?

CHARLIE: I'm with friends! Mostly.

STELLA: Charlie. Are you homeless?

CHARLIE: No, I'm with friends! I said, I'm with friends. It's OK. If you don't have any on you, that's all right. I'll pay you back.

STELLA: Why didn't you come home?

CHARLIE: (A beat, then.) I wrecked it. It wasn't there anymore. It wasn't what I wanted. I thought nothing would be better.

STELLA: Is it?

(Lewis appears, with Stella's wrap. He doesn't see Charlie at first.)

LEWIS: Sorry that took so long. To get to the wraps I had to get by three girls who were throwing up, and one who was shooting up.

CHARLIE: Edward's parties are great, aren't they?

LEWIS: A total blast.

CHARLIE: Hey, Lewis.

(He reaches over; they shake.)

LEWIS: Charlie. (To Stella.) You OK?

CHARLIE: *(Distracted.)* Yeah, great! I mean, I was hoping to find Clea here, but she's, who knows where she is . . . I'm telling you, she's really a piece of work. You were so better off out of that. I did you a favor, man, I really did.

LEWIS: *(To Stella, quiet.)* Do you want to go? We can go, right now.

STELLA: I don't know.

CHARLIE: No, God, come on, I can find Clea later, it's so great to see you guys! You look great. Stell, you look terrific.

LEWIS: *(To Stella.)* We should go.

CHARLIE: *(Snapping.)* She's my wife! Would you stop telling her what to do! I mean what the fuck are you . . . what . . . what the fuck is this?

(A beat.)

STELLA: We're going to China, Charlie. Next week. Lewis and I are going to China to get my baby.

CHARLIE: Together?

STELLA: Yes. Lewis and I are going to China together.

CHARLIE: Well, that's just — classic. How long did you wait, huh, Lewis? A week, two weeks, how long did it take you to start moving in on my wife?

STELLA: You have no right to even ask —

CHARLIE: How long did it take you, Lewis?

LEWIS: Three weeks.

CHARLIE: Three weeks! Wow, that's, you know, admirable self-restraint. You know, you really gave it time then. Good for you. Three weeks. That was loyal.

LEWIS: You're not allowed to expect loyalty after what you did!

CHARLIE: Not from you, clearly!

LEWIS: This is such a distortion.

CHARLIE: Make your excuses! You stole my wife.

STELLA: He didn't steal me.

CHARLIE: Oh yeah, he loves you. He really really loves you, that's really what's going on here. Love will find a way. I'm so happy for you both.

STELLA: *(Furious at this.)* Well, what was I supposed to do, wait for you? Wait for you to to — come to your senses and and — what was I supposed to do? You just threw me away like it was nothing, Charlie! How could you? How could you. Neither of us were perfect, but what we had was real.

CHARLIE: I DON'T WANT ANYTHING REAL. Where do you, where where do you think you are, anyway? Have you been out of the house lately? Have you been to Times Square? It's fantastic! You look up, and they're everywhere. Movie stars. TV stars. Underwear models. Those crazy rap people nobody understands, they're everywhere. Three and four stories tall, hovering over everything, like gods. Laughing. All of them, laughing at us. Because they know. All these fake people are having a more real life than we are! Real? Why should I want to be real? Fuck reality.

(*She turns, away from him, upset. Charlie starts toward her; Lewis steps between them.*)

LEWIS: Leave her alone Charlie. Leave us alone.

(*He takes her hand, leads her off, back to the party.*)

CHARLIE: Wait. Wait wait wait.

(*Silence. He paces, restless, tries to go back into the party, fails. Completely alone now, he looks out at the night. After a moment, Clea enters, in a beautiful black dress.*)

CLEA: I heard you were looking for me. I saw the Nazi priestess and your friend; they looked pretty cozy. Anyway, they told me in front of Nick that you were out here looking for me and I have to say it's really a problem, OK? I mean, Nick is completely allergic to you now because that lunch you had, you weren't exactly subtle. So make it fast.

CHARLIE: I need that money.

CLEA: What?

CHARLIE: We racked up a lot on my credit cards. I need that money back. Fifteen hundred, at least. To start.

CLEA: Fifteen hundred dollars? I don't even know you!

CHARLIE: You know me. You spent all my money. You took me from my wife. You're here with my ex-friend Nick —

CLEA: "Ex-friend," who you always called "the asshole — "

CHARLIE: (*Anger rising.*) He is an asshole!

CLEA: (*Sharp.*) Well, that asshole is my boss. I am his personal assistant.

CHARLIE: And what did you have to do to get that plum job?

CLEA: I did pretty much the same thing I did for you, only this time, it got me somewhere. And Nick has been really great to me. I can't be seen with you.

(*She starts to go. He steps in front of her.*)

CHARLIE: Wait wait wait —

CLEA: Get out of my way, Charlie —

CHARLIE: No wait! Forget about the money. Please, I just need to talk to someone for a second, I'm out there by myself all day and I I, Lewis and

Stella were here and they left, and I just can't go back down there by myself. I can't go back down.

(He doesn't move. She sighs, frustrated.)

CLEA: Oh boy. Look. I'm sorry you're like not having a good time right now, I really really am. Now get out of my way.

CHARLIE: Because, to be that alone. People everywhere, and no one who sees you. With recognition. It's you!

CLEA: OK. Earth to Charlie

(He takes her by the arm and leads her back to the railing.)

CHARLIE: And I'm just starting to see, just now even, what's wrong with all of this, this fall into narcissism —

CLEA: CHARLIE.

CHARLIE: Is how lonely it is. Aren't you lonely?

CLEA: *(Startled.)* Am I what?

CHARLIE: Lonely. That's the problem. That's what's wrong with it. All of it. We're not meant to be this lonely, and you and I, we, we went to this lonely place together, and I just think that, I know, there's nothing between us, but maybe — we could, we could help each other out of it. If we just had a cup of coffee. Or even, not even a cup of coffee. Maybe just a glass of water. If we started that simply, and had a glass of water. Together.

CLEA: You want me to have a glass of water with you?

CHARLIE: It might help. Holy beggars did this. They just ate and drank the simplest, people would give them what they could, from the earth, and it was like a connection.

CLEA: This isn't funny.

CHARLIE: To the self, and others, connection for people who have no place in the world. Which none of us, really, none of us do.

CLEA: Let go of my hand.

CHARLIE: No, listen — To my heart. Listen —

CLEA: I said LET GO! *(She shoves him away, steely.)* Get it together, would you? God, you're a mess, you're really just a total wreck and there's a party going on in there, Charlie! Get a clue! There's four casting agents in there! Plus Nick — OK I'm going to tell you this I don't know why because you so don't deserve it but the fact is, he still needs somebody to play the homeless guy in the third act and it's only two lines and I could get him to just give it to you if you would just — just tell Nick how much you love the pilot, he will really like that. You know part of the reason he gets so edgy with you is because he thinks you're really talented, like fucked up but talented and honestly, if you just said some nice things it would solve everything! Just don't talk about having a glass of water with him, OK? That is too nuts. Holy beggars, also off the table, OK? OK, Charlie? Honestly, you are so much work, I'm going to have to have a massage for a week to get over this. I mean it. It's a party! OK, Charlie? It's a party.

(She pushes by him, back into the party. Charlie watches her go, then looks out over the water.)

CHARLIE: It is surreal. That's exactly what it is.

(He leans back, looking into the doorway, considering whether or not he will reenter the fray. Blackout.)

END OF PLAY